UNDERSTANDING AND USING

ENGLISH GRAMMAR

Third Edition

Workbook

Betty Schrampfer Azar

Chief contributor: Rachel Spack Koch
Contributors: Susan Jamieson
Barbara Andrews
Jeanie Francis
Donald A. Azar

Longman

Editorial director: *Allen Ascher*
Executive editor: *Louisa Hellegers*
Development editor: *Janet Johnston*
Director of design and production: *Rhea Banker*
Associate director of electronic publishing: *Aliza Greenblatt*
Managing editor: *Shelley Hartle*
Electronic production editor: *Rachel Baumann*
Associate art director: *Carey Davies*
Senior manufacturing manager: *Patrice Fraccio*
Production manager: *Ray Keating*
Manufacturing buyer: *Dave Dickey*
Production assistant: *Donna Stevenson*
Illustrator: *Don Martinetti*

Published by Pearson Education
10 Bank Street, White Plains, N.Y. 10606

Printed in the United States of America
10 9

ISBN 0-13-958687-3

CONTENTS

Chapter 5   ADVERB CLAUSES OF TIME AND SUMMARY OF VERB TENSES

Chapter 6   SUBJECT–VERB AGREEMENT

Chapter 7   NOUNS

Chapter 8   PRONOUNS

Chapter 9   MODALS, PART 1

Chapter 13 ADJECTIVE CLAUSES

Chapter 14 GERUNDS AND INFINITIVES, PART 1

Chapter 15 GERUNDS AND INFINITIVES, PART 2

Chapter 16 COORDINATING CONJUNCTIONS

Chapter 17 ADVERB CLAUSES

Chapter 18 REDUCTION OF ADVERB CLAUSES TO MODIFYING ADVERBIAL PHRASES

Chapter 19 CONNECTIVES THAT EXPRESS CAUSE AND EFFECT, CONTRAST, AND CONDITION

Chapter 20 CONDITIONAL SENTENCES AND WISHES

Appendix **SUPPLEMENTARY GRAMMAR UNITS**

Special Workbook Section **PHRASAL VERBS**

Preface

This ELT *Workbook* is a place for students to explore and practice English grammar on their own. It is a place where they can test and fine-tune their understandings of English structures and improve their abilities to use English meaningfully and correctly.

It is keyed to the explanatory grammar charts found in *Understanding and Using English Grammar, Third Edition,* a classroom teaching text for students of English as a second or foreign language, as well as in the accompanying *Chartbook,* a reference grammar with no exercises.

The *Workbook* is designed not only for students who desire the opportunity for independent study of English grammar, but also as a resource for teachers who need exercise material for additional classwork, homework, testing, or individualized instruction.

The answers to ALL of the practices are given in the back of the book in an *Answer Key.* The *Answer Key* is on perforated pages so that it can be detached to construct a separate booklet. If teachers desire to use the *Workbook* as a classroom teaching text, the *Answer Key* can be removed at the beginning of the term.

A note on changes from the previous edition: The *Workbook* that accompanied the previous edition of *Understanding and Using English Grammar* had both self-study (answers given) and guided study (no answers given) practices. This *Workbook* has only self-study practices. The guided study practices that involved communicative, interactive, and/or task-based activities are now in the main teaching text, and other guided study practices from the previous edition have been adapted to a self-study format in this edition. Another change is that the presentation of phrasal verbs was deleted from the main text and is now found in a special supplementary section in this *Workbook.*

Acknowledgments

The multi-talented Shelley Hartle, my associate in all work matters, and the masterful Janet Johnston, my longtime editor, are indispensable to the production of the Azar texts. I owe them great gratitude — and also thoroughly enjoy their friendship. In particular, they have expertly handled all the many editorial and production tasks demanded by this *Workbook* and its accompanying *Chartbook*.

Longtime users of my textbooks may have noted the change in publisher. My textbooks had a Prentice Hall imprint for nineteen years; that imprint is now changing to Longman due to a recent corporate acquisition. Both imprints represent quality academic publication.

I am pleased to have my work join Longman's long history of publishing excellence in the area of teaching English to speakers of other languages. My own commitment to quality publication matches well with the Longman tradition.

I wish to thank those at Prentice Hall Regents who helped make my association with that publisher one of mutual respect and enjoyment in recent years, in particular Robin Baliszewski and Mary Jane Peluso.

I also wish at this time to thank those at Pearson Education, the owners of the Longman imprint, who have eased my transition to a new publishing company. In particular I wish to thank Joanne Dresner, Allen Ascher, and Louisa Hellegers for their open, professional, and friendly management styles. I look forward to a long and rewarding relationship.

Others at Pearson Education I wish to thank are Rachel Baumann, Carey Davies, Aliza Greenblatt, and Ray Keating. Thanks are also due to Donna Stevenson, who input the entire *Workbook* on disk from a giant cut-and-paste puzzle.

Last, I wish to thank Larry Harris, my husband, for teaching me how to play. Hard work has always come easily to me, but not how to play. Now there's balance.

CHAPTER 1
Overview of Verb Tenses

◇ **PRACTICE 1. Verb tenses. (Charts 1-1 → 1-5)**

Directions: Following are some dialogues between Speaker A and Speaker B. Complete the dialogues by using the correct form of the words in parentheses.

1. A: I'm going to ask you some questions so that we can practice verb tenses. What *(you, do)* ___do you do___ every day before you come to class? Name one thing.

   B: I *(eat)* __eat__ breakfast.

2. A: What *(you, do)* _____ last night? Name three separate activities.

   B: Last night I *(eat)* _____ dinner. Then I *(visit)* _____ some friends, and later I *(write)* _____ a couple of letters.

3. A: What *(you, do)* _____ right now? What activity is in progress right now, at this exact moment?

   B: Right now I *(talk)* _____ to you. I *(answer)* _____ your questions.

4. A: Where were you at this exact time yesterday? And what activity was in progress then?

   B: Let me think. At this time yesterday, I was at the bookstore. I *(look)* _____ for the books I needed to buy for this class.

5. A: How many questions *(I, ask)* _____ since we began this exercise?

   B: I think you *(ask)* _____ me five or six questions since we began this exercise.

6. A: What *(you, do)* _____ for the past five minutes? In other words, what activity began five minutes ago and has been in progress from then until now?

   B: I *(talk)* _____ to you for the past five minutes. I started talking to you five minutes ago, and I am still talking to you.

7. A: Where *(you, be)* _____ tomorrow morning?

   B: I *(be)* _____ in class tomorrow morning.

8. A: What *(you, do)* _____ at this exact time tomorrow? In other words, what activity will be in progress at this exact same time tomorrow?

   B: Right now I am sitting in the classroom. And at this exact time tomorrow, I *(sit)* _____ in the classroom.

9. A: What *(you, do)* _____ by the time you got to class today? In other words, what is one activity that you had completed before you arrived in class today?

   B: Well, for one thing, I *(eat)* _____ breakfast by the time I got to class today.

10. A: What *(you, do)* _____ by the time you go to bed tonight? Name one activity that you will have completed before you go to bed tonight.

    B: I *(eat)* _____ dinner by the time I go to bed tonight.

Directions: Complete the sentences with the correct form of the words in parentheses.

SIMPLE

PROGRESSIVE

PRESENT

1. Tom has regular habits. He *(eat)* _____ dinner every day. He has eaten dinner every day since he was a child. He ate dinner every day last month. He ate dinner yesterday. He will eat dinner tomorrow. He will probably eat dinner almost every day until the end of his life.

eats

4. At 7:00 this evening, Tom started to eat dinner. It is now 7:15. Tom is on the phone because Mary called him. He says, "Can I call you back? I *(eat)* _____ dinner right now. I'll finish soon and will call you back. I don't want my dinner to get cold." Tom's dinner is in progress when Mary calls.

am eating

PAST

2. Tom eats dinner every day. Usually he eats at home, but yesterday, he *(eat)* _____ dinner at a restaurant.

ate

5. Last week Tom went to a restaurant. He began to eat at 7:00. At 7:15 Mary came into the restaurant, saw Tom, and walked over to say hello. Tom's dinner was still in front of him. He hadn't finished it yet. In other words, when Mary walked into the restaurant, Tom *(eat)* _____ dinner. Tom's dinner was in progress when Mary arrived.

was eating

FUTURE

3. Tom ate dinner yesterday. He eats dinner every day. In all probability, he *(eat)* _____ dinner tomorrow.

will eat

6. Tom will begin his dinner at 7:00 tonight. Mary will arrive at 7:15. It takes Tom 30 minutes to eat his dinner. In other words, when Mary arrives tonight, Tom *(eat)* _____ his dinner. Tom's dinner will be in progress when Mary arrives.

will be eating

be + present participle

sleep slept   slept   sleeping
base   past   past participle   present participle

PERFECT   PERFECT PROGRESSIVE

7. Tom finished eating dinner at 7:30 tonight. It is now 8:00, and his mother has just come into the kitchen. She says, "What would you like for dinner? Can I cook something for you?" Tom says, "Thanks Mom, but I (eat, already) _____ dinner."

7:00–7:30 (dinner) 8:00 (mother)

10. Tom began to eat dinner at 7:00 tonight. It is now, at this moment, 7:15. Tom (eat) _____ _____ his dinner for 15 minutes, but he hasn't finished yet. In other words, his dinner has been in progress for 15 minutes.

7:00 (dinner began) 7:15 now

15 minutes

8. Yesterday Tom cooked his own dinner. He began at 7:00 and finished at 7:30. At 8:00 his mother came into the kitchen. She offered to cook some food for Tom, but he (eat, already) _____ _____. In other words, Tom had finished his dinner before he talked to his mother.

7:00–7:30 (dinner) 8:00 (mother)

11. Last week Tom went to a restaurant. He began to eat at 7:00. At 7:15 Mary came into the restaurant, saw Tom, and walked over to say hello. Tom's dinner was still in front of him. He hadn't finished it yet. In other words, when Mary walked into the restaurant, Tom (eat) _____ _____ dinner. Tom's dinner was in progress when Mary arrived.

7:00 (dinner began) 7:15 (Mary)

15 minutes

9. Tomorrow Tom will begin dinner at 7:00 and finish at 7:30. His mother will come into the kitchen at 8:00. In other words, Tom (eat, already) _____ dinner by the time his mother walks into the kitchen.

7:00–7:30 (dinner) 8:00 (mother)

12. Tonight Tom will go to a restaurant. He will begin to eat at 7:00. At 7:15 Mary will come into the restaurant, see Tom, and walk over to say hello. Tom's dinner will still be in front of him. He won't have finished it yet. In other words, when Mary walks into the restaurant tomorrow, Tom (eat) _____ _____ dinner for 15 minutes. Tom's dinner will have been in progress for 15 minutes by the time Mary arrives.

7:00 (dinner began) 7:15 (Mary)

15 minutes

◇ **PRACTICE 3. Spelling of *-ing* and *-ed* forms. (Chart 1-6)**

PART A. Write the correct *-ing* and *-ed* form for each verb.

1. shout _____
2. slope _____
3. stop _____
4. stoop _____
5. ánswer _____

6. refér _____
7. return _____
8. enjoy _____
9. copy _____
10. die _____

PART B. Write the correct *-ing* form for each verb.

11. point _____
12. beat _____
13. bet _____
14. excite _____
15. éxit _____

16. regrét _____
17. attempt _____
18. shout _____
19. flit _____
20. interest _____

PART C. Write the correct *-ed* form for each verb.

21. bóther _____
22. blur _____
23. scare _____
24. scar _____
25. fear _____

26. star _____
27. stare _____
28. órder _____
29. súffer _____
30. occúr _____

PART D. Write the correct *-ing* form for each verb.

31. dream _____
32. file _____
33. fill _____
34. fail _____
35. annoy _____

36. deny _____
37. scrub _____
38. drain _____
39. fan _____
40. interrupt _____

PART E. Write the correct *-ed* form for each verb.

41. comb _____
42. wrap _____
43. groan _____
44. occupy _____
45. spray _____
46. wipe _____

47. whip _____
48. accept _____
49. permít _____
50. mérit _____
51. whísper _____
52. infér _____

CHAPTER 2

Present and Past, Simple and Progressive

◇ **PRACTICE 1. The simple present and the present progressive. (Charts 2-1 and 2-2)**
Directions: Complete the sentences by using either the simple present or the present progressive of the verbs in the list. Include any words given in parentheses. Use each verb only once.

belong	fail	scream	tape
bite	fight	✓shine	try
bleed	mean	shrink	whisper
blow	✓own	sleep	

1. It's a gray day today. The sun (*not*) _____isn't shining_____.

2. The bank lent us money for a down payment, so now we (*own*) ___own___ the house we used to rent.

3. Shhh! I _____ to concentrate. I can't hear myself think with all that noise going on.

4. This book is mine. That one _____ to Pierre.

5. Shhh! The baby _____. We don't want to wake him up.

6. A: Juan! What's the matter with your hand? It _____,

   B: I just cut it when I was using a knife. It's not serious. I'll wash it and put a bandage on it.

7. A: My marks in school are terrible this term. I _____ three of my courses.

   B: Maybe you can improve your grades before the end of the term if you start studying harder.

8. That sweater won't fit you if you wash it in hot water. Wool _____ in hot water.

9. Look at Joan. She _____ her fingernails. She must be nervous.

10. The children can't get their kite high up in the air because the wind (*not*) _____ _____ hard enough today.

11. My two children don't get along. It seems they (*always*) _____ about something. Is that typical of siblings?

12. You can hear Tommy all over the house. Why (he) _____?
    I'd better see what's wrong.

13. "Singular" _____ "one."

14. Alice and John! Why (you) _____ to each other? If you have
    something important to say, say it aloud to all of us.

15. Kareem has his tape recorder on his desk. He _____ the professor's
    lecture today.

◇ **PRACTICE 2. Stative vs. progressive verbs. (Charts 2-3 and 2-4)**
  Directions: Use either the simple present or the present progressive of the verbs in parentheses.

  1. Tim *(have)* ___has___ a car.

  2. Tim *(have)* ___is having___ trouble with his car, so he has to take the bus to work these days.

  3. This box *(weigh)* _____ a lot. It's too heavy for me to lift.

  4. I just handed the box to the postal worker. Right now she *(weigh)* _____
     it to see how much postage it *(need)* _____.

  5. I *(do)* _____ this practice at the moment. It *(consist)* _____
     of both nonprogressive and progressive verbs.

  6. I *(think)* _____ about the verbs in this grammar practice right now. I
     (think) _____ all of my answers are correct, but I'll use the answer key to
     check them when I finish, just to make sure.

  7. Mrs. Edwards is at the market. Right now she *(look)* _____ at the
     apples. They *(look)* _____ fresh.

  8. My cousin is an actor. She *(appear, currently)* _____ in the
     popular TV series called "Doctors of Mystery." Have you seen that show?

  9. Jack *(appear)* _____ happy this morning. He's smiling.

 10. A: This tooth is killing me!
     B: It's a good thing you *(see)* _____ a dentist today.

 11. Susan is looking at some people across the street, but she *(see, not)* _____
     anyone she knows.

 12. A: What are you thinking about? You have such a pleasant expression on your face.
     B: I *(imagine)* _____ what it would be like to be on a tropical beach
        right now.

 13. A: Why isn't Richard here?
     B: I *(imagine)* _____ he'll be here soon. Don't worry about him.

14. A: Bye, Alex.

   B: Wait! *(you, forget, not)* _____ something?

   A: What do you mean?

   B: Isn't this your backpack?

   A: Gosh. Yes. How could I forget that? Thanks.

15. A: When is Jessica's birthday?

   B: I *(forget)* _____ when her birthday is. Sometime in November, isn't it?

16. A: Are you happy with the school you decided to send your daughter to?

   B: Yes, indeed. But it's pretty expensive. It *(cost)* _____ us an arm and a leg to send her there, but we think it's worth it. And it won't last forever.

17. A: What's the price on that lamp? I really like it.

   B: Let me see. Well, no wonder. It *(cost)* _____ three times as much as the other one. You certainly have expensive tastes.

18. A: What are you doing?

   B: I *(smell)* _____ the scent of this candle. It *(smell)* _____ good.

19. A: Watch out, Tommy! Those scissors are sharp. *(you, be)* _____ careful? Don't cut yourself.

   B: It's okay. I won't hurt myself.

20. A: Do you let Tommy use scissors? He's very young.

   B: It's not a problem. He *(be)* _____ very careful when he cuts something with scissors. He knows how to use scissors carefully.

21. A: That's a big stack of bills on your desk, Sam. Haven't you paid your bills this month?

   B: No. Nor last month. I know I *(be)* _____ irresponsible about paying my bills right now, but I've been really busy. I'll take care of them soon. Generally, I *(be, not)* _____ an irresponsible person.

◇ **PRACTICE 3. The simple present and the present progressive. (Charts 2-1 → 2-4)**
   Directions: Use either the simple present or the present progressive of the verbs in parentheses.

   1. Dennis *(drink, usually)* ___usually drinks___ coffee with his breakfast, but this morning he *(drink)* ___is drinking___ tea instead.

   2. Janet *(take)* _____ the bus to work every day. She *(wait, usually)* _____ for the bus at the corner of 5th and Pine.

   3. This morning it *(rain)* _____. I can see Janet from my window. She *(stand)* _____ at the corner of 5th and Pine. She *(hold)* _____ her umbrella over her head. She *(wait)* _____ for the bus.

4. Mike *(take)* _____ three classes this semester. Every morning he *(study)* _____ for two hours before he goes to school. He *(have)* _____ French class at 9 o'clock. He *(take, also)* _____ _____ chemistry and accounting. He *(like)* _____ chemistry best of all, but he *(have)* _____ better grades in accounting and French.

5. MOTHER: Susie! Get your fingers out of the dessert! What *(you, do)* _____?

   SUSIE: I *(taste)* _____ the cake. It *(taste)* _____ good.

6. JANICE: What *(you, write)* _____ in your notebook?

   DIANE: I *(make)* _____ notes about the questions I want to ask the teacher.

   JANICE: *(you, prepare, always)* _____ so thoroughly for every class?

   DIANE: I *(try, always)* _____ to.

7. LARRY: Why *(the children, be)* _____ so good today? They *(clean)* _____ their rooms and *(pick)* _____ up all their toys and clothes from the rest of the house.

   CAROL: I promised to take them to the water slide this afternoon if they did all their chores first.

8. ALFONSO: What's that?

   NURSE: A needle. I *(prepare)* _____ to give you a shot.

   ALFONSO: I *(need, not)* _____ a shot!

   NURSE: Just relax and breath deeply. Everything will be fine.

   ALFONSO: Ouch!

◇ **PRACTICE 4. Pronunciation of -ed. (Chart 2-6)**
   Directions: Write the pronunciation of the *-ed* ending after each word.

   1. greeted ___/əd/___   7. attempted _____   13. cooked _____

   2. wished ___/t/___   8. dropped _____   14. prepared _____

   3. listened ___/d/___   9. served _____   15. introduced _____

   4. crossed _____   10. included _____   16. allowed _____

   5. lifted _____   11. reported _____

   6. joined _____   12. promised _____

◇ **PRACTICE 5. Irregular verbs. (Chart 2-7)**
　　Directions: The following is a review of the forms of irregular verbs. The simple form is given.
　　You are to provide the simple past and the past participle.

GROUP 1: ALL THREE FORMS ARE DIFFERENT					

Group 1A: The vowel changes from "i" to "a" to "u."

begin	began	begun	sink	_____	_____
drink	_____	_____	spring	_____	_____
ring	_____	_____	stink	_____	_____
shrink	_____	_____	swim	_____	_____
sing	_____	_____			

Group 1B: The vowel changes in the simple past. The past participle ends in "n."

blow	blew	blown	get	_____	_____
draw	_____	_____	forget	_____	_____
grow	_____	_____			
know	_____	_____	mistake	_____	_____
throw	_____	_____	shake	_____	_____
fly	_____	_____	take	_____	_____
break	_____	_____	bite	_____	_____
choose	_____	_____	hide	_____	_____
drive	_____	_____			
freeze	_____	_____	be	_____	_____
ride	_____	_____	eat	_____	_____
rise	_____	_____	fall	_____	_____
speak	_____	_____	forgive	_____	_____
steal	_____	_____	give	_____	_____
swear	_____	_____	lie	_____	_____
tear	_____	_____	see	_____	_____
wear	_____	_____			
weave	_____	_____	do	_____	_____
write	_____	_____	go	_____	_____

GROUP 2: TWO FORMS ARE THE SAME: THE SIMPLE PAST AND THE PAST PARTICIPLE

Group 2A: The simple past and the past participle end in "d."

sell	sold	sold	lay	_____	_____
tell	_____	_____	pay	_____	_____
			say	_____	_____
flee	_____	_____			
bleed	_____	_____	find	_____	_____
breed	_____	_____	grind	_____	_____
feed	_____	_____	wind	_____	_____
lead	_____	_____			
read	_____	_____	have	_____	_____
speed	_____	_____	hear	_____	_____

Group 2B: The simple past and the past participle end in "t."

creep	crept	crept	bring	_____	_____
deal	_____	_____	buy	_____	_____
feel	_____	_____	catch	_____	_____
keep	_____	_____	fight	_____	_____
kneel	_____	_____	seek	_____	_____
leave	_____	_____	teach	_____	_____
mean	_____	_____	think	_____	_____
meet	_____	_____			
sleep	_____	_____	bend	_____	_____
sweep	_____	_____	build	_____	_____
weep	_____	_____	lend	_____	_____
			send	_____	_____
lose	_____	_____	spend	_____	_____

Group 2C: The vowel changes to form the simple past and the past participle.

cling	clung	clung	hold	_____	_____
dig	_____	_____	shoot	_____	_____
hang	_____	_____	sit	_____	_____
spin	_____	_____	stand	_____	_____
stick	_____	_____	understand	_____	_____
sting	_____	_____	win	_____	_____
strike	_____	_____			
swing	_____	_____			

Group 2D: Only the simple past is different.		
become	became	become
come	_____	_____
run	_____	_____

GROUP 3: ALL THREE FORMS ARE THE SAME

bet	bet	bet	put	_____	_____
bid	_____	_____	quit	_____	_____
broadcast	_____	_____	shed	_____	_____
burst	_____	_____	shut	_____	_____
cost	_____	_____	slit	_____	_____
cut	_____	_____	split	_____	_____
hit	_____	_____	spread	_____	_____
hurt	_____	_____	upset	_____	_____
let	_____	_____			

◇ **PRACTICE 6. Simple past of irregular verbs. (Chart 2-7)**

Directions: Complete the sentences with the simple past of the irregular verbs in the list. Pay special attention to spelling. Use each verb only once.

burst	draw	slide	stick
buy	hide	slit	✓swear
dig	shake	spread	win

1. All of the witnesses ___swore___ to tell the truth in the court of law.

2. Mike was so cold that his whole body _____.

3. Using only a pen with blue ink, Sue _____ a beautiful picture of a bird.

4. When the balloon _____, everyone was startled by the sudden noise.

5. Paul _____ his money because he was afraid it would get stolen while he was away.

6. Emily accidentally _____ her finger with a needle while she was sewing.

7. Janice _____ the top of the envelope with a knife instead of ripping it open.

8. I lost control of my car, and it _____ across the ice.

9. Mary _____ butter all over her piece of toast with her knife.

10. Our team finally _____ the soccer game by one goal.

11. The small animal _____ a hole in the ground to make her nest.

12. When Fred went shopping yesterday, he _____ some car wax and a garden hose.

◇ **PRACTICE 7. Simple past of irregular verbs. (Chart 2-7)**
Directions: Complete the sentences with the simple past of the irregular verbs in the list. Pay special attention to spelling. Use each verb only once.

bite	*cling*	*pay*	*sting*
blow	*feel*	*quit*	*swim*
catch	*mean*	*shed*	*weave*

1. I broke a tooth when I _____ into a piece of hard candy.

2. The little boy _____ to his mother's hand as they walked toward the school bus.

3. Maria promised to help us. I hope she _____ what she said.

4. Arthur _____ out all of the candles on his birthday cake.

5. We both _____ smoking three months ago, and we already feel much better.

6. Douglas _____ the outside of his pocket to make sure his wallet was still there.

7. A bee _____ me on the hand while I was working in the garden.

8. Matthew Webb was the first person who _____ across the English Channel.

9. Paul _____ much more for his bike than I spent for mine.

10. Rita threw the ball high in the air. Daniel _____ it when it came down.

11. Each year as the snake grew larger, it formed a new skin and _____ its old skin.

12. Everyone in Ali's family has a special skill. His sister _____ that beautiful carpet.

◇ **PRACTICE 8. Simple past of irregular verbs. (Chart 2-7)**
   Directions: Complete the sentences with the simple past of the irregular verbs in the list. Pay special attention to spelling. Use each verb only once.

bet	*freeze*	*sink*	*split*
choose	*lead*	*spend*	*upset*
fly	*ring*	*spin*	*weep*

1. Dr. Perez _____ ten hours in the operating room performing delicate surgery.

2. On my first day at the university, Sally _____ the way to our classroom. I followed.

3. We made a friendly wager on the game. I _____ a dollar on my team.

4. I _____ when I heard the tragic news. Everyone else cried too.

5. As she stood, she _____ the table, and everything on top of it fell to the floor.

6. Paul wanted to make a fire, but the logs were too big. So he _____ them with his axe.

7. When I threw a piece of wood from the shore, it floated on top of the water. When I threw a
   rock, it _____ immediately to the bottom of the lake.

8. In 1927, Charles Lindbergh _____ from New York to Paris in 33 hours and
   30 minutes. How long does it take today on an SST? *(SST = supersonic transport)*

9. When the children _____ around and around, they became dizzy.

10. The telephone _____ several times and then stopped before I could answer it.

11. William had trouble deciding which one he liked best, but he finally _____ the
    blue sweater.

12. When my cat heard a noise in the bushes, she _____ in her tracks (i.e., stopped
    moving completely) and listened intently.

◇ **PRACTICE 9. Simple past of irregular verbs. (Chart 2-7)**
   Directions: Complete the sentences with the simple past of the irregular verbs in the list. Pay special attention to spelling. Use each verb only once.

broadcast	fall	lose	steal
cost	flee	seek	strike
deal	hold	shoot	sweep

1. Ron had a small accident. He _____ to the floor when his foot got caught in the rug.

2. The car that Barb was driving went out of control and _____ a stop sign. That's the first time Barb ever hit anything with her car.

3. All of the radio and TV stations _____ the news of the peace plan yesterday.

4. When Mrs. Grant was having trouble, she _____ help from her neighbors. She asked them for support and advice.

5. The team played badly. They _____ the game by seven points. Oh, well. You can't win 'em all.

6. When we played cards, Jane _____ five cards to each player.

7. Sue _____ the knife in her right hand and the fork in her left hand.

8. The hunter slowly raised his rifle and _____ at the deer, but he missed.

9. Jenny wanted a color TV for her apartment, but the least expensive one _____ too much for her budget, so she decided to wait until she could save enough money.

10. When I spilled rice on the floor, I got the broom and _____ it up.

11. A thief broke into Carlos's apartment and _____ his TV and his stereo set.

12. Tommy wanted to play a little joke on his friend Marcia. He ran up to Marcia's front door, rang the doorbell, and then _____ quickly down the street. When Marcia answered the door, no one was there.

◇ **PRACTICE 10. Troublesome verbs: *raise/rise, set/sit, lay/lie*. (Chart 2-8)**
   Directions: Select the correct verb in parentheses.

1. Mr. Wong *(raises, rises)* many different kinds of vegetables in his garden.

2. The man *(raised, rose)* to his feet and walked to the front of the room.

3. Mike *(set, sat)* a large vase of roses on the coffee table.

4. Claudia and Paulo *(set, sat)* next to each other at the lecture last night.

5. Jackie always *(lays, lies)* her wedding ring on the kitchen counter when she washes dishes.

6. Wouldn't you prefer to be *(lying, laying)* on the beach right now instead of sitting in this class?

7. When Alex *(lay, laid)* down to take a nap, he ended up sleeping for the whole afternoon.

8. Where is my wallet? I *(lay, laid)* it here on the dresser five minutes ago.

9. Dr. Singh *(hung, hanged)* his diploma from medical school on the wall in his office.

10. Nepal *(lies, lays)* to the north of India.

◇ **PRACTICE 11. The simple past and the past progressive. (Charts 2-9 → 2-12)**
Directions: Fill in the blanks with the simple past or the past progressive of the verbs in parentheses. Include any other words in parentheses.

1. We *(have)* _____had_____ a wonderful dinner last night to celebrate our 25th wedding anniversary.

2. We *(have, at home)* __were at home having__ our anniversary dinner when my uncle called to congratulate us last night.

3. A: Why is Henry in the hospital?
   B: He *(work, in his garage)* _____ on his car when the gas tank *(explode)* _____.
   A: What *(cause)* _____ the explosion?
   B: Henry *(Δlight)* _____ a cigarette.

4. A: I'm sorry, Officer. I *(see, not)* _____ the stop sign. I *(think)* _____ _____ about something else.
   B: What *(you, think)* _____ about? You should have been thinking about your driving.

5. Bill asked me to go over to his apartment, but I *(want, not)* _____ to leave the house because I *(wait)* _____ for a phone call.

6. Amy *(hear, not)* _____ her parents having an argument last night. She *(listen, in her room)* _____ to music.

7. When Richard *(stop)* _____ his car suddenly, the groceries *(fall)* _____ out of the bag they were in and *(spill)* _____ all over the floor of the car.

8. When the door-to-door salesperson *(come)* _____ yesterday, Claudia *(hear, not)* _____ the doorbell because she *(dry, in her room)* _____ _____ her hair with her electric hair dryer.

9. When I was a child, my mother always *(serve)* _____ cookies and milk to my friends and me when we *(go)* _____ to my house after school.

10. When we *(look)* _____ in on the baby last night, he *(sleep)* _____ _____. I think he *(dream)* _____ about something nice because he *(smile)* _____.

◇ **PRACTICE 12. The simple past and the past progressive. (Charts 2-9 → 2-12)**

Directions: Fill in the blanks with the simple past or the past progressive of the verbs in parentheses.

1. Yesterday David *(cross)* ___was crossing___ a street when a truck *(turn)* ___turned___ the corner very fast and almost *(hit)* ___hit___ him.

2. During the study period in class yesterday, it *(be)* _____ hard for me to concentrate because the student next to me *(hum)* _____ .

3. Last Monday while we *(watch, in our living room)* _____
   _____ an exciting game on television, the electricity
   (go) _____ out. So we *(go)* _____ outside, *(get)* _____ into the car,
   (turn) _____ on the radio, and *(listen)* _____ to the rest of the
   game. The next day the car battery *(be)* _____ dead.

4. The police *(outwit)* _____ a thief yesterday. They *(surround)*
   _____ the jewelry store while he *(stuff, still inside)* _____
   _____ his pockets with diamonds.

5. Yesterday we had a houseful of children for my son's sixth birthday party. In the middle of
   the party, the phone *(ring)* _____ , so I had to leave the children alone for a
   moment. When I *(come)* _____ back into the room, most of the children
   (play, still) _____ together nicely. But over in the corner, Bobby
   (pull) _____ Annie's hair. I quickly *(run)* _____ over and *(tell)*
   _____ Bobby to stop.

6. TEACHER: You're late again. You were supposed to be here ten minutes ago. Where were you?
   MICHAEL: I *(look)* _____ for a place to park.
   TEACHER: *(you, find)* _____ one?
   MICHAEL: Yes, but it's at a parking meter that has a 15-minute limit. So every 15 minutes
   I'll have to go out and put some more money in the meter.
   TEACHER: Maybe you should start taking the bus to school.
   MICHAEL: I *(take)* _____ the bus a couple of days ago and ended up
   miles from school. That's why I was absent from class.
   TEACHER: Oh.

7. BOB: My office mate, Jack, really makes me angry!
   SUE: Why?
   BOB: Well for one thing, he *(interrupt, always)* _____ me. I
   can barely get a sentence out of my mouth.
   SUE: Is that all?
   BOB: No. He *(ask, always)* _____ me to write his reports for him.
   I have enough reports of my own without doing his reports too!

8. SUE: So how did you and Bob get along at work today?

BOB: Same old stuff. While I *(try)* _____ to explain something to him, he *(interrupt)* _____ me, not just once but repeatedly. And once again he *(ask)* _____ me to write a report that the boss had asked him to write. I *(refuse)* _____ .

SUE: Good for you. Jack needs to write his own reports.

◇ **PRACTICE 13. The simple past and the past progressive. (Charts 2-9 → 2-12)**
Directions: Complete the sentence with the simple past or the past progressive. Use any verb that seems right to you.

1. Last Saturday while Sandy ___was cleaning___ out the attic, she ___found___ her grandmother's wedding dress.

2. Two days ago, Peter _____ all of his money out of the bank and _____ a new car. Yesterday, while he _____ to work, he lost control of his steering and _____ another car. He wasn't hurt, but the accident completely _____ his new car.

3. Last night we suddenly _____ up from a sound sleep when we _____ a noise about 3:00 A.M. I thought it was a burglar, but it was only a cat that _____ _____ along the window sill.

4. Two days ago I _____ my friends Ann and Andy at their apartment. They _____ the dishes when I _____ . They _____ quickly, and we all _____ down and _____ about old times.

5. When I _____ to/at the airport, Lisa _____ for me in the baggage claim area. As soon as she _____ me, she _____ her arms and _____ something I couldn't hear because the people around me _____ so much noise.

6. Mary _____ outside _____ the flowers when it _____ to rain. So of course she _____ off the hose and let nature take care of her garden.

CHAPTER 3

Perfect and Perfect Progressive Tenses

◇ **PRACTICE 1. The present perfect. (Chart 3-1)**
Directions: Complete the sentences with the present perfect of the appropriate verb from the list. Use each verb only once. Include any words in parentheses.

cost	grow	ride	swim
drive	improve	save	win
✔eat	know	start	write
forget	make	sweep	

1. A: How about more pie?

   B: No, but thanks. I can't swallow another bite. I *(already)* ___have already eaten___ too much.

2. Our football team is having a great season. They _____ all but one of their games so far this year and will probably win the championship.

3. Jane is expecting a letter from me, but I *(not)* _____ to her yet. Maybe I'll call her instead.

4. Jack is living in Spain now. His Spanish used to be terrible, but it _____ greatly since he moved there.

5. Our baby *(not)* _____ to talk yet. My friend's baby, who is several months older, can already say a few words in English and a few words in French.

6. A: I hear your parents are coming to visit you. Is that why you're cleaning your apartment?

   B: You guessed it! I *(already)* _____ the floor, but I still need to dust the furniture. Want to help?

7. A: I understand Tom is a good friend of yours? How long *(you)* _____ _____ him?

   B: Since we were kids.

8. Everyone makes mistakes in life. I _____ lots of mistakes in my life. The important thing is to learn from one's mistakes. Right?

9. A: I *(never)* _____ on the subways in New York City. Have you?

   B: I've never even been in New York City.

10. A: *(you, ever)* _____ in the Atlantic Ocean?

   B: No, only the Pacific — when I was in Hawaii. I even went snorkeling when I was there.

11. Little Freddie _____ a lot since I last saw him. He's going to be tall just like his father, isn't he?

12. Let's stop at the next motel. We _____ 500 miles so far today, and that's enough.

13. Alex spoke Arabic when he lived in Lebanon as a young child, but now he _____ _____ almost all of his Arabic. He remembers only a few words.

14. Maintaining this old car for the past five years _____ us much less than we would have spent if we had bought a new one. We _____ a lot of money by not buying a new car, haven't we?

◇ **PRACTICE 2. Using *since* and *for*. (Chart 3-1)**
   Directions: Write either *since* or *for* in the blanks.

1. I haven't seen my brother _____*for*_____ 6 months. I haven't seen my sister ____*since*____ April.

2. My wife and I have moved three times _____ we got married.

3. We've lived here _____ three years, but we're going to move again soon.

4. The Smiths have lived here _____ a long time. They've lived here _____ 1980.

5. My sister's husband got a job on a fishing boat in Alaska. He's been there _____ eleven weeks, but he should be coming home soon.

6. The International Olympic Games have continued almost without interruption _____ 1896.

7. The world has enjoyed Beethoven's music _____ nearly 200 years.

8. They have been married _____ last summer.

9. The first sections of the Great Wall of China have endured _____ a long time. They have endured _____ more than 2,200 years.

10. Overall, Ed hasn't learned very much _____ the term began. He needs to study harder.

11. The clock on the campus tower hasn't moved _____ 3:13 on March 2, 1966. Nobody has been able to fix the clock _____ that time.

12. Argentina won the World Cup in 1986 for the second time _____ the cup was first awarded in 1930. Soccer is a popular sport there.

◇ **PRACTICE 3. The simple past and the present perfect.** (Charts 2-9 and 3-1)
Directions: Complete the sentences with the simple past or the present perfect of the verbs in parentheses.

1. I _____knew_____ Tim when he was a child, but I haven't seen him for many years. I __have known__ Larry, my best friend, for more than 20 years. *(know)*

2. The company and the union finally _____ on salary raises two days ago. Since then, they _____ on everything, and the rest of the negotiations have gone smoothly. *(agree)*

3. Mark _____ a trip to Asia last October. He _____ many trips to Asia since he started his own import-export business. *(take)*

4. Ivan _____ the violin with the London Symphony since 1990. Last year he _____ Beethoven's violin concerto at one of the concerts. *(play)*

5. When she was in college, Julia _____ home at least once a week. Now she has a job and is living in Chicago. In the last six months she _____ only three letters to her parents. *(write)*

6. Our university _____ 121 students to study in other countries last year. In total, we _____ 864 students abroad over the last ten years. *(send)*

7. Masaru is a pilot for JAL. He _____ nearly 8 million miles during the last 22 years. Last year, he _____ 380,000 miles. *(fly)*

8. Mark missed his physics examination this morning because he _____. He _____ a lot since the beginning of the semester. He'd better buy a new alarm clock. *(oversleep)*

◇ **PRACTICE 4. The present perfect and the present perfect progressive.** (Charts 3-1 and 3-2)
Directions: Use either the present perfect or the present perfect progressive of the given verbs.

1. The children are at the park. They *(play)* __have been playing__ ball for the last two hours, but they don't seem tired yet.

2. Jim *(play)* __has played__ soccer only a couple of times, so he's not very good at it. He's much better at tennis.

3. A: Janice *(sleep)* _____ for almost eleven hours. Don't you think we should wake her up?
   B: I guess we probably should.

4. Tim *(sleep)* _____ in the downstairs bedroom only once. He usually sleeps upstairs in the bedroom he shares with his brother.

5. I *(fly, not)* _____ on a plane since last year when I was on a plane that had a fire in one of its engines. Now I'm afraid to even think about getting on an airplane.

6. A: How much longer until we arrive at the Singapore airport?

   B: Let me see. It's about 9:15. We *(fly)* _____ for almost six hours. We should be there in another couple of hours.

7. A: Is the rescue crew still looking for survivors of the plane crash?

   B: Yes, they *(search)* _____ the area for hours, but they haven't found anybody else. They'll keep searching until night falls.

8. Karl *(raise)* _____ three children to adulthood. Now they are educated and working in productive careers.

9. Sally is falling asleep at her desk. Dr. Wu *(lecture)* _____ since ten, and it's now past noon.

10. Virginia is a law student. Ever since she enrolled in law school, she *(miss, never)* _____ _____ a class due to illness.

11. The club members *(make, finally)* _____ their decision. The election is over, and they *(choose)* _____ a new president. Ann Andrews is now the club leader.

◇ **PRACTICE 5. The present perfect and the present perfect progressive. (Charts 3-1 and 3-2)**
   Directions: Complete the sentences by using the present perfect or the present perfect progressive of the words in the list. Use each verb only once. Include any words in parentheses.

cook	hear	spend	✓understand
dig	meet	stand	wait
grow	paint	travel	want

1. They have never gotten along with each other. I *(never)* <u>have never understood</u> why they agreed to be roommates in the first place.

2. Al just introduced me to his sister. Now I _____ everyone in his family.

3. Ms. Erickson is a sales clerk in a large department store. It's almost closing time. Her feet hurt, as they do every day, because she _____ at the sales counter since eight o'clock this morning.

4. A: I am so happy! I finally got the one thing that I *(always)* _____.

   B: What's that?

5. My uncle _____ the outside of his house for three weeks, and he's still not finished. He's being very careful. He wants his house to look just right.

6. The Smiths are presently in Tunisia. They _____ throughout North Africa since the middle of May. They'll return home in another month.

7. My brother's daughter _____ nearly six inches (15 cm) since I last saw her two years ago.

8. A: How much money do you have to buy clothes with?

   B: Sixty dollars.

   A: I thought you had a hundred dollars.

   B: I did. But I (already) _____ forty.

9. A: Isn't the rice ready to eat yet? It _____ for over an hour, hasn't it? Are you sure you know how to cook rice?

   B: Of course I do! I've watched my mother make rice for years.

10. I'm surprised that George apologized for what he said. As far as I can remember, I (never) _____ him say "I'm sorry" before.

11. A: We _____ to hear about the new baby since 5 A.M. Isn't there any word yet?

    B: Not yet.

12. A: I've been watching Mr. Tuttle in his front yard across the street. He _____ _____ a long trench across the middle of his yard for the last two hours. I wonder why.

    B: He's uncovering the water pipes so he can repair a leak and put in new plumbing.

◇ **PRACTICE 6. The simple past and the past perfect. (Charts 2-9 and 3-3)**
   Directions: Use the simple past or the past perfect of the verbs in the list to complete the sentences. Include any words in parentheses. Use each verb only once.

be	✓finish	invent	sting
burn	fly	leave	teach
design	help	spend	✓turn on

   1. By the time Jason arrived to help, we (already) _____had already finished_____ moving everything.

   2. The apartment was hot when I got home, so I _____turned on_____ the air conditioner.

   3. Alexander Graham Bell (already) _____ the telephone by the time I was born.

   4. The farmer's barn caught on fire some time during the night. By the time the firefighters arrived, the building _____ to the ground. It was a total loss.

5. The suit I bought cost more than a week's salary. Until then, I (never) _____ _____ so much on one outfit.

6. Yesterday a hornet _____ me under my arm. That really hurt! When I put on my shirt after working in the garden, I didn't notice that there was a hornet in it.

7. We were not happy with the plans that the architect showed us for our new house. Obviously, he (never) _____ a home like the one we wanted.

8. When I saw that Mike was having trouble, I _____ him. He was very appreciative.

9. My wife and I went to Disneyland when we visited Los Angeles last spring. Prior to that time, we (never) _____ to such a big amusement park. It was a lot of fun.

10. Last year I experienced how tedious long plane trips can be. I _____ in an airplane for fairly long distances before, but never as long as when I went to Australia in June.

11. Mr. Khan has had experience teaching chemistry and physics, but he (never) _____ _____ mathematics until this year. He's found that he enjoys teaching math.

12. Promptly at five, I went to Iris' office to offer her a ride home from work, but I couldn't find her. She (already) _____ .

◇ **PRACTICE 7. The simple past and the past perfect. (Charts 2-9 and 3-3)**
Directions: Use the simple past or the past perfect of the verbs in parentheses. In some cases, both forms are correct.

1. Yesterday I (go) ___went___ to my daughter's dance recital. I (be, never) ___had never been___ to a dance recital before. I (take, not) ___didn't take___ dancing lessons when I (be) ___was___ a child.

2. Last night, I (eat) _____ four servings of food at the "all-you-can-eat" special dinner at The Village Restaurant. Until that time, I (eat, never) _____ so much in one meal. I've felt miserable all day today.

3. A: I (see) _____ you in the school play last night. You (do) _____ a terrific acting job. (you, act, ever) _____ in a play before this one?
   B: Yes. I (start) _____ acting when I was in elementary school.

4. Last year, I *(go)* _____ mountain climbing for the first time. It was exciting and terrifying at the same time. We *(move)* _____ slowly and carefully, and it *(take)* _____ three days to get to the top. Imagine our surprise when we climbed onto the summit and found another group of climbers. They *(arrive)* _____ several hours ahead of us. They were having dinner and listening to Beethoven. We *(laugh)* _____ , and they *(invite)* _____ us to join them. The climb *(be)* _____ , to say the least, an unforgettable experience.

5. A friend of mine, Judith Nelson, is presently working in the international sales division at an electronics firm. She's just returned from a trip to Japan. She was asked to go there because she can speak Japanese. When she *(be)* _____ a business student at Boston University, she *(study)* _____ Japanese for four years. She *(have, never)* _____ the opportunity to use her Japanese until she went to Tokyo last month. While she was there, she *(speak)* _____ Japanese every day and *(enjoy)* _____ every minute of it. She's eager to return.

6. When I first *(travel)* _____ abroad to study, I *(live, never)* _____ _____ in a dormitory before. During the first year, I *(have)* _____ a roommate from Switzerland who *(become)* _____ a very good friend. Prior to that time, I *(live, never)* _____ with anyone from another culture.

◇ **PRACTICE 8. The present perfect progressive and the past perfect progressive.**
(Charts 3-2 and 3-4)

Directions: Use the present perfect progressive or the past perfect progressive to complete these sentences.

1. Anna *(listen to)* __had been listening to__ loud rock music when her friends arrived, but turned it off so all of them could study together. When they finished, she turned it back on, and they *(dance)* __have been dancing__ and *(sing)* __singing__ for two hours now.

2. We *(wait)* _____ for Ali for the last two hours, but he still hasn't arrived.

3. We *(wait)* _____ for Ali for over three hours before he finally arrived yesterday.

4. Oscar *(train)* _____ for the Olympics for the last three years and wants to make the national team next year.

5. The marathon runner *(run)* _____ for almost two hours when he collapsed to the pavement. He received immediate medical attention.

6. Tom had a hard time finding a job. He *(try)* _____ to get a new job for six months before he finally found a position at a local community college. Now he has a two-year contract. He *(teach)* _____ there for only a few weeks, but he likes his new job very much.

7. Dr. Sato *(perform)* _____ specialized surgery since she began working at the university hospital ten years ago. She still does many operations each year, but now her work is so famous that she travels all over the world lecturing to other surgeons on her technique.

8. The Acme Construction Company is having problems. They *(work)* _____ _____ on a new office building for the last seven months, and everything seems to be going wrong. Earlier, they stopped work on a smaller structure that they *(build)* _____ so they could take on this job. Now both projects are in jeopardy.

CHAPTER 4
Future Time

◇ **PRACTICE 1.** *Will* vs. *be going to.* (Charts 4-1 and 4-2)
Directions: Complete the sentences with *will* or *be going to,* as appropriate. Include any words in parentheses.

1. A: Excuse me, waiter! This isn't what I ordered. I ordered a chicken salad.

   B: Sorry, sir. I ___will___ take this back and get your salad.

   A: Thank you.

2. A: Would you like to join Linda and me tomorrow? We ___are going to___ visit the natural history museum.

   B: Sure. I've never been there.

3. A: Where's the mustard?

   B: In the refrigerator, on the middle shelf.

   A: I've looked there.

   B: Okay. I _____ find it for you.

4. A: What's all this paint for? *(you)* _____ paint your house?

   B: No, we _____ paint my mother's house.

5. A: Paul, do you want to go with me to the shopping mall?

   B: No thanks. I have some things I have to do today. I _____ wash my car and then clean out the basement.

6. A: Someone needs to take this report to Mr. Day's office right away, but I can't leave my desk.

   B: I _____ do it.

   A: Thanks.

7. A: Let's make something easy for dinner. Got any ideas?

   B: I _____ make some rice. Why don't you make a salad?

   A: Sounds good.

8. A: Why did you buy so many tomatoes?

   B: I _____ make a lot of spaghetti sauce.

9. A: Who'd like to take the VCR back to the visual aids room? Any volunteers?

   B: I _____ do it.

10. A: Why did you buy so many vegetables?

   B: I _____ make a large salad for the potluck dinner tonight.

11. A: Why is Carlos wearing a suit and tie? He usually wears jeans to class.

   B: He _____ give a speech at the faculty lunch today.

   A: Really? What *(he)* _____ speak about?

   B: About university study in his country.

12. A: I wonder what the weather is like in Chicage now. I need to know what kind of clothes to pack for my trip there.

   B: I don't know, but it just so happens that I have a cousin who lives in Chicago, and I have to call her tonight. I _____ ask her about the weather and tell you what she says.

13. A: I need some help.

   B: What can I do, Andy?

   A: I _____ go to a job interview this afternoon, and I don't have a decent tie to wear.

   B: I _____ lend you one of mine.

   A: Thanks.

14. A: You're going out?

   B: Yes. I _____ go to the grocery store for some fruit, meat, and rice. Can you think of anything else we need?

   A: How about some chocolate-covered nuts?

   B: I said "need"!

◇ **PRACTICE 2. Expressing the future in time clauses. (Chart 4-3)**
Directions: Complete the sentences with the simple present or with **will** and/or the correct form of **be going to**. (In some blanks, both **will** and **be going to** may be possible.)

1. The strike has been going on for over two months now. The strikers *(return, not)*
   ___will not / are not going to return___ to work until they *(get)* __get__ a raise
   and the benefits they are demanding.

2. A: Have you heard any news about Barbara since her car accident?

   B: No, I've heard nothing. As soon as I *(hear)* _____ something, I *(let)* _____ you know.

3. A: I see you're reading *The Silk Road*. I'd really like to read it sometime.

   B: I *(lend)* _____ it to you as soon as I *(finish)* _____ it.

   A: Really? Thanks!

4. When Rita *(get)* _____ her driver's license next week, she *(be)* _____
   _____ able to drive to school every day.

5. A: Mr. Jackson called. He'll be here at the garage to pick up his car in a few minutes. He
   (be, not) _____ very happy when he *(learn)* _____
   about the bill for repairs on his car. Do you want to talk to him when he *(come)*
   _____ in and *(ask)* _____ about his bill?

   B: Not especially, but I will.

6. After Ali *(return)* _____ to his country next month, he *(start)* _____
   _____ working at the Ministry of Agriculture.

7. According to the newspaper, the Department of Transportation *(build)* _____
   _____ a new four-lane highway into the city. In my opinion, it *(be)*
   _____ obsolete before they *(complete)* _____ it. It seems to
   me that a six-lane highway is needed to handle the heavy traffic.

8. Relax. The plumber is on his way. He *(be)* _____ here before there *(be)*
   _____ a flood in the kitchen. Let's just keep mopping up the water the best we can.

◇ **PRACTICE 3. Using the present progressive to express future time. (Chart 4-4)**
   Directions: Change the verbs in *italics* to the present progressive for those sentences that express a planned event or definite intention. In some sentences, no change is possible.

   1. A: The package has to be there tomorrow. Will it get there in time?
      B: Don't worry. I'm *going to send* it by express mail.
         › *I'm sending it by express mail.*

   2. A: What's the weather report?
      B: It is going to rain tomorrow morning. *(no change)*
         → *(Not possible: It's raining tomorrow morning.)*

   3. A: Would you like to have dinner with me tonight, Pat?
      B: Thanks, but I'm *going to have* dinner with my sister and her husband.

   4. A: What *are you going to do* this evening?
      B: I'm *going to study* at the library.

   5. A: The phone is ringing.
      B: I'll *got* it.

   6. A: Did you know that Bill and Sue are engaged?
      B: No. That's great! When *are* they *going to get* married?
      A: In September.

   7. A: You're *going to laugh* when I tell you what happened to me today!
      B: Oh? What happened?

   8. A: Have you lived here long?
      B: No, not long. Only about a year. But we're *going to move* again next month. My father's company has reassigned him to Atlanta, Georgia.

   9. A: I tried to register for Professor Stein's economics class, but it's full. *Is* he *going to teach* it again next semester?
      B: I think so.

   10. A: Son, I'm *not going to send* you any money this month. You're spending far too much. You need to learn to be more careful.
       B: But Dad . . . !
       A: Just do the best you can. Your mother and I *are going to come* to visit you next month. We can talk about it then.

◇ **PRACTICE 4. Future progressive. (Chart 4-5)**
   Directions: Complete the sentences with the future progressive or the simple present of the verbs in parentheses.

   1. Just relax, Antoine. As soon as your sprained ankle *(heal)* __heals__ , you can play soccer
      again. At this time next week, you *(play)* __will be playing__ soccer again.

   2. I'll meet you at the airport tomorrow. After you *(clear)* _____ customs, look
      for me just outside the gate. I *(stand)* _____ right by the door.

3. Ingrid and Ruth won't be at this school when classes *(start)* _____ next semester. They *(attend)* _____ a new school in Taiwan.

4. Please come and visit today when you *(have)* _____ a chance. I *(shop)* _____ from 1:00 to 2:30, but I'll be home after that.

5. I won't be here next week. I *(attend)* _____ a seminar in Los Angeles. Ms. Gomez will substitute-teach for me. When I *(return)* _____ , I will expect you to be ready for the midterm examination.

◇ **PRACTICE 5. The future perfect and the future perfect progressive. (Charts 4-6 and 4-7)**
Directions: Complete the sentences with the future perfect or the future perfect progressive of the verbs in the list. Include any words in parentheses. Use each verb only once.

arrive	listen	✔rise	smoke
fly	ride	save	teach

1. By the time I get up tomorrow morning, the sun *(already)* <u>will already have risen /</u> <u>will have already risen</u> .

2. This is a long trip! By the time we get to Miami, we _____ on this bus for over 15 hours.

3. We're going to be late meeting my brother's plane. By the time we get to the airport, it *(already)* _____ .

4. He's never going to stop talking. In 15 more minutes, we _____ _____ to him lecture for three solid hours. I don't even know what he's saying anymore.

5. What? You're smoking another cigarette? At this rate you _____ _____ a whole pack by lunchtime. Don't you think you should cut down a little?

6. This is the longest flight I have ever taken. By the time we get to New Zealand, we _____ for 13 hours. I'm going to be exhausted.

7. Douglas has been putting some money away every month to prepare for his trip to South America next year. By the end of this year, he _____ enough. It looks like he's going to make it.

8. Can you believe it? According to our grammar teacher, by the end of this semester she _____ more than 3,000 students from 42 different countries. She has been teaching for nearly 20 years — and she still loves it!

CHAPTER 5
Adverb Clauses of Time and Summary of Verb Tenses

◇ **PRACTICE 1. Adverb clauses of time. (Charts 5-1 and 5-2)**

Directions: Change the position of the adverb clause in the sentence. Underline the adverb clause in the given sentence, and underline the adverb clause in the new sentence. Punctuate carefully.

1. I didn't feel any older <u>when I reached my 21st birthday</u>.

   → *When I reached my 21st birthday, I didn't feel any older.*

2. <u>I had a cup of tea</u> before I left for work.

3. After I get home from work, I <u>like to read the evening newspaper</u>.

4. Since my watch broke, I <u>have been late to work three times</u>.

5. <u>My cat hides under the house</u> whenever it rains.

6. <u>I'm going to get a job</u> once I finish school.

7. While I was waiting for my bus, I <u>heard a gunshot</u>.

8. <u>The village will have no electric power</u> until a new generator is installed.

9. The last time I was in Taipei, <u>I saw Mr. Wu</u>.

10. As soon as we saw the tornado heading toward our town, <u>we ran to the basement of the town hall</u>.

◇ **PRACTICE 2. Adverb clauses of time. (Charts 5-1 and 5-2)**
Directions: Using the words in parentheses, make logical connections between the ideas in Column A with the ideas in Column B. Punctuate carefully and pay attention to verb tenses. Underline the adverb clauses in the new sentences.

Examples: 1. <u>As soon as the taxi **gets** here</u>, we can leave.
        2. I turned off the TV <u>before I left the room</u>.

Column A
1. Our taxi will get here. *(as soon as)*
2. I turned off the TV. *(before)*
3. I parachuted from a plane. *(the first time)*
4. My boss stormed into my office *(while)*
5. Ceylon had been independent for 24 years. *(after)*
6. Jack fell off his bicycle. *(since)*
7. Ms. Johnson will return your call. *(as soon as)*
8. John will learn how to use a computer. *(once)*
9. I won't return this book to the library. *(until)*
10. Sue dropped a carton of eggs. *(as)*
11. Anna will go to class. *(the next time)*
12. The flooding river raced down the valley. *(when)*
13. The rice will be done. *(just as soon as)*
14. When I go to bed at night, I like to read. *(until)*

Column B
A. She was leaving the store.
B. It destroyed everything in its path.
✔ C. We can leave.
D. I get sleepy.
✔ E. I left the room.
F. Its name was changed to Sri Lanka.
G. We can eat.
H. She'll have some free time.
I. I'll finish my research project.
J. I was both terrified and exhilarated.
K. I was talking on the phone to an important client.
L. He'll be able to work more efficiently.
M. He's had to use crutches to walk.
N. She'll remember to take her grammar book.

◇ **PRACTICE 3. Verb tenses in adverb clauses of time. (Chapters 1 → 5)**
Directions: Choose the letter of the correct answer.

1. After Jessica ___C___ her degree, she intends to work in her father's company.
   A. will finish   B. will have finished C. finishes   D. is finishing

2. By the time I go to bed tonight, I _____ my work for the day.
   A. will finish   B. have finished   C. will have finished D. finish

3. When my parents _____ for a visit tomorrow, they will see our new baby for the first time.
   A. will arrive   B. arrived   C. will have arrived D. arrive

4. Fatemah looked down to discover a snake at her feet. When she saw it, she _____ .
   A. was screaming B. had screamed   C. screamed   D. screams

5. By the time Alfonso finally graduated from high school, he _____ seven different schools because his parents moved frequently.
   A. attended   B. was attending   C. had attended   D. had been attending

6. Until you learn to relax more, you _____ your ability to speak English.
   A. haven't improved   C. don't improve
   B. aren't improving   D. won't improve

7. I borrowed four books on gardening the last time I _____ to the library.
   A. go   B. went   C. had gone   D. have gone

8. Before I started the car, all of the passengers _____ their seat belts.
   A. will buckle   B. had buckled   C. buckle   D. have buckled

9. It seems that whenever I travel abroad, I _____ to take something I need.
   A. forgot   B. am forgetting   C. forget   D. had forgotten

10. When I see the doctor this afternoon, I _____ him to look at my throat.
    A. will ask   B. asked   C. will have asked   D. ask

11. After ancient Greek athletes won a race in the Olympics, they _____ a simple crown of olive leaves.
    A. received   B. had received   C. were receiving   D. have received

12. After the race _____ , the celebration began.
    A. had been won   B. is won   C. will be won   D. has been won

13. I'll return Bob's pen to him the next time I _____ him.
    A. see   B. will see   C. will have seen   D. have seen

14. I _____ all of the questions correctly since I began this grammar exercise on verb tenses.
    A. am answering   B. answer   C. have answered   D. answered

15. A small stone struck the windshield while we _____ down the gravel road.
    A. drive   B. were driving   C. had driven   D. had been driving

◇ **PRACTICE 4. Verb tense review. (Chapters 1 → 5)**
Directions: Use any appropriate tense for the verbs in parentheses.

1. My grandfather (*fly, never*) _____ in an airplane, and he has no intention of ever doing so.

2. Jane isn't here yet. I (*wait*) _____ for her since noon, but she still (*arrive, not*) _____ _____ .

3. In all the world, there (*be*) _____ only 14 mountains that (*reach*) _____ _____ above 8,000 meters (26,247 feet).

4. I have a long trip ahead of me tomorrow, so I think I'd better go to bed. But let me say good-bye now because I won't see you in the morning. I (*leave, already*) _____ _____ by the time you (*get*) _____ up.

5. Right now we (*have*) _____ a heat wave. The temperature (*be*) _____ in the upper 90s (upper 30s Celsius) for the last six days.

6. Last night I (*go*) _____ to a party. When I (*get*) _____ there, the room was full of people. Some of them (*dance*) _____ , and others (*talk*) _____ . One young woman (*stand*) _____ by herself. I (*meet, never*) _____ her, so I (*introduce*) _____ myself to her.

7. About three yesterday afternoon, Jessica *(lie)* _____ in bed reading a book. Suddenly she *(hear)* _____ a loud noise and *(get)* _____ up to see what it was. She *(look)* _____ out the window. A truck *(back, just)* _____ into her new car!

8. Next month I have a week's vacation. I *(plan)* _____ to take a trip. First, I *(go)* _____ to Madison, Wisconsin, to visit my brother. After I *(leave)* _____ Madison, I *(go)* _____ to Chicago to see a friend who *(study)* _____ at the university there. She *(live)* _____ in Chicago for three years, so she *(know)* _____ her way around the city. She *(promise)* _____ to take me to many interesting places. I *(be, never)* _____ in Chicago, so I *(look)* _____ forward to going there.

9. Yesterday while I *(sit)* _____ in class, I *(get)* _____ the hiccups. The person who *(sit)* _____ next to me told me to hold my breath. I *(try)* _____ that, but it didn't work. The instructor *(lecture)* _____ _____, and I didn't want to interrupt him, so I just sat there trying to hiccup quietly. Finally, after I *(hiccup)* _____ for almost five minutes, I *(raise)* _____ my hand and *(excuse)* _____ myself from class to go get a drink of water.

10. The weather has been terrible lately. It *(rain)* _____ off and on for two days, and the temperature *(drop)* _____ drastically. It *(be)* _____ really cold today. Just three days ago, the sun *(shine)* _____ _____ and the weather *(be)* _____ pleasant. The weather certainly *(change)* _____ quickly here. I never know what to expect. Who knows? When I *(wake)* _____ up tomorrow morning, maybe it *(snow)* _____ .

◇ **PRACTICE 5. Verb tense review. (Chapters 1 → 5)**
Directions: Complete the sentences with the verbs in parentheses. Use any appropriate tense.

On June 20th, I returned home. I *(1. be)* _____ away from home for two years. My family *(2. meet)* _____ me at the airport with kisses and tears. They *(3. miss)* _____ me as much as I had missed them. I *(4. be)* _____ very happy to see them again. When I *(5. get)* _____ the chance, I *(6. take)* _____ a long look at them. My little brother *(7. be)* _____ no longer little. He *(8. grow)* _____ a lot. He *(9. be)* _____ almost as tall as my father. My little sister *(10. wear)* _____ a green dress. She *(11. change)* _____ quite a bit, too, but she *(12. be, still)* _____ mischievous and inquisitive. She *(13. ask)* _____ me a thousand questions a minute, or so it seemed. My father *(14. gain)* _____ some weight, and his hair *(15. turn)* _____ a little grayer, but otherwise he was just as I had remembered him. My mother *(16. look)* _____ a little older, but not much. The wrinkles on her face *(17. be)* _____ smile wrinkles.

◇ **PRACTICE 6. Verb tense review. (Chapters 1 → 5)**
   Directions: Complete the sentences with the verbs in parentheses. Use any appropriate tense.

On June 20th, I will return home. I *(1. be)* _____ away from home for two years by that time. My family *(2. meet)* _____ me at the airport with kisses and tears. They *(3. miss)* _____ me as much as I have missed them. I *(4. be)* _____ very happy to see them again. When I *(5. get)* _____ a chance, I *(6. take)* _____ a long look at them. My little brother *(7. be, no longer)* _____ so little. He *(8. grow)* _____ at least a foot. He *(9. be)* _____ almost as tall as my father. My little sister *(10. wear, probably)* _____ a green dress because that's her favorite color. She *(11. change)* _____ quite a bit, too, but she *(12. be, still)* _____ mischievous and inquisitive. She *(13. ask)* _____ me a thousand questions a minute, or so it will seem. My father *(14. gain, probably)* _____ some weight, and his hair *(15. turn)* _____ a little grayer, but otherwise he will be just as I remember him. My mother *(16. look)* _____ a little older, but not much. The wrinkles on her face *(17. be)* _____ smile wrinkles.

◇ **PRACTICE 7. Verb tense review. (Chapters 1 → 5)**
   Directions: Complete the sentences with the verbs in parentheses. Use any appropriate tense.
   PART I.

A: What *(1. seem)* _____ to be the trouble, Ms. Jones?

B: I *(2. send)* _____ in my money for a subscription to your magazine, *Computer Data*, two months ago, but to date I *(3. receive, not)* _____ any issues.

A: I'm sorry to hear that. Unfortunately, one of our main computers *(4. function, not)* _____ at the moment. However, our computer specialists *(5. work)* _____ very hard to fix it at the present time. We *(6. start)* _____ your new subscription as soon as possible.

B: Thank you.

PART II

A: Where's Sonia? I *(1. see, not)* _____ her lately.

B: She *(2. recuperate, at home)* _____ .

A: Oh? What *(3. recuperate, she)* _____ from?

B: She *(4. hurt)* _____ her back while she *(5. play)* _____

volleyball last week in the game against South City College.

A: What happened? How *(6. she, hurt)* _____ her back?

B: She *(7. try)* _____ to spike a ball when she *(8. collide)*

_____ with another player and *(9. fall)* _____ to the ground.

She *(10. land)* _____ hard and *(11. twist)* _____ her back.

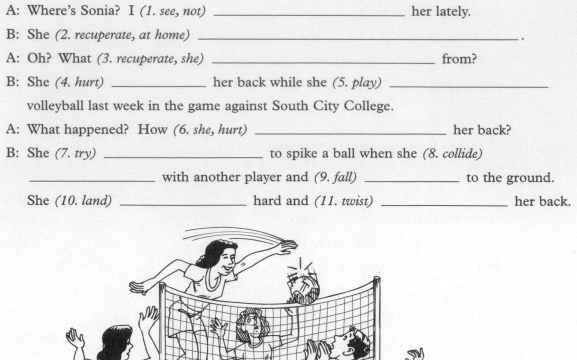

A: Gosh, that's too bad. I'm sorry to hear that. How's she doing?

B: Well, she's pretty uncomfortable. She *(12. wear)* _____

a special brace on her back for the last five days. Needless to say, she *(13. be, not)*

_____ able to play volleyball since her injury. She probably

(14. be, not) _____ able to play again for at least a month.

A: *(15. her doctor, allow)* _____ her to play in the

national tournament at the end of the summer?

B: She *(16. have)* _____ the brace on her back for more than

seven weeks by then, so I think he will.

A: I hope so. I know how much she likes to compete in volleyball games. And the team

really needs her.

PART III.

A: Hi, Jim. How's it going?

B: Great.

A: *(1. you, enjoy)* _____ the rock concert last night?

B: You bet! I had a terrific time.

A: Tell me about it. I *(2. go, never)* _____ to a rock concert.

B: Well, I *(3. go, never)* _____ to a rock concert before either, so I

(4. know, not) _____ what to expect. I've been to symphony concerts

lots of times, but never a rock concert. Ten minutes before the concert was supposed to

start, hundreds of teenagers *(5. try, still)* _____ to find their

seats. The place was a madhouse. I thought that things would settle down once the

concert began. Boy, was I wrong! As soon as the lead singer *(6. appear)* _____

on the stage, everyone *(7. start)* _____ screaming at the top of their lungs.

I couldn't hear myself think. But after a while things calmed down. And the music was

great. At one time during the concert, while the lead singer *(8. sing)* _____

_____ a famous hit song, many people in the audience knew the song so

well that they sang along with him. All in all, the concert *(9. be)* _____ a lot of

fun, but very noisy.

A: It does sound like it was a lot of fun!

PART IV.

Mark Twain, the author of the *The Adventures of Tom Sawyer,* is one of America's best-

loved storytellers. He *(1. grow up)* _____ in a small town on the Mississippi River.

As a young boy, he *(2. admire, greatly)* _____ _____ the pilots of the

riverboats and dreamed about being a riverboat pilot on the mighty river. He pursued his

dream, and by the age of 22, he himself *(3. become)* _____ _____ a riverboat

pilot. Later in life, when he *(4. become)* _____ a writer, many of his stories

(5. contain) _____ elements of his own experiences. He wrote many

humorous stories and articles about life on the Mississippi River before he *(6. die)*

_____ in 1910 at the age of 74. Sadly, Twain *(7. work)* _____

on a new story for several months before his death, but he *(8. finish, never)* _____

_____ it. Over the years since his death, his boyhood home in

Hannibal, Missouri, *(9. become)* _____ a favorite place for Americans

to visit to learn about Twain and life on the Mississippi at the turn of the 19th century.

◇ **PRACTICE 8. Test A: Verb tenses. (Chapters 1 → 5)**
   Directions: Choose the correct answer.

Example: I've been in this city for a long time. I __C__ here sixteen years ago.
   A. have come   B. was coming   C. came   D. had come

1. "Hurry up! We're waiting for you. What's taking you so long?"
   "I _____ for an important phone call. Go ahead and leave without me."
   A. wait   B. will wait   C. am waiting   D. have waited

2. "Robert is going to be famous someday. He _____ in three movies already."
   "I'm sure he'll be a star."
   A. has been appearing   C. has appeared
   B. had appeared   D. appeared

3. "Where's Polly?"
   "She _____."
   A. is in her room studying   C. studies in her room
   B. in her room is studying   D. has in her room studied

4. "Hello? Alice? This is Jeff. How are you?"
   "Jeff? What a coincidence! I _____ about you when the phone rang."
   A. was just thinking   C. have just been thinking
   B. just thought   D. was just thought

5. "What _____ about the new simplified tax law?"
   "It's more confusing than the old one."
   A. are you thinking   C. have you thought
   B. do you think   D. have you been thinking

6. "When is Mr. Fields planning to retire?"
   "Soon, I think. He _____ here for a long time. He'll probably retire either next year or the
   year after that."
   A. worked   C. has been working
   B. had been working   D. is working

7. "Why did you buy all this sugar and chocolate?"
   "I _____ a delicious dessert for dinner tonight."
   A. make   C. am going to make
   B. will make   D. will have made

8. "Let's go! What's taking you so long?"
   "I'll be there as soon as I _____ my keys."
   A. found   B. will find   C. find   D. am finding

9. Next week when there _____ a full moon, the ocean tides will be higher.
   A. is being   B. is   C. will be   D. will have been

10. While I _____ TV last night, a mouse ran across the floor.
    A. watch   B. watched   C. was watching   D. am watching

11. Fish were among the earliest forms of life. Fish _____ on earth for ages and ages.
    A. existed   B. are existing   C. exist   D. have existed

12. The phone _____ constantly since Jack announced his candidacy for president this morning.
    A. has been ringing   C. had rung
    B. rang   D. had been ringing

13. The earth _____ on the sun for its heat and light.
    A. is depend   B. depending   C. has depend   D. depends

14. I don't feel good. I _____ home from work tomorrow.
    A. am staying   B. stay   C. will have stayed   D. stayed

15. Today there are weather satellites that beam down information about the earth's atmosphere.
    In the last two decades, space exploration _____ great contributions to weather forecasting.
    A. is making   B. has made   C. made   D. makes

16. On July 20, 1969, Astronaut Neil Armstrong _____ down onto the moon, the first person
    ever to set foot on another celestial body.
    A. was stepping   B. stepped   C. has stepped   D. was step

17. The plane's departure was delayed because of mechanical difficulties. When the weary
    passengers finally boarded the aircraft, many were annoyed and irritable because they _____
    in the airport for three and a half hours.
    A. are waiting   C. have been waiting
    B. were waiting   D. had been waiting

18. If coastal erosion continues to take place at the present rate, in another fifty years this beach
    _____ anymore.
    A. doesn't exist   C. isn't existing
    B. isn't going to exist   D. won't be existing

19. Homestead High School's football team _____ a championship until last season, when the
    new coach led them to win first place in their league.
    A. has never won   C. had never been winning
    B. is never winning   D. had never won

20. Non-native speakers need many years of intensive language study before they can qualify as
    interpreters. By the end of this year, Chen _____ English for three years, but he will still
    need more training and experience before he masters the language.
    A. will be studying   C. will have been studying
    B. has studied   D. has been studying

◇ **PRACTICE 9. Test B: Verb tenses. (Chapters 1 → 5)**
   Directions: Choose the correct answer.

Example: I've been in this city for a long time. I __c__ here sixteen years ago.
   A. have come   B. was coming   C. came   D. had come

1. "May I speak to Dr. Paine, please?"
   "I'm sorry, he _____ a patient at the moment. Can I help you?"
   A. is seeing   B. sees   C. has been seeing   D. was seeing

2. "When are you going to ask your boss for a raise?"
   " _____ to her twice already! I don't think she wants to give me one."
   A. I've talked   B. I've been talking   C. I was talking   D. I'd talked

3. "Do you think Harry will want something to eat after he gets here?"
   "I hope not. It'll probably be after midnight, and we _____ ."
   A. are sleeping   C. have been sleeping
   B. will be sleeping   D. be sleeping

4. Paul, could you please turn off the stove? The potatoes _____ for at least thirty minutes.
   A. are boiling   C. have been boiling
   B. boiling   D. were boiling

5. "Is it true that spaghetti didn't originate in Italy?"
   "Yes. The Chinese _____ spaghetti dishes for a long time before Marco Polo brought it back to Italy."
   A. have been making   C. had been making
   B. have made   D. make

6. "I once saw a turtle that had wings. The turtle flew into the air to catch insects."
   "Stop kidding. I _____ you!"
   A. don't believe   C. didn't believe
   B. am not believing   D. wasn't believing

7. "Could someone help me lift the lawnmower into the pickup truck?"
   "I'm not busy. I _____ you."
   A. help   B. will help   C. am going to help   D. am helping

8. My family loves this house. It _____ the family home ever since my grandfather built it 60 years ago.
   A. was   B. has been   C. is   D. will be

9. Here's an interesting statistic: On a typical day, the average person _____ about 48,000 words. How many words did you speak today?
   A. spoke   B. was speaking   C. speaks   D. is speaking

10. I know you feel bad now, Tommy, but try to put it out of your mind. By the time you're an adult, you _____ all about it.
   A. forget   C. will forget
   B. will have forgotten   D. forgot

11. It's against the law to kill the black rhinoceros. They ____ extinct.
    A. became   B. have become   C. become   D. are becoming

12. After ten unhappy years, Janice finally quit her job. She ____ along with her boss for a long time before she finally decided to look for a new position.
    A. hadn't been getting   C. didn't get
    B. isn't getting   D. hasn't been getting

13. The National Hurricane Center is closely watching a strong hurricane over the Atlantic Ocean. When it ____ the coast of Texas sometime tomorrow afternoon, it will bring with it great destructive force.
    A. reaches   B. will reach   C. is reaching   D. reaching

14. At one time, huge prehistoric reptiles dominated the earth. This Age of Dinosaurs ____ much longer than the present Age of Mammals has lasted to date.
    A. lasted   B. was lasting   C. has lasted   D. had lasted

15. Jim, why don't you take some time off? You ____ too hard lately. Take a short vacation.
    A. worked   B. work   C. were working   D. have been working

16. The city is rebuilding its dilapidated waterfront, transforming it into a pleasant and fashionable outdoor mall. Next summer when the tourists arrive, they ____ 104 beautiful new shops and restaurants in the area where the old run-down waterfront properties used to stand.
    A. will found   B. will be finding C. will have found D. will find

17. A minor earthquake occurred at 2:07 A.M. on January 3. Most of the people in the village ____ at the time and didn't even know it had occurred until the next morning.
    A. slept   B. had slept   C. were sleeping   D. sleep

18. The little girl started to cry. She ____ her doll, and no one was able to find it for her.
    A. has lost   B. had lost   C. was losing   D. was lost

19. According to research reports, people usually ____ in their sleep 25 to 30 times each night.
    A. turn   B. are turning   C. have turned   D. turned

20. Jane's eyes burned and her shoulders ached. She ____ at the computer for five straight hours. Finally, she took a break.
    A. is sitting   B. has been sitting C. was sitting   D. had been sitting

CHAPTER 6
Subject–Verb Agreement

◇ **PRACTICE 1. Preview: subject–verb agreement. (Chapter 6)**
Directions: Correct the mistakes in the use of singular and plural forms.

1. My mother wear$_\wedge$ glasses. [*s* inserted]

2. Elephant is large animals.

3. Your heart beat faster when you exercise.

4. Healthy hearts needs regular exercise.

5. Every child in the class know the alphabet.

6. Some of the magazine at the dentist's office are two year old.

7. A number of the students in my class is from Mexico.

8. One of my favorite subject in school is algebra.

9. There's many different kind of insects in the world.

10. Writing compositions are difficult for me.

11. The United State have a population of more than 250 million.

12. Most of the people in my factory division likes and gets along with one another, but a few of

    the worker doesn't fit in with the rest of us very well.

◇ **PRACTICE 2. Pronunciation and spelling of final -s/-es. (Chart 6-1)**
Directions: Add **-s** or **-es** to these words to spell them correctly, and give the pronunciation of the ending.

1. ball __s__ /z/

2. wish __es__ /əz/

3. aunt __s__ /s/

4. flower ____ ____

5. park ____ ____

6. touch ____ ____

7. month ____ ____

8. tree ____ ____

9. keep ____ ____

10. dress ____ ____

11. valley ____ ____

12. industry ____ ____

13. swallow ____ ____

14. cliff ____ ____

15. bath ____ ____

16. bathe ____ ____

◇ **PRACTICE 3. Basic subject–verb agreement. (Chart 6-2)**
   Directions: Choose the correct verb, singular or plural, for each subject.

   1. The weather *is, are* cold.

   2. Vegetables *is, are* good for you.

   3. A dog *barks, bark.*

   4. Dogs *barks, bark.*

   5. Ann *is, are* at home.

   6. Ann and Sue *is, are* at home.

   7. Every boy and girl *is, are* here.

   8. A boy and a girl *is, are* in the street.

   9. The furniture in that room *is, are* comfortable.

   10. The chairs in that room *is, are* comfortable.

   11. The furniture in those rooms *is, are* comfortable.

   12. The chair, as well as the table, *is, are* made of wood.

   13. The chairs, as well as the table, *is, are* made of wood.

   14. The chair, as well as the tables, *is, are* made of wood.

   15. Eating vegetables *is, are* good for you.

◇ **PRACTICE 4. Subject–verb agreement: using expressions of quantity. (Chart 6-3)**
   Directions: Choose the correct verb, singular or plural, for each subject.

   1. Some of the road *is, are* closed due to flooding.

   2. Some of the roads *is, are* closed due to flooding.

   3. A lot of that movie *is, are* full of violence.

   4. A lot of movies *is, are* full of violence.

   5. Three-fourths of the pizza *has, have* already been eaten.

   6. Three-fourths of the pizzas *has, have* already been eaten.

   7. Most of the houses *was, were* destroyed by fire.

   8. Most of the house *was, were* destroyed by fire.

   9. One of the houses *was, were* destroyed by fire.

   10. Each of the houses *is, are* in ruins.

   11. Each house *is, are* in ruins.

   12. Every one of the houses *has, have* serious damage.

   13. Every house *has, have* serious damage.

   14. None of the houses *has, have* escaped damage.

15. None of the city *is, are* safe at night.

16. None of the cities *is, are* safe at night.

17. The number of desks in that classroom *is, are* thirty-five.

18. A number of stores *is, are* closed today because of the holiday.

◇ **PRACTICE 5. Subject–verb agreement: using *there* + *be* and some irregularities.**
   (Charts 6-4 and 6-5)
   Directions: Choose the correct verb, singular or plural, for each subject.

1. There *is, are* a cup on the table.

2. There *is, are* some cups on the table.

3. Why *isn't, aren't* there any windows in the classroom?

4. Why *isn't, aren't* there any chalk for the chalkboard?

5. States *is, are* political units.

6. The United States *is, are* in North America.

7. The news in that newspaper *is, are* biased.

8. Economics *is, are* an important area of study.

9. Diabetes *is, are* an illness. Mumps *is, are* another kind of illness. Rabies *is, are* a disease
   you can get from being bitten by an infected animal.

10. 100 meters *isn't, aren't* a long distance to travel by car.

11. Five minutes *isn't, aren't* too long to wait.

12. Six and four *is, are* ten.

13. People *is, are* interesting.

14. English *is, are* a common language.

15. The English *is, are* friendly people.

16. The elderly in my country *is, are* given free medical care.

◇ **PRACTICE 6. Subject–verb agreement. (Charts 6-2 → 6-5)**
   Directions: Choose the correct completion for each sentence.

1. Nearly 40 percent of the people in our town never *votes, vote* in local elections.

2. A number of students *has, have* participated in intensive language programs abroad.

3. The number of students who knew the answer to the last question on the exam *was, were*
   very low.

4. Every one of the boys and girls in the school *knows, know* what to do if the fire alarm rings.

5. *Isn't, Aren't* Portuguese spoken in Brazil?

6. A lot of Brazilians *speaks and understands, speak and understand* Spanish.

7. Why *is, are* the police standing over there?

8. Why *does, do* most of the television stations broadcast news at the same hour?

9. Some of the most important books for my report *is, are* not available in the school library.

10. There *has, have* been times when I have seriously considered dropping out of school.

11. Not one of the women in my office *has, have* received a promotion in the past two years. All of the promotions *has, have* gone to men.

12. The news on the radio and TV stations *confirms, confirm* that a serious storm is approaching our city.

13. Geography *is, are* fascinating. Mathematics *is, are* fascinating.

14. Mathematics and geography *is, are* my favorite subjects.

15. By law, every man, woman, and child *is, are* guaranteed the right to free speech.

16. *Isn't, Aren't* sugar and pineapple the leading crops in Hawaii?

17. Why *is, are* there a shortage of certified school teachers at the present time?

18. How many states in the United States *begins, begin* with the letter "A"?*

19. The United States *consists, consist* of 50 states.

20. What places in the world *has, have* no snakes?

21. Politics *is, are* a constant source of interest to me.

22. *Was, Were* there ever any doubt in your mind about the outcome of the election?

*Look in the *Answer Key* for the answer to this question.

CHAPTER 7
Nouns

◇ **PRACTICE 1. Final -s/-es. (Chapter 6 and Chart 7-1)**
Directions: Add final **-s/-es** where necessary. Do not change, add, or omit any other words in the sentences.

1. A bird care $\overset{s}{\wedge}$ for its feather $\overset{s}{\wedge}$ by cleaning them with its beak.

2. There are many occupation in the world. Doctor take care of sick people. Pilot fly airplane. Farmer raise crop. Shepherd herd sheep.

3. An architect design building. An archeologist dig in the ground to find object from past civilizations.

4. The first modern computer were developed in the 1930s and 1940s. Computer were not commercially available until the 1950s.

5. There are several factory in my hometown. The glass factory employ many people.

6. Kangaroo are Australian animal. They are not found on any of the other continent, except in zoo.

7. Mosquito are found everywhere in the world, including the Arctic.

8. At one time, many people believed that tomato were poisonous.

9. Bird, fish, insect, and mammal are different species. Each group of these life form shares physical characteristic.

10. Most of the creature in the world possess the five sense of sight, hearing, touch, taste, and smell. However, these sense are often more highly developed in one species than another. Bird have a highly developed sense of sight. For instance, an eagle can spot a small lizard from high in the air. The lizard would be undetectable by a human being from the same distance. Animal that hunt by following a trail on the ground may have poor eyesight but a keen sense of smell. For example, dog see a blurred, gray world because they are nearsighted and cannot see colors. However, they can smell thousands of times better than human being can.

◇ **PRACTICE 2. Plural nouns. (Chart 7-1)**
Directions: Write the plural form of each noun.

1. foot _____feet_____
2. hero _____heroes_____
3. knife _____
4. quality _____
5. doorway _____
6. gentleman _____
7. wolf _____
8. quiz _____
9. custom _____
10. video _____
11. potato _____

12. deer _____
13. ox _____
14. donkey _____
15. mystery _____
16. chief _____
17. thief _____
18. flash _____
19. memo _____
20. memorandum _____
21. crisis _____
22. mouth _____

◇ **PRACTICE 3. Irregular foreign plurals. (Chart 7-1)**
Directions: Use the correct plural forms of the nouns in the list to complete the sentences.
Use each word only once.

bacterium	datum	oasis
crisis	hypothesis	phenomenon
criterion	medium	stimulus
curriculum	memorandum	✓thesis

1. Graduate students are often required to write long papers in which they state an opinion and give evidence to support it. These papers are often referred to as ___theses___.

2. Thunder and lightning are _____ of nature.

3. Before the students began their chemistry experiments, they stated theories to explain what was going to happen in their experiments. In other words, they made _____.

4. The government of that country is unstable. The country has faced many political _____ in the last ten years. It has had to face one problem after another.

5. The office supervisor, Ms. Hall, is well known for the large number of _____ she sends to her staff. She believes it is necessary to write many notes to remind the staff of things that need to be taken care of.

6. The mass _____ include radio, television, newspapers, magazines, and the Internet.

7. The teacher wanted to make sure the students understood the standards by which she would make her judgments. She carefully explained the _____ she would use to judge the students' work.

8. All of the departments at the university provide descriptions of their _____ in the school catalog. Look there to find out what courses each department offers.

9. Certain factors cause plants to grow. These _____ are light, water, and fertile soil.

10. Very small living things that can cause disease are called germs. Germs are forms of _____ .

11. In a desert, there are places where water is available and a few plants grow. These areas are called _____ .

12. The researcher assembled numerous facts through months of investigation. She used the _____ she had gathered to write a report for a scientific journal.*

◇ **PRACTICE 4. Possessive nouns. (Chart 7-2)**
Directions: Make the *italicized* nouns possessive by adding apostrophes and final *-s/-es*.

1. He put the mail in the *secretary*'s mailbox.

2. There are three secretaries in our office. The *secretaries*' mailboxes are in the hallway.

3. Tom has two cats. The *cat*   food and water dishes are on a shelf in the laundry room.

4. I have one cat. My *cat*   feet are white, but the rest of her is black.

5. My *child*   name is Olaf.

6. Their *children*   names are Pablo and Gabriella.

7. My *supervisor*   names are Ms. Anderson and Mr. Gomez.

8. Your *supervisor*   name is Mrs. Wright.

9. I'm interested in other *people*   ideas.

10. This *month*   issue of that magazine has several interesting articles.

---

*In very formal English, **data** is considered plural, but more typically it is used as a singular noncount noun.
Typical use: **This data is** *not correct.*
Formal use: **These data are** *not correct.*

11. All of the performers in the play did well. The audience applauded the *actor*   excellent
    performances.

12. An *actor*   income is uncertain.

◇ **PRACTICE 5. Using apostrophes. (Charts 7-2 and 8-1)**
    Directions: Add apostrophes as necessary to mark a possessive noun or a contraction with a pronoun.

    1. Mary's father works at the Northgate Medical Center. He's a dentist.

    2. Jacks parents live in Georgia. His parents home is in Atlanta.

    3. Our teachers last name is Wells. Shes one of the best teachers in the school.

    4. Our teachers last names are Wells, Hunt, and Moore. Theyre all good teachers.

    5. Ms. Wells husband is also a teacher. Ms. Hunts husband is an engineer.

    6. Its well known that a bear likes sweet food. Its favorite food is honey.

    7. Anns telephone number is 555-8989. Ours is 555-8998. People often confuse hers with
       ours, so we get frequent calls for her.

    8. The tiger is a beautiful animal. Its coat is orange and white with black stripes. Although its
       found in the wild only in Asia, people throughout the world appreciate its beauty and power.
       Even though tigers are protected by laws, many scientists predict their extinction within
       twenty to thirty years. How much poorer our childrens and grandchildrens lives will be
       when the earth no longer has a place for tigers, elephants, wolves, and numerous other
       animals whose fates rely upon the wisdom and compassion of humankind.

◇ **PRACTICE 6. Using nouns as modifiers. (Chart 7-3)**
    PART I. Complete the sentences with the nouns in the parentheses. Use the singular or plural
    form as appropriate.

    1. They sell __toys__ at that store. It is a __toy__ store. *(toy)*

    2. I like _____ salads. I like salads that contain _____ . *(tomato)*

    3. I have a _____ garden. I grow many different kinds of _____ .
       (vegetable)

    4. Some people are addicted to _____ . They are _____ addicts. *(drug)*

    5. *(two + lane)* We drove down an old, narrow highway that had only _____ .
       We drove down a _____ highway.

    6. *(five + minute)* I gave a _____ speech in class. My speech lasted
       for _____ .

7. *(sixty + year + old)* The Watkins live in a _____ house. Any house that is _____ usually needs a lot of repairs.

PART II. **PART II.** Complete the sentences, using the *italicized* noun as a modifier.

8. That handbook is for *students*. It is a ___ student handbook. ___

9. Their baby is *ten months old*. They have a _____

10. Our trip lasted for *three days*. We took a _____

11. She is a psychologist for *children*. She is a _____

12. I wrote a check for *fifty dollars*. I wrote a _____

13. I will get *three credits* for that course. It is a _____

14. Their house has *nine rooms*. It is a _____

15. That food is for *dogs*. It is _____

16. That room is for *guests*. It is a _____

17. The professor asked us to write a paper of *five pages*. She asked us to write a _____
_____

18. I have a sister who is *ten years old* and a brother who is *twelve years old*. I have a _____
_____

◇ **PRACTICE 7. Using nouns as modifiers. (Chart 7-3)**
Directions: What do you call the following?

1. someone who robs banks → *a bank robber*

2. someone who fights bulls → *a bullfighter* ⋆

3. someone who collects stamps → *a stamp collector* ⋆⋆

4. someone who trains animals

5. someone who tells stories⋆

6. someone who collects taxes⋆⋆

7. something that opens cans

8. something that wipes a windshield

_____

⋆Usually spelled as one word.

⋆⋆Spelled with **-or** instead of **-er**.

9. someone who earns wages

10. someone who manages an office

11. someone who programs computers

12. someone who keeps books*

13. something that removes spots

14. something that holds pots

15. someone who makes trouble*

16. someone who reads minds

17. something that dries hair

18. something that peels potatoes

19. someone who plays tennis

20. someone who fights fires*

21. somcone who carries mail

◇ **PRACTICE 8. Count and noncount nouns. (Charts 7-4 → 7-6)**
  Directions: Add final *-s/-es* to the *italicized* noun if necessary. Do not add, omit, or change any other words.

1. Jackie has brown *hair* (no change) and gray *eye*S.

2. My parents gave me some good *advice* .

3. I always drink *water* when I'm hot and thirsty.

4. We ate some *sandwich* for lunch.

5. A gambler needs a lot of *luck* .

6. I have a lot of *homework* to do tonight.

7. Maria took some good *photograph* at the wedding party.

8. Our country has made a lot of *progress* in the last 25 years.

9. That book has a lot of good *idea* .

10. An encyclopedia contains a lot of *information* .

11. I've learned a lot of new *vocabulary* .

12. Olga knows a lot of American *slang* .

---

*Usually spelled as one word.

13. Every day, I learn some more new *word*   in English.

14. Pioneer women had a lot of *courage*   .

15. We bought some new *clothing*   .

16. I bought a pair of leather *glove*   .

17. At rush hour there are a lot of *car*   on the highway. Although normally it takes us twenty *minute*   to drive from home to work, at rush hour it can take an hour because of the heavy *traffic*   .

18. Ann likes to wear *jewelry*   . Today she is wearing four *ring*   , six *bracelet*   , and a *necklace*   .

19. I had *meat*   , *rice*   , *vegetable*   , and some *tea*   for dinner.

20. *Butterfly*   begin as *caterpillar*   and then are transformed into beautiful *insect* with vividly colored *wing*   .

21. *Traveling*   can impart a great deal of *education*   as well as *enjoyment*   . When *people*   travel to another *country*   , they can learn about its *history*   , *economy*   , and *architecture*   , as well as become acquainted with its various *custom*   .

22. Although everyone believed the accused man was guilty of murder, he was acquitted. The prosecuting attorney did not have enough *evidence*   to convict him, nor even any *proof* that he had been able to enter the murdered man's house.

23. You need more *calcium*   in your diet, Mrs. Abbott. It is found in milk and milk *product*   , in dark green *vegetable*   such as broccoli, and in *fish*   such as *sardine*   . You need *vitamin*   , too. Do you take *vitamin pill*   ?

24. Last night we heard about a new political crisis in our country. Do you have any more *information*   about it? Are there any reports of *violence*   ? We've heard a lot of rumors about what may be happening, but we're anxious to know the *truth*   . We need *fact*   , not *gossip*   .

25. We received a postcard from Melissa today. She's on vacation in the country, staying in a two-hundred-*year*   -old inn. She says that the area has fantastic *scenery*   and a wonderful golf course. She's having a lot of *fun*   .

◇ **PRACTICE 9. Using articles. (Charts 7-7 and 7-8)**
   Directions: Complete the sentences with *a/an, the,* or *Ø*.

1. __Ø__ lightning is __a__ flash of light. It is usually followed by __Ø__ thunder.

2. Last night we had __a__ terrible storm. Our children were frightened by __the__ thunder.

3. _____ circles are _____ round geometric figures.

4. _____ circle with _____ slash drawn through it is an international symbol meaning "Do not do this!" For example, _____ circle in _____ illustration means "No Smoking."

5. _____ milk I put on my cereal this morning was sour because someone forgot to put it in _____ refrigerator after dinner last night.

6. _____ milk is an important source _____ of protein and _____ calcium.

7. _____ wisdom comes more from _____ understanding than from _____ knowledge.

8. I always appreciate _____ wisdom of my mother's advice.

9. In class yesterday, I sat next to two women. _____ woman on my right had _____ right answer to _____ teacher's question about verb forms.

10. Maria is _____ independent young woman who knows her own mind.

11. Have you met Mr. and Mrs. Smith? Mrs. Smith used to be _____ teacher, but now she is _____ computer programmer. Mr. Smith is _____ architect. The Smiths used to live in _____ apartment, but recently they have built _____ house.

12. Frank Lloyd Wright is _____ name of _____ famous architect. He is _____ architect who designed the Guggenheim Museum in New York. He also designed _____ hotel in Tokyo. _____ hotel was designed to withstand _____ earthquakes.

13. According to today's paper, the mayor has appointed _____ committee to study what improvements need to be made in the city. _____ committee, which plans to continue its study through the rest of this year, will discuss _____ following proposals: (1) to build _____ new sewage disposal plant and (2) to create _____ new park. In _____ present proposal, _____ new park would have _____ swimming pool.

14. The large oak tree growing at _____ southeast corner of Vine Avenue and Pine Street has been _____ landmark since pioneer days. Unfortunately, it was shattered by _____ bolt of lightning during the thunderstorm last night.

15. My uncle's hobby is restoring _____ old cars. Right now he's working on _____ 1922 automobile. It's _____ antique car and has great value.

16. My aunt's new car has _____ power windows, _____ cassette player, and _____ multi-adjustable driver's seat.

17. Patty is my ten-year old daughter. She likes to play _____ jokes on people. Yesterday she put _____ frog into _____ lunchbox she saw sitting on _____ table in _____ school lunchroom.

18. Long-term exposure to _____ sun between 10 A.M. and 3 P.M. can be harmful. _____ person's skin will eventually become wrinkled and more susceptible to _____ cancer.

19. Yesterday I locked my keys in my car. Using _____ coat hanger, I tried to reach _____ lock inside _____ window next to _____ driver's seat, but I couldn't get _____ door to unlock. I thought about calling _____ police, but finally decided to call my wife. I suggested she take _____ taxi and bring her keys to open _____ car for me.

20. We flew to Dallas and then rented _____ car. On _____ second day we had _____ car, it wouldn't start, so the rental agency provided us with another one.

21. Mary is wearing _____ beautiful ring today. It is made of _____ gold and _____ rubies. _____ gold in her ring was mined in Canada. _____ rubies came from Burma.

22. One of the first things you need to do when you move to _____ new city is to find _____ place to live. Most _____ newspapers carry _____ advertisements (called "want ads") for _____ apartments that are for rent. If you find _____ ad for _____ furnished apartment, _____ apartment will probably contain _____ stove and _____ refrigerator. It will also probably have _____ furniture such as _____ beds, _____ tables, chairs, and maybe _____ sofa.

23. My wife and I have recently moved to this city. Since we're going to be here for only _____ short time, we're renting _____ furnished apartment. We decided that we didn't want to bring our own furniture with us. _____ apartment is in _____ good location, but that's about the only good thing I can say about it. Only one burner on _____ stove works. _____ refrigerator is noisy, and _____ refrigerator door won't stay closed unless we tape it shut. _____ bed sags in the middle and creaks. All of the rest of _____ furniture is old and decrepit too. Nevertheless, we're still enjoying living in this city. We may have to look for _____ another apartment, however.

24. This sentence is _____ last sentence in this exercise. This is _____ end of the exercise.

Directions: Complete the sentences with *much* or *many*. Give the plural forms of the nouns as necessary. Choose the correct singular or plural verb as necessary.

1. How _____many_____ watch _es___ does the average person own?

2. How _____much_____ jewelry __∅___ do you usually wear?

3. How _____many_____ ~~tooth~~ ___teeth___ do babies usually have when they're born?

4. How _____much_____ bread __∅___ is \ ~~are~~ there in the bread drawer?

5. I don't know _____ American slang _____ .

6. Tending young children takes too _____ patience _____ for me. I'm better at spending time with young adults.

7. How _____ video _____ do you usually rent during a month?

8. My hair is all frizzy today. There *is \ are* _____ humidity _____ in the air.

9. The lawyers interviewed _____ witness _____ to the crime.

10. I haven't done _____ traveling _____ in the last few years.

11. We visited _____ village _____ on our trek that were without running water.

12. They didn't have _____ fun _____ when they were children because they were forced to work from sunup to sundown.

13. Pedro hasn't made _____ progress _____ in improving his English because he speaks Spanish with his friends all day long.

14. Our cat is old and lazy. He doesn't catch _____ mouse _____ .

15. There *isn't \ aren't* _____ news _____ in the paper this morning about the hurricane in Costa Rica.

16. Captain Cook had _____ adventure _____ during his sailing trips.

17. There *was \ were* so _____ smog _____ in Los Angeles yesterday that you couldn't see any of the hills or mountains from the city.

18. I didn't know _____ grammar _____ before taking this course. I'm not familiar with _____ grammar textbook _____ .

19. The streets in the downtown area of my city are no longer safe. There *is \ are* too _____ car thief _____ , mugger _____ , and pickpocket _____ .

20. There *isn't \ aren't* _____ information _____ of _____ importance in some daily newspapers.

21. How _____ active volcano _____ is \ are there in the world today?

22. Politicians give _____ speech _____ during their careers.

◇ **PRACTICE 11. Using *a few/few; a little/little*. (Chart 7-10)**
Directions: Without substantially changing the meaning of the sentences, replace the *italicized* words with *a few, (very) few, a little*, or *(very) little*.

1. I think that ~~some~~ *a little* lemon juice in a salad makes it taste better.

2. Many people have graduate degrees, but ~~not many~~ *(very) few* people have more than two graduate degrees.

3. You might reach your goal if you put forth *some* more effort.

4. Even though the mountain is very steep and the climb is hazardous, *several* strong-willed people have managed to reach the top.

5. The number of people in the world who are willing to risk their lives climbing a dangerous mountain is small. *Not very many* people will actually face death to climb a mountain.

6. The professor lectured very clearly. As a result *not man*y students had questions at the end of the class period.

7. I have to go to the post office because I have *some* letters to mail.

8. Every day Max goes to his mailbox, but it is usually empty. He gets *not much* mail.

9. My friend arrived in the United States *several* months ago.

10. I think you could use some help. Let me give you *some* advice.

11. *Not many* days ago I met a very interesting person.

12. Margaret likes sweet tea. She usually adds *some* honey to her tea. Sometimes she adds *some* milk, too.

13. Has anyone ever called you on the phone and tried to sell you something you didn't want? I have *not much* patience with people who interrupt my dinner to try to sell me a magazine.

14. He's a lucky little boy. Because his parents have taken good care of him, he has had *not many* problems in his young life.

◇ **PRACTICE 12. Using *of* in expressions of quantity. (Charts 7-11 and 7-12)**
Directions: Add *of* or write Ø in the blanks.

1. When I went shopping yesterday, there were several __Ø__ jackets in my size.

2. Several __of__ the jackets were made of 100 percent wool.

3. Many _____ students work part-time while they are attending school.

4. Many _____ my classmates have part-time jobs.

5. Some _____ dairy products are high in cholesterol.

6. Some _____ my favorite kinds of food are not good for me to eat.

7. The teacher didn't fail any _____ the students in his class.

8. Any _____ passengers who have first-class tickets can board the plane first.

9. I picked a few _____ flowers from my garden and made a bouquet.

10. A few _____ the flowers in the bouquet have already wilted.

11. Everyone needs a little _____ luck in life.

12. Most _____ babies learn to walk before their first birthday.

13. Our company imports products from abroad. Most _____ these new products are

    testmarketed in selected cities.

14. Most _____ people enjoy picnics.

15. Some _____ the people we want to invite for our anniversary dinner will be on vacation.

16. Not all _____ trees lose their leaves in winter.

17. All _____ deciduous trees lose their leaves during the cold part of the year, whereas

    evergreen trees do not.

18. All _____ the trees in that orchard have been sprayed with pesticides.

19. Both _____ my sisters attended Harvard University.

20. Both _____ women are talented in music and drama.

21. The concert was delayed because two _____ the musicians had left their instruments on

    the bus.

22. A trio consists of three _____ musicians.

23. I have two _____ sisters and three _____ brothers.

24. Two _____ my brothers live in St. Louis.

25. A hundred _____ people bought tickets to the lecture.

26. Two hundred _____ people came to the public meeting.

27. Hundreds _____ people visit the Lincoln Memorial every day.

28. A thousand _____ years ago, the power of electricity had not been discovered.

29. Three thousand _____ years ago, the number of planets in our solar system was unknown.

30. Thousands _____ years ago, the wheel was invented.

◇ **PRACTICE 13. Using *one, each, every*. (Chart 7-13)**
   Directions: Choose the correct word in *italics*.

   1. Each *student, students* in the class is required to take the final examination.

   2. Each of the *student, students* in the class is required to take the final examination.

   3. Every one of the *room, rooms* in our apartment has at least one window.

   4. There is at least one window in every *room, rooms* in our apartment.

   5. My bedroom has only one, very small *window, windows*.

   6. One of the smallest *window, windows* in our apartment is in my bedroom.

   7. When John bought some supplies at the hardware store, he thought the total amount on the bill was incorrect, so he checked each *item, items* on his bill very carefully.

   8. Each of the *item, items* on the bill was correct.

   9. Alex took an extended vacation in northern Europe last summer. Sweden was one of the *country, countries* he visited when he was in Scandinavia.

   10. Susan has traveled widely, but she has visited only one Scandinavian *country, countries*.

   11. Tom believes that there are no strangers. He views each *person, people* in the world as a friend he hasn't met yet.

   12. I answered every *question, questions* on the examination. I didn't skip any.

   13. Each one of the *child, children* in the class was given a piece of paper and a crayon. Each *child, children* drew a picture.

   14. Hunger is one of the biggest *problem, problems* in the world today.

   15. Each of the *applicant, applicants* for the scholarship is required to furnish five references (that is, names of people who are willing to write letters of recommendation).

CHAPTER 8
Pronouns

◇ **PRACTICE 1. Personal pronouns. (Chart 8-1)**
   Directions: Choose the correct pronoun in *italics*.

   1. Please take these papers and give *it, them* to Mike.

   2. Tom asked Ann and *I, me* about the new theater.

   3. Janice and *I, me* live in an apartment.

   4. Just between you and *I, me,* I think Tom is going to lose *him, his* job.

   5. When a player committed a foul, the referee blew *him, his* whistle and pointed at *she, her.*

   6. A boa constrictor, which is a very large snake, kills *its, it's* victims by strangling *it, them.*

   7. People can easily send a letter to another city. *It, They* simply have to drop *it, them* into a

      collection box.

   8. The teacher said to the students, "Throughout the semester, please write *your, yours*

      compositions on every other line, and be sure to write *it, them* in ink."

   9. Both Ron and *I, me* are expecting some mail. Are those letters for *he, him* or *I, me?*

   10. *My, Mine* roommate and *I, me* have to share a bookshelf. *She, Her* keeps *her, hers* books

       on the top two shelves, and I keep *my, mine* on the bottom two shelves.

   11. A monkey spends most of *its, it's* time in trees.

   12. I studied English when I was in high school. But I haven't studied *it, them* since I

       graduated from high school ten years ago, so I've forgotten a lot of *it, them.*

   13. I looked everywhere in my room for my keys, but I couldn't find *it, them.*

   14. After work, Mr. Gray asked to speak to Tim and *I, me* about the company's new policies.

       He explained *it, them* to *we, us* and asked for *our, ours* opinions.

   15. The first person I saw when I got off the plane was my sister. My father and *she, her* had

       come to the airport to greet *I, me.* My father was waiting for *we, us* in *his, him* car

       outside the airport.

Directions: Complete the sentences with pronouns. In some of the blanks there is more than one possibility. Choose the appropriate singular or plural verb in parentheses where necessary.

1. A student should always hand in ___his/her; his or her; his; her___ work on time.

2. Students should always hand in ___their___ work on time.

3. Teachers determine _____ students' course of study.

4. A teacher determines _____ students' course of study.

5. Each student is expected to hand in _____ work on time.

6. All students are expected to hand in _____ work on time.

7. If someone calls, please ask _____ to leave a message.

8. Somebody left _____ raincoat in the classroom.

9. The flight crew on our long plane trip were very attentive. _____ efforts to make us comfortable were greatly appreciated.

10. My family is wonderful. _____ *(has, have)* always helped me in any way _____ could.

11. The crowd enjoyed the game. _____ got excited whenever the home team scored.

12. The crowd at the last concert broke attendance records. _____ *(was, were)* the largest audience ever to have been in that stadium to listen to a rock concert.

◇ **PRACTICE 3. Reflexive pronouns. (Chart 8-4)**

Directions: Complete the sentences by using appropriate reflexive pronouns.

1. John overslept and missed his plane to San Francisco. He was angry at ___himself___ for not checking his alarm clock before going to bed.

2. I was a stranger at the party. I stood alone for a while, then walked over to an interesting-looking person and introduced _____ .

3. Jason has only _____ to blame for the mistake he made.

4. Sue, please help _____ to some more cake. And would you like some more coffee?

5. All of you who are successful Olympic athletes should be very proud of _____ . Your achievements inspire people all over the world.

6. The math team from our high school won the state competition. They should pat _____ on the back for a job well done.

7. When I was younger, I would get embarrassed by my mistakes. Now I am more relaxed and have found it is easier to laugh at _____ .

8. Children need to learn to rely upon _____ .

9. My father always told me to handle my problems _____ and not to expect others to solve them for me.

10. The little girl lost her teddy bear in the park. She tried to be brave, but at bedtime she cried _____ to sleep.

11. Edward lived a lonely life as a young boy. With no one to play with, he would often sit on the front steps talking to _____ or to an imaginary friend.

12. What delicious cheesecake, Amelia! Did you make this _____ ?

13. Whenever we have problems in life, we have to be careful not to waste too much time feeling sorry for _____ .

14. After a busy day at work, I always enjoy a little time by _____ .

15. Fred wanted to be able to do something unusual, so he taught _____ to drink a glass of water while standing on his head.

16. I can't help you, Bob. You'll have to solve your problem by _____ .

17. Jane did not join the rest of us. She sat in the back of the room by _____ .

18. You may think Stan is telling the truth, but I _____ don't believe him.

19. It is important for all of us to be honest with _____ .

20. Now that their children are grown, Mr. and Mrs. Grayson live by _____ .

21. You _____ have to make a decision, Ann. No one can make it for you.

22. I don't know what to tell you, Sue and Jack. You will have to take care of that problem _____ .

23. When everybody else forgot his birthday, Ralph decided to give _____ a birthday present. He bought a new shirt for _____ .

◇ **PRACTICE 4. Pronoun agreement. (Charts 8-1 → 8-5)**
Directions: Complete the sentences with appropriate pronouns. Choose the correct words in *italics* as necessary.

1. We should ask ___ourselves___ if ___we are___ *(is, are)* doing everything in ___our___ power in order to solve the problem of hunger in the world.

2. Each of you should ask _____ if _____ *(is, are)* doing everything in _____ power in order to solve the problem of hunger in the world.

3. All of you should ask _____ if _____ *(is, are)* doing everything in _____ power in order to solve the problem of hunger in the world.

4. People should ask _____ if _____ *(is, are)* doing everything in _____ power in order to solve the problem of hunger in the world.

5. One should ask _____ if _____ *(is, are)* doing everything in _____ power in order to solve the problem of hunger in the world.

6. Everyone should ask _____ if _____ *(is, are)* doing everything in _____ power in order to solve the problem of hunger in the world.

◇ **PRACTICE 5. Forms of *other*. (Chart 8-7)**
Directions: Use a form of ***other*** to complete the sentences.

1. I had a red pen, but I seem to have lost it. I guess I'd better buy ___another___ one.

2. Some people are lazy. _____ are energetic. Most people are a mixture of both.

3. Two countries share the island of Hispañola. One is Haiti. _____ is the Dominican Republic.

4. Excuse me, waiter? Could you please bring me _____ fork? I dropped mine on the floor.

5. Only two countries in South America, Bolivia and Paraguay, are inland. All of _____ _____ have coastlines.

6. Washington is one of the five states of the United States with borders on the Pacific Ocean. What are _____ states?*

7. A successful harvest depends largely on the weather. In some years, there is an abundant harvest. In _____ years, the harvest is lean, especially when there is a drought.

_____

*Look in the *Answer Key* for the answer to this question.

8. I enjoyed watching everyone at the beach. Some people were playing volleyball, while _____ were picnicking. Some were listening to music, some were sleeping, and _____ were just lying in the sun. _____ people were swimming in the surf.

9. I'll be finished with this report soon. Give me _____ twenty minutes and I'll be ready to go with you.

10. Ali has been here studying for almost three years. In _____ six months he will have his degree and return to his country.

11. Only three of the forty-two applicants for the job possess the necessary qualifications. None of _____ will be considered.

12. I work for Mr. Anderson every _____ Saturday. I help him with chores around his house.

13. Scandinavia consists of four countries. One is Denmark. _____ are Finland, Norway, and Sweden.

14. Budapest, Hungary, is actually two cities. On one side of the Danube River lies Buda, and directly across from it, on _____ side of the river, lies Pest

15. Most of the candidates who will take the qualifying examination in May will probably pass the first time. _____ will have _____ chance next month.

16. Some people like to take vacations in the mountains. _____ prefer the seashore. Some people like to drive from place to place; _____ people prefer to get to their destinations as quickly as possible. Although many people like to travel on their vacations, many _____ prefer to just stay at home.

17. The Wolcott twins are identical. In _____ words, they look alike. But they also think alike. Sometimes when one begins a sentence, _____ one finishes it.

18. One of the most important inventions in the history of the world was the printing press. _____ was the electric light. _____ were the telephone, the television, and the computer.

19. To avoid competitive disadvantages, professional boxers are classified by weight groups. There are over a dozen different weight classes. One is called the flyweight group. _____ are the featherweight, middleweight, and heavyweight groups.

20. The committee meets every _____ Monday.

21. Joe and Frank, detectives in the police department, work as a team. They work well with each _____ .

14. Many of the _____ not used today. They are remnants of the past.
   A. railroad tracks around here are   C. railroad tracks around here is
   B. railroad's tracks around here is   D. railroads' tracks around here are

15. As we walked through the jungle, the _____ unusually quiet.
   A. monkeys were   B. monkeys was   C. monkies were   D. monkies was

16. At the news conference, several reporters didn't get clear answers to _____ questions.
   A. theirs   B. their   C. his and hers   D. his and her

17. I have a _____ sister.
   A. seven years old   B. seven-years-old   C. seven-year-old   D. seven years olds

18. There _____ in the world today.
   A. is many new computer company   C. are many new computers companies
   B. is many new computer companies   D. are many new computer companies

19. Self-esteem is important. It's important for people to like _____.
   A. oneself   B. yourself   C. him/herself   D. themselves

20. What _____ you used in picking a winner in the art contest?
   A. is the criteria   B. are the criteria   C. are the criterion   D. are the criterions

◇ **PRACTICE 8. Test B: Nouns and pronouns. (Chapters 6 → 8)**
Directions: Choose the correct completion.

Example: I don't get ___B___ .
   A. many mail   B. much mail   C. many mails   D. much mails

1. One of the dinner _____ broken.
   A. plate is   B. plates are   C. plates is   D. plate are

2. Most _____ hard.
   A. of students work B. students work   C. student works   D. of student works

3. Can you help me? I need _____ information.
   A. a little   B. little   C. a few   D. few

4. All of the athletes who took part in the international games should be very proud of _____ .
   A. himself   B. oneself   C. themselves   D. yourselves

5. Snow and rain _____ of nature.
   A. are phenomenon B. are phenomena   C. is phenomena   D. is phenomenon

6. I accidentally broke the _____ by stepping on it. I apologized to them for my carelessness.
   A. child's toy   B. child's toys   C. children's toy   D. childrens' toys

7. Our weather is cloudy in the winter. We don't have _____ .
   A. many sunshines B. many sunshine   C. much sunshines   D. much sunshine

8. Several of my friends are _____ reporters.
   A. newspaper   B. newspapers   C. newspaper's   D. newspapers'

9. Construction workers need _____ to build a highway.
   A. an heavy equipment   C. heavy equipments
   B. a heavy equipment   D. heavy equipment

10. Our classroom is supplied with _____ .
   A. plenty of chalks B. plenty of chalk   C. several chalks   D. several chalk

11. Knowing several _____ helpful if you work for an international corporation.
   A. languages are   B. language is   C. languages is   D. language are

12. Two-thirds of my _____ from the Middle East.
   A. classmates is   B. classmate are   C. classmate is   D. classmates are

13. There _____ in my country.
   A. are a lot of problem   C. is a lot of problems
   B. are a lot of problems   D. is a lot of problem

14. Winning a lottery is a rare occurrence. _____ very small.
   A. A number of winners is   C. A number of winners are
   B. The number of winners is   D. The number of winners are

15. There are several means of mass communication. The newspaper is one. Television is
    _____ .

    A. other   B. the other   C. another   D. the another

16. Each of the _____ own cage.

    A. birds has their   B. bird has its   C. birds have their   D. birds has its

17. I really need _____ . Can we talk?

    A. some advice   B. an advice   C. some advices   D. advices

18. Every _____ a license plate.

    A. cars have   B. cars has   C. car has   D. car have

19. The swimming team has done well this year. All of _____ have trained very hard.

    A. their members   B. its members   C. it's members   D. theirs members

20. Next week, we're going to take a _____ .

    A. three day trips   B. three-day trip   C. three days trip   D. three days' trip

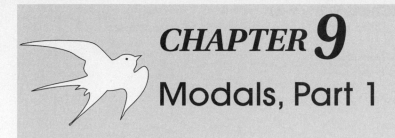

CHAPTER 9
Modals, Part 1

◇ **PRACTICE 1. Verb forms with modal auxiliaries. (Chart 9-1)**
   Directions: Choose the correct completion.

   1. Mary can _____ to the meeting.
      A. comes   B. to come   C. come

   2. Jack should _____ harder.
      A. studies   B. to study   C. study

   3. The whole team must _____ together in order to win the game.
      A. worked   B. to work   C. work

   4. We ought _____ before we drop in on Peter and Marcia. They may be busy.
      A. called   B. to call   C. call

   5. Paul can _____ Chinese very well because he studied it for six years.
      A. speaks   B. to speak   C. speak

   6. May I _____ you?
      A. can help   B. to help   C. help

   7. The construction crew might _____ the bridge in time for the holiday traffic.
      A. finished   B. to finish   C. finish

   8. We had better _____ an umbrella when we go out. It looks like it's going to rain.
      A. taken   B. to take   C. take

   9. I couldn't _____ that book because I didn't take any money with me.
      A. bought   B. to buy   C. buy

   10. The children should _____ "thank you" when you gave them their gifts.
       A. has said   B. to have said   C. have said

   11. Tom could _____ us to help him move.
       A. had asked   B. to have asked   C. have asked

   12. I can't find the grocery list. Gail must _____ it with her when she went out.
       A. has taken   B. to have taken   C. have taken

◇ **PRACTICE 2. Making polite requests. (Charts 9-2 → 9-4)**
　　Directions: Change the sentences into polite requests using the words in parentheses.

　　　1. I want you to hand me that book. *(would)*
　　　　→ *Would you (please) hand me that book?*

　　　2. I want you to give me some advice about buying a computer. *(could)*

　　　3. I want to borrow your wheelbarrow. *(could)*

　　　4. I want to have a cup of coffee. *(may)*

　　　5. I want to use your bicycle tomorrow. *(can)*

　　　6. I want you to read over my composition for spelling errors. *(would)*

　　　7. I want you to open the door for me. *(would you mind)*

　　　8. I want to leave early. *(would you mind)*

◇ **PRACTICE 3. Using *would you mind*. (Chart 9-4)**
　　Directions: Using the verb in parentheses, fill in the blank either with *if I* + PAST tense or with the
　　-ing form of the verb, as appropriate.

　　　1. A: It's cold in here. Would you mind *(close)* ____closing____ the window?
　　　　B: Not at all. I'd be glad to.

　　　2. A: It's cold in here. Would you mind *(close)* ____if I closed____ the window?
　　　　B: Not at all. Go right ahead. I think it's cold in here, too.

　　　3. A: Would you mind *(take)* _____ the book back to the library for me?
　　　　B: Not at all.

　　　4. A: This story you wrote is really good. Would you mind *(show)* _____ it to
　　　　　my English teacher?
　　　　B: Go right ahead. That'd be fine.

　　　5. A: I'll wash the dishes. Would you mind *(dry)* _____ them? That would
　　　　　help me a lot.
　　　　B: I'd be happy to.

　　　6. A: I'm feeling kind of tired and worn out. This heavy work in the hot sun is hard on me.
　　　　　Would you mind *(finish)* _____ the work yourself?
　　　　B: No problem, Grandpa. Why don't you go in and rest? I'll finish it up.

　　　7. A: Would you mind *(use)* _____ your name as a reference on this job
　　　　　application?
　　　　B: Not at all. In fact, ask them to call me.

8. A: Would you mind *(wait)* _____ here for just a minute? I need to run back to the classroom. I forgot my notebook.

   B: Sure. Go ahead. I'll wait right here.

9. A: I need to look up the meaning of the word "stationery." Would you mind *(borrow)* _____ your dictionary?

   B: No, I don't mind. I'm not using it right now.

10. A: Since this is the first time you've owned a computer, would you mind *(give)* _____ you some advice?

    B: Not at all. I'd appreciate it.

◇ **PRACTICE 4. *Must (not)* and *(do not) have to*. (Charts 9-5 and 9-6)**
   Directions: Choose the correct completion according to the meaning.

   1. Soldiers ___B___ disobey a superior officer.
      A. must/have to   B. must not   C. don't have to

   2. To stay alive, people _____ breathe oxygen.
      A. must/have to   B. must not   C. don't have to

   3. You _____ finish your work on this project before you go on vacation. You'll probably lose your job if you don't.
      A. must/have to   B. must not   C. don't have to

   4. If you have an aquarium, you _____ give your tropical fish too much food or they'll die.
      A. must/have to   B. must not   C. don't have to

   5. To be a successful mountain climber, you _____ have a great deal of stamina.
      A. must/have to   B. must not   C. don't have to

   6. Thank goodness we _____ eat fish again tonight. Dad didn't catch any today.
      A. must/have to   B. must not   C. don't have to

   7. You _____ exert yourself. You're still not fully recovered from your surgery.
      A. must/have to   B. must not   C. don't have to

   8. My room is a mess, but I _____ clean it before I go out tonight. I can do it in the morning.
      A. must/have to   B. must not   C. don't have to

   9. We really _____ help Marge move to her new apartment over the weekend. Not only is it too difficult for one person, but she still has her arm in a sling from her shoulder sprain a week ago.
      A. must/have to   B. must not   C. don't have to

   10. Bill is in the darkroom developing the negatives of the photos he took on his last trip to Peru. You _____ open the door while he's there because the light will ruin the pictures.
       A. must/have to   B. must not   C. don't have to

◇ **PRACTICE 5. Verb form review: _have to_. (Charts 9-5 and 9-6)**
  Directions: Complete the sentences with any appropriate form of *have to*. Include any words in parentheses.

1. A: *(you)* ___Do you have to___ leave so early?

   B: I'm afraid I do. I have some work I ___have to___ finish before I go to bed tonight.

2. Last night Jack ___had to___ go to a meeting. *(you)* ___Did you have to___ go to the meeting last night too?

3. Joan travels to the Soviet Union frequently. Luckily, she speaks Russian, so she *(not)* _____ rely on an interpreter when she's there.

4. I *(not)* _____ water the garden later today. Joe has agreed to do it for me.

5. I _____ write three term papers since the beginning of the semester.

6. Why *(Tom)* _____ leave work early yesterday?

7. I found some milk in the refrigerator, so we *(not)* _____ go to the store after all. There is plenty.

8. *(John)* _____ buy a round-trip ticket when he went to Egypt?

9. Matt is nearsighted. He _____ wear glasses ever since he was ten years old.

10. By the time this week is finished, I _____ take eight examinations in five days. The life of a student isn't easy!

11. *(you, not)* _____ return these books to the library today? Aren't they due?

12. If Jean stays in Brazil much longer, she _____ teach English part-time so that she'll have enough money to support herself. *(she)* _____ apply for a special work visa? Or can she work part-time on a student visa?

13. Because it was Emily's birthday yesterday, she *(not)* _____ do any of her regular chores, and her mother let her choose anything she wanted to eat for dinner.

14. When I arrived in Rome last week, I was looking forward to practicing my Italian. I'm disappointed because I *(not)* _____ speak Italian very much since I got here. Everyone keeps talking to me in English.

◇ **PRACTICE 6.** *Should, ought to, had better.* (Charts 9-7 and 9-8)

Directions: Give advice to the people in the following situations. Use ***should, ought to,*** or ***had better***. Choose from the suggested completions in the list, or use your own words.

> call home and talk to his family
> change clothes before he goes
> clean it up right away
> find a chemistry major to tutor her
> get his roommate a pair of earphones
> ✓join some clubs to meet people with similar interests
> listen to Tom before he fired him
> make her own decisions about her career and go to architecture school
> not eat so much
> not leave the room; apologize immediately; signal to a waiter for help
> stop for gas
> take it back sooner

1. Ann would like to make some new friends. → *I think she should/ought to join some clubs to meet people with similar interests.*

2. Ellen is having a lot of trouble in her chemistry class. She's failed the last two tests.

3. You didn't stop for gas, and then you ran out of gas on the highway.

4. Sam and Tim, both teenagers, have messed up the house, and their parents are coming home soon.

5. You had to pay a fine because your library book was overdue.

6. Ron is wearing jeans. He's expected at a formal reception this evening.

7. Mary's parents expect her to work in the family business, a shoe store, but she wants to be an architect.

8. Richard's roommate stays up very late studying. While his roommate is studying, he listens to loud music, and Richard can't get to sleep.

9. Pierre is feeling really homesick these days.

10. You have a stomach ache because you ate too much.

11. Tom didn't show up for work yesterday because he and his friend were in an auto accident. Tom was okay, but his friend was badly hurt, so Tom had to stay with him at the hospital. Tom didn't call his boss to tell him he wouldn't be at work. When Tom arrived at work today, his boss fired him immediately, refusing to listen to any of Tom's explanations for missing work.

12. A man was having dinner in a restaurant with a co-worker. When he got up, he accidentally bumped the table, spilling a plate of food onto the woman's lap. He looked at her in horror and left the room.

◇ **PRACTICE 7. *Be supposed to*. (Chart 9-9)**
Directions: Correct any errors in the use of ***be supposed to***.

1. The students are suppose to write a composition.

2. They supposed write it about a person they admire.

3. They're supposing to write it in ink.

4. They don't supposed to write it in pencil.

5. When are they suppose to hand it in?

◇ **PRACTICE 8. *Be supposed to*. (Chart 9-9)**
Directions: Restate the following rules in sentences with ***be supposed to***.

1. NO SMOKING → *You are not supposed to smoke.*

2. KEEP OFF THE GRASS.

3. NO EATING OR DRINKING IN THIS ROOM.

4. MOVE TO THE REAR OF THE BUS.

5. DO NOT JOKE WITH AIRPORT PERSONNEL WHILE YOUR HAND LUGGAGE IS BEING INSPECTED.

6. USE THE STAIRS IN CASE OF FIRE. DO NOT USE THE ELEVATOR.

7. NO LITTERING.

8. SLOWER TRAFFIC KEEP RIGHT.

◇ **PRACTICE 9. Let's, why don't, shall I/we. (Chart 9-10)**
Directions: Complete the dialogues with appropriate pronouns. If nothing is needed in the blank, write Ø.

1. A: We'll never find an apartment we can afford in the middle of the city. Why don't
   __we__ look for one in the suburbs. It's farther, but the apartments are probably less
   expensive.
   B: Okay. I'll drive. Let's __Ø__ drive to the suburbs right now.
   A: Why don't __we__ look in the newspaper first? We should look in the classified ads
   for that area. Do you have this morning's paper?
   B: No. Shall __I__ go get one?
   A: Good idea. I'll come with you.

2. A: I'm worried about Barbara. She's never this late.
   B: Let's not _____ worry. She's probably just held up in traffic.
   A: Why don't _____ call her parents? At least then we'll know if she left home on
   time.
   B: Okay, if it will make you feel better, but why don't _____ just try not to get upset?
   I'm sure she's okay.

3. A: This pasta is delicious! Why don't _____ try some?
   B: No, thank you. I'm full. Let's _____ ask for the check.
   A: What? No dessert? This place is famous for its pies. Why don't _____ stay and
   have some dessert?
   B: I couldn't eat another bite, but I'll wait for you. Shall _____ get the waiter for you?
   A: Yes, please, when you see him. Thanks. You sure you don't want any dessert?

4. A: I think it's time for us to fix up the apartment.
   B: Okay. Why don't _____ do something to the living room?
   A: That's a good idea. Shall _____ paint the walls?
   B: Sure. Sounds great.
   A: Okay. I'll go to the paint store. Shall _____ get the same color that's on there now,
   or a different one?
   B: Something different.
   A: Why don't _____ get an off-white?
   B: No. How about a light yellow?
   A: Okay. And while I'm gone, why don't _____ cover the furniture and floor so we
   won't drip paint on anything.
   B: Well, I'd really like to help, but I have to get back to work.
   A: What?!

◇ **PRACTICE 10. Using *could* and *should* to make suggestions. (Chart 9-11)**
  Directions: For each of these situations, give three suggestions with ***could***. Then give definite
  advice with ***should***.

1. It's late at night. Tony is home by himself. He hears a window break. He thinks it's a
   burglar. Now what? What could or should he do now?

   He **could** _hide under his bed._

   He **could** _pick up his baseball bat and go looking for the intruder._

   He **should** _leave the house and go to his neighbor's to call the police._

2. Bruce has helped his mother onto the train and escorted her to a seat. While he is saying
   goodbye, the train begins pulling away from the station. By the time he gets through the
   crowded aisles to the exit, the train is traveling fast. Now what?

   He **could** _____

   He **could** _____

   He **should** _____

3. Kim is an insomniac. Every night she tosses and turns until 2 or 3 A.M. and gets only a few
   hours of sleep. It's beginning to affect her work, as she has to be in her office at 8:00 A.M.
   She's always tired. She needs some advice.

   She **could** _____

   She **could** _____

   She **should** _____

4. You were driving in the countryside late at night, and you noticed that you were almost out of gas. You managed to make it to a small town nearby but discovered that the only gas station in town was closed. You decided to hitchhike to the next town and look for an open station, but the person who picked you up robbed you and left you stranded on a country road. Hitchhiking was a bad idea. What were some other possible courses of action you could have taken?

I could _____

I could _____

I should _____

CHAPTER 10
Modals, Part 2

◇ **PRACTICE 1. Degrees of certainty: *must* and *may/might/could*. (Chart 10-1)**
Directions: Which of the two completions is the speaker most likely to say? Choose the best completion.

1. "Look at all the children waiting for the bus. What time is it?"
   "It _____ be after 3:00. That's when school is out."
   A. must   B. might

2. "George says that we're going to have a very high inflation rate next year."
   "He _____ be right. I think his view is as good as anybody's. I've heard strong opinions on all sides of that issue."
   A. must   B. could

3. "Have you heard anything from Ed? Is he still in Africa?"
   "He _____ be, or he _____ already be on his way home. I'm just not sure."
   A. must . . . must   B. could . . . could

4. "Is that a famous person over there in the middle of that crowd?"
   "It _____ be. Everyone's trying to get her autograph."
   A. must   B. might

5. "Isn't Peter Reeves a banker?"
   "Yes. Why don't you talk to him? He _____ be able to help you with your loan."
   A. must   B. may

6. "Isn't Margaret's daughter over sixteen?"
   "She _____ be. I saw her driving a car, and you have to be at least sixteen to get a driver's license."
   A. must   B. might

7. "Overall, don't you think the possibility of world peace is greater now than ever before?"
   "It _____ be. I don't know. Political relationships can be fragile."
   A. must   B. may

8. "The speedometer on my car is broken."
   "Do you think you're driving over the speed limit?"
   "I don't know. I _____ ."
   A. must be   B. might be   C. am

9. "You've been on the go all day. Aren't you exhausted?"
   "Yes, I _____ . I can't remember when I've ever been this worn out."
   A. must be   B. may be   C. am

10. "Have you seen the new movie playing at the Bijou?"
    "No, but it _____ sad. Many people leaving the theater seem to have been crying."
    A. must be   B. might be   C. is

11. "Do you hear that squeak? What is it?"
    "I don't know. It _____ a mouse. Isn't that what a mouse sounds like?"
    A. must be   B. may be   C. is

12. "How old do you think Roger is?"
    "I just looked at his driver's license. He _____ 33."
    A. must be   B. might be   C. is

◇ **PRACTICE 2. Forms of modals. (Charts 10-1 → 10-5)**
   Directions: Complete the sentences with the appropriate form of the words in parentheses. Add *not* if necessary for a sentence to make sense.

1. A: Where's Ann?

   B: I don't know. She *(could + visit)* _____ her aunt and
      uncle right now. She usually visits them every Friday evening.

2. You *(should + watch)* _____ the movie on TV tonight. I
   highly recommend it. It's a classic.

3. I heard a loud crash in the next room. When I walked in, I found a brick on the floor, and
   the window was broken. Someone *(must + throw)* _____ the brick
   through the window.

4. Jack is in the employee lounge drinking coffee. He *(should + work)* _____
   _____ on his report right now. It's due at 3:00 this afternoon. He
   (should + waste) _____ his time in the employee lounge.

5. Do you hear the guitar music? Carla *(must + play)* _____ her guitar.

6. A: I need to see Tom. Where is he?

   B: In his room. Knock on his door softly. He *(might + take)* _____
      _____ a nap.

7. Michael wanted to go to the opera, but he put off buying a ticket, and now they're all sold.
   He *(should + buy)* _____ his ticket weeks ago. He
   (should + wait) _____ until now to try to get a ticket.

8. Bob was stopped by a police officer last night. He *(must + drive)* _____
   _____ too fast when she clocked him on her radar. She gave him
   a speeding ticket.

9. The staff *(must + plan)* _____ very well for the luncheon.
   There are still about ten people waiting to eat, and there's not enough food left.

10. A: Where's your bicycle?

    B: I don't know. One of my friends (*may + borrow*) _____ it.
       Gee, I hope it wasn't stolen. Maybe Sally borrowed it.

    A: Sally? She (*could + borrow*) _____ it. She has a
       broken leg. Why would she want to borrow your bicycle?

11. George didn't do very well on the test because he didn't understand what he was supposed
    to do. He (*could + listen*) _____ very carefully
    when the teacher gave the directions.

12. A: Joan was really upset when she found out that someone had told Alan about the surprise
       birthday party she gave him last night. She thinks Joe told him.

    B: Joe (*could + tell*) _____ him about it. He was out of town
       until just before the party. He barely got there in time from the airport.

13. A: Art has two full-time jobs this summer to make some money for school in the fall. He
       (*must + have*) _____ very much time to rest and do other things.

    B: That might explain why no one answered the door when I stopped by his house a little
       while ago. He (*must + sleep*) _____ .

14. A: Kathy just bought a new car, and now she's looking for a new apartment.

    B: She (*must + make*) _____ a lot of money in her new job.

◇ **PRACTICE 3. Making conclusions: *must* and *must not*. (Charts 10-1 → 10-5)**
   Directions: Make logical conclusions about these situations. Use ***must*** or ***must not*** for your
   "best guess."

   1. The Adams' house is dark and quiet. Their car isn't in the driveway.
      → *They must not be at home.*

   2. We had a test in class yesterday. Charles, who rarely studies and usually fails the tests, got a
      score of 95% this time.
      → *He must have studied for the test.*

   3. The man sitting behind us has been talking throughout the movie. He knows what's going
      to happen before it happens.

   4. Anita is in bed. The lights are out, and I can hear someone snoring.

   5. Mrs. Jenkins has lost some of her hearing. Yesterday the children asked her several times for
      some cookies, but she didn't answer.

   6. Jeremy's car radio is always set on the classical music station. He also keeps a supply of
      classical music tapes in the car.

   7. When Jeremy's wife is in the car with him, she always asks him to change the station or the
      tape.

   8. Diane never seems to have enough money. I tried to call her last night and got a recording
      telling me that her phone had been disconnected.

9. Four people had dinner together. Two of them ate wild mushrooms, and two of them didn't. The two who ate the mushrooms are now critically ill.

10. I heard a loud crash in the next room. I rushed in immediately and found our antique vase on the floor. It was broken. Five-year-old Bobby was playing quietly with his toy truck. The cat was leaping frantically from table to table. The window was open, and the breeze was blowing gently through the room. I wondered what had happened to the antique vase.

◇ **PRACTICE 4. Ability: *can* and *could*. (Chart 10-6)**
    Directions: Complete the sentences with ***can, can't, could***, or ***couldn't***.

1. Fish _____ talk.

2. I used to be a good swimmer. I _____ swim long distances when I was a teenager.

3. Why _____ all the nations of the world just get along in peace? Why are there always wars somewhere on the earth?

4. When I was younger, I _____ stay up past midnight and get up at dawn feeling refreshed and ready to go. I _____ do that any longer now that I'm middle-aged.

5. I _____ get to sleep last night because it was too hot in my room.

6. An illiterate person is someone who _____ neither read nor write.

7. My uncle was a wonderful craftsman. He made beautiful things out of wood. But he _____ read or write because he never went to school.

8. I had to put together my daughter's tricycle. It came from the factory unassembled. At first
I _____ figure out what to do, but finally, after hours of work, I managed to
get it assembled.

◇ **PRACTICE 5. Repeated action: *would*. (Chart 10-7)**
Directions: Complete the sentences using ***would*** and the verbs in the list. Use each verb only
once. Include any words in parentheses.

bring	drive	listen	throw
call	fall	take	wipe
✓come	knock	tell	✓yell

1. My father never liked to talk on the phone. Whenever it rang, he *(always)* __would always__
   __yell__ , "I'm not here!" Usually, he was only joking and __would come__ to the
   phone when it was for him.

2. I'll always remember Miss Emerson, my fifth grade teacher. Sometimes a student
   _____ asleep in her class. Whenever that happened, Miss Emerson
   _____ a piece of chalk at the student!

3. Until we finally had a long talk about it, my Aunt Pat *(never)* _____
   before coming over. In fact, she *(not even)* _____ on the
   door. She would just walk right in and catch us all by surprise.

4. I have fond childhood memories of my Uncle Joe. Whenever he came to visit, he *(always)* _____ me a little present.

5. When our kids were still living at home, I liked to go out to eat with my family. On every payday, I _____ the family to some restaurant for dinner.

6. People acquire strange habits. For example, my Uncle Oscar, who lived with us when I was a child, *(always)* _____ his plate with his napkin whenever he sat down to a meal.

7. I'll never forget evenings spent with my grandparents when I was a child. My grandmother _____ stories of her childhood seventy years ago, and we _____ intently and question her for every detail.

8. When I was a salesman, it seemed to me that I was in my car most of the time. I _____ to work to pick up my schedule, and then go from place to place all day, calling on small businesses.

◇ **PRACTICE 6. *Would rather.* (Chart 10-8)**
Directions: Complete the sentences with the suggestions in the list or your own words.

> be an environment lawyer   study Chinese
> go home   stay home
> not go out   not tell you
> ✔go to an opera
> go out with their friends . . . stay home with their parents

1. I went to a movie last night. I prefer operas to movies. I would rather **have gone to an opera**.

2. I studied French when I was in high school only because my parents wanted me to. I would rather _____.

3. Jack's parents want him to become a doctor. He'd rather _____, but he feels he has to respect his parents' wishes, so he has enrolled in medical school.

4. I know you want to know, but I'd rather _____. I told Marge that I'd keep it a secret.

5. Sometimes teenagers would rather _____ than _____.

6. I would rather _____ right after dinner at the restaurant last night, but my friends insisted on going back to John's apartment to listen to some music and talk. Tonight, I'd really rather _____. I want to get a good night's sleep for the first time all week.

◇ **PRACTICE 7. Test A: Modals and phrasal modals. (Chapters 9 and 10)**
   Directions: Choose the correct completion.

   Example: Peter __C__ rather sleep on a mattress than on the floor.
   A. shall   B. could   C. would   D. must

   1. Al painted his bedroom black. It looks dark and dreary. He _____ a different color.
      A. had to choose   C. must have chosen
      B. should have chosen   D. could have been choosing

   2. Tom is sitting at his desk. He's reading his chemistry text because he has a test tomorrow.
      He _____ .
      A. could study   C. will study
      B. should be studying   D. must be studying

   3. When Mr. Lee was younger, he _____ work in the garden for hours, but now he has to
      take frequent rests because he has emphysema.
      A. has got to   C. should be able to
      B. can   D. could

   4. Whenever my parents went out in the evening, I _____ the job of taking care of my
      younger brother.
      A. would get   C. must have gotten
      B. should get   D. had better get

   5. Yesterday I _____ to a furniture store. I bought a new lamp there.
      A. could go   C. could have gone
      B. went   D. ought to have gone

   6. Tom wasn't at the party last night. He must not _____ a ride. I know he wanted to
      come, but he didn't have a ride.
      A. be able to have gotten   C. have been able to get
      B. to have been able to get   D. be able to get

   7. Robert has a new car. He _____ it for a very good price. He paid 30 percent less than
      the regular retail cost.
      A. could buy   C. was supposed to buy
      B. had to buy   D. was able to buy

   8. "Did you enjoy the picnic?"
      "It was okay, but I'd rather _____ to a movie."
      A. go   B. be going   C. have gone   D. went

   9. "Why are you so sure that Ann didn't commit the crime she's been accused of committing?"
      "She _____ that crime because I was with her, and we were out of town that day."
      A. may not have committed   C. committed
      B. wasn't supposed to commit D. couldn't have committed

   10. "Since we have to be there in a hurry, we _____ take a taxi."
       "I agree."
       A. had better   C. have been used to
       B. may   D. are able to

11. "It _____ rain this evening. Why don't you take an umbrella?"
    "That's a good idea. May I borrow yours?"
    A. had better   B. could be   C. must   D. might

12. "_____ you hand me that pair of scissors, please?"
    "Certainly."
    A. May   B. Shall   C. Will   D. Should

13. Larry drove all night to get here for his sister's wedding. He _____ exhausted by the time he arrived.
    A. ought to be   C. must have been
    B. could be   D. will have been

14. "What are you doing here now? You _____ be here for another three hours."
    "I know. We got an early start, and it took less time than we expected. I hope you don't mind."
    A. couldn't   C. had better not
    B. might not   D. aren't supposed to

15. "_____ taking me downtown on your way to work this morning?"
    "Not at all."
    A. Can you   C. Would you mind
    B. Why don't you   D. Could you please

16. "I locked myself out of my apartment. I didn't know what to do."
    "You _____ your roommate."
    A. could have called   C. would have called
    B. may have called   D. must have called

17. "You haven't eaten anything since yesterday afternoon. You _____ be really hungry!"
    "I am."
    A. might   B. will   C. can   D. must

18. "How long have you been married?"
    "We _____ have been married for twenty-three years on our next anniversary."
    A. must   B. should   C. will   D. could

19. "I _____ there at 6 P.M. for the meeting, but my car won't start. Could you please give me a lift in your car?"
    "Sure. Are you ready to go now?"
    A. will be   B. may be   C. supposed to be   D. have got to be

20. "I left a cookie on the table, but now it's gone. What happened to it?"
    "I don't know. One of the children _____ it."
    A. may have eaten   C. had to eat
    B. could eat   D. should have eaten

◇ **PRACTICE 8. Test B: Modals and phrasal modals. (Chapters 9 and 10)**

Directions: Choose the correct completion.

Example: Peter ___C___ rather sleep on a mattress than on the floor.

    A. shall   B. could   C. would   D. must

1. "My boss is always looking over my shoulder whenever I do anything."
   "That _____ bother you."
   "But it does."
       A. shouldn't   B. might not   C. may not   D. won't

2. "This movie is boring and too violent."
   "I agree. _____ leave?"
       A. Will we   B. Why don't we   C. Must we   D. Would we

3. "Chris, you _____ the fish in the refrigerator before it spoils."
   "You're right. I didn't know it was still in the shopping bag."
       A. had better put   C. would rather put
       B. had to put   D. may put

4. "What does Mr. Griffin do for a living?"
   "Nothing. He's very rich. He _____ work for a living."
       A. must not   C. doesn't have to
       B. shouldn't   D. hadn't better

5. "Why are you so late?"
   "I _____ my aunt to the airport. The traffic was terrible!"
       A. could take   C. should take
       B. must have taken   D. had to take

6. "I heard that Laura was offered a job at a top computer firm in Chicago."
   "Oh? That's wonderful! She _____ very pleased."
       A. is supposed to be   C. must be
       B. might be   D. is

7. "My boss expects me to work this weekend."
   "You shouldn't _____ work on weekends."
       A. must   B. be going to   C. ought to   D. have to

8. "They towed my car away from the executive parking lot yesterday."
   "You _____ have parked there."
       A. may not   B. should not   C. must not   D. might not

9. "Are you going to have a big birthday party for your father?"
   "Not this year, but next year. He _____ 50 years old then."
       A. should be   B. must be   C. will be   D. has to be

10. "I need some help with this table. _____ you lift the other end, please?"
    "Sure, just a second."
        A. May   B. Should   C. Could   D. Shall

11. "How did you get my telephone number? It's not listed in the phone book, so you _____ have found it in the directory."
    "I got it from your mother."
        A. may not   B. won't   C. might not   D. couldn't

12. "Is that volcano dormant or active?"
    "Active. According to the experts, it _____ erupt again in the very near future."
    A. would   B. may be   C. could   D. had better

13. "Last year I _____ this fine print in these contracts, but now I can't."
    "You'd better go to the eye doctor."
    A. could read   C. should have read
    B. must have read   D. had to read

14. "Is littering against the law?"
    "Yes. There's a law that says that you _____ throw trash on the streets."
    A. don't have to   C. couldn't
    B. must not   D. might not

15. "Do you want to go to the seashore for vacation?"
    "I think I'd rather _____ to the mountains."
    A. to go   B. going   C. go   D. have gone

16. "Barbara just told me that she can't go to the meeting tonight."
    "She _____ go! We need her there for the financial report."
    A. has got to   B. has gotten to   C. have to   D. must be

17. "_____ letting me use your bicycle for a little while?"
    "Not at all."
    A. Please to   C. Will you
    B. Would you mind   D. Could you please

18. "We _____ be here. That sign says No Trespassing."
    "It's too late now. We're already here."
    A. couldn't   C. might not
    B. don't have to   D. aren't supposed to

19. "Harry's new jacket doesn't seem to fit him very well."
    "He _____ it on before he bought it."
    A. must have tried   C. should have tried
    B. was able to try   D. may have tried

20. "Do you like to play tennis?"
    "Yes. When I worked at the embassy, I _____ meet a friend at five every afternoon for a game."
    A. would   B. should   C. had better   D. would rather

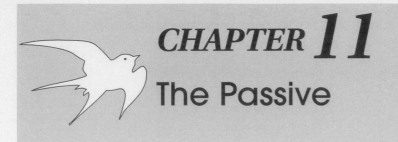

CHAPTER 11
The Passive

◇ **PRACTICE 1. Forming the passive. (Chart 11-1)**
   Directions: Change the active to the passive by writing the correct form of *be* in the blanks. Use the same tense for *be* in the passive sentence that is used in the active sentence.

Example: Mrs. Bell answered my question. .... My question __was__ **answered** by Mrs. Bell.

1. *simple present:*
   Authors write books. .... Books _____ **written** by authors.
2. *present progressive:*
   Mr. Brown is writing that book. .... That book _____ **written** by Mr Brown.
3. *present perfect:*
   Ms. Lee has written the report. .... The report _____ **written** by Ms Lee.
4. *simple past:*
   Bob wrote that letter. .... That letter _____ **written** by Bob.
5. *past progressive:*
   A student was writing the report. .... The report _____ **written** by a student.
6. *past perfect:*
   Lucy had written a memo. .... A memo _____ **written** by Lucy.
7. *simple future:*
   Your teacher will write a report. .... A report _____ **written** by your teacher.
8. *be going to:*
   Tom is going to write a letter. .... The letter _____ **written** by Tom.
9. *future perfect:*
   Alice will have written the report. .... The report _____ **written** by Alice.

10. The judges have made a decision. .... A decision _____ **made** by the judges.

11. Several people saw the accident. .... The accident _____ **seen** by several people.

12. Ann is sending the letters. .... The letters _____ **sent** by Ann.

13. Fred will plan the party. .... The party _____ **planned** by Fred.

14. The medicine had cured my illness. .... My illness _____ **cured** by the medicine.

15. The cat will have caught the mouse. ...... The mouse _____ **caught** by the cat.

16. Engineers design bridges. .... Bridges _____ **designed** by engineers.

17. The city is going to build a bridge. .... A bridge _____ **built** by the city.

18. A guard was protecting the jewels. .... The jewels _____ **protected** by a guard.

◇ **PRACTICE 2. Forming the passive: questions, negative, and affirmative.**
     (Chart 11-1 and Appendix Units B and D)

Directions: Change these sentences to the passive.

1. a. QUESTION: Did Tom write that report? → *Was that report written by Tom?*
   b. NEGATIVE: No, he didn't write it. → *No, it wasn't written by him.*
   c. AFFIRMATIVE: Alice wrote it. → *It was written by Alice.*

2. a. QUESTION: Is Mr. Brown painting your house?
   b. NEGATIVE: No, he isn't painting it.
   c. AFFIRMATIVE: My uncle is painting it.

3. a. QUESTION: Will Steve wash the dishes?
   b. NEGATIVE: No, he won't wash them.
   c. AFFIRMATIVE: The children will wash them.

4. a. QUESTION: Has Sue planned the meeting?
   b. NEGATIVE: No, she hasn't planned it.
   c. AFFIRMATIVE: The committee has planned it.

5. a. QUESTION: Does Mr. Parr play that violin?
   b. NEGATIVE: No, he doesn't play it.
   c. AFFIRMATIVE: His son plays it.

6. a. QUESTION: Is Jack going to return the books to the library?
   b. NEGATIVE: No, he isn't going to return them.
   c. AFFIRMATIVE: His sister is going to return them.

7. a. QUESTION: Did the archeologists discover the ancient skeleton?
   b. NEGATIVE: No, they didn't discover it.
   c. AFFIRMATIVE: A farmer discovered it.

8. a. QUESTION: Was Sally preparing the food?
   b. NEGATIVE: No, she wasn't preparing it.
   c. AFFIRMATIVE: Her mother was preparing it.

9. a. QUESTION: Will Ms. Anderson have typed the letters?
   b. NEGATIVE: No, she won't have typed them.
   c. AFFIRMATIVE: The secretary will have typed them.

◇ **PRACTICE 3. Forming the passive. (Chart 11-1 and Appendix Units B and D)**

Directions: In the following, active sentences are changed to passive sentences. Complete the passive sentences with the appropriate verb form. Keep the same tense. Use question and negative forms as necessary.

1. Did Ann discover the mistake?

   → __Was__ the mistake __discovered__ by Ann?

2. A famous author wrote that book.

   → That book __was written__ by a famous author.

3. Jack won't pay the bill.

   → The bill __won't be paid__ by Jack.

4. The waiter refilled my glass.

→ My glass _____ by the waiter.

5. Did Sue knock that vase to the floor?

→ _____ that vase _____ to the floor by Sue?

6. Tommy didn't break the chair.

→ The chair _____ by Tommy.

7. Alan's knowledge of art doesn't impress me.

→ I _____ by Alan's knowledge of art.

8. One of the parents is taping the children's song.

→ The children's song _____ by one of the parents.

9. Is a student pilot flying that airplane?

→ _____ that airplane _____ by a student pilot?

10. The best chess player will win the match.

→ The match _____ by the best chess player.

11. Your emotional appeals will not influence the judge.

→ The judge _____ by your emotional appeals.

12. The voters are going to decide that issue.

→ That issue _____ by the voters.

13. The city attorney has discovered new evidence.

→ New evidence _____ by the city attorney.

14. Mr. Snow hasn't taught that course since 1985.

→ That course _____ by Mr. Snow since 1985.

15. Had a special messenger delivered the package before you got to the office?

→ _____ the package _____ by a special messenger before you got to the office?

16. The pollution in the city was affecting Tim's breathing.

→ Tim's breathing _____ by the pollution in the city.

Directions: In these sentences, some of the verbs are transitive and some are intransitive. Identify the verb of the sentence. Then identify the object of the verb if there is one. If the verb has an object, change the sentence to the passive. Use the symbol Ø to indicate "none."

	VERB	OBJECT OF VERB	PASSIVE SENTENCE
1. Al will pay the bill.	will pay	the bill	The bill will be paid by Al.
2. Sue will come tomorrow.	will come	Ø	Ø
3. The hotel supplies towels.			
4. Accidents happen every day.			
5. Everyone noticed my mistake.			
6. The train arrived at three.			
7. The news didn't surprise me.			
8. Did the news surprise you?			
9. The sun wasn't shining.			
10. Ann interrupted my story.			
11. Do ghosts exist?			
12. Birds fly in the sky.			
13. Will Ed come tomorrow?			
14. Mr. Lee died last year.			
15. Did Bob throw the ball?			
16. Sue laughed loudly.			
17. An old man told the story.			
18. It hasn't rained lately.			

◇ **PRACTICE 5. Forming the passive. (Chart 11-1)**

Directions: Change these active sentences to passive if possible. Some of verbs are intransitive and cannot be changed. Keep the same tense.

1. My uncle will meet you at the airport. → *You will be met at the airport by my uncle.*

2. Our plane will land at 6:03. *(no change)*

3. John is working at the bakery.

4. We walked downtown after work yesterday.

5. The chef will prepare the food.

6. The baby was crying in his crib.

7. I don't agree with you.

8. Thousands of people ride the subway every day.

9. Joe fell down on his way to school this morning.

10. George seemed unhappy yesterday.

11. Our houseguests are going to arrive sometime tomorrow afternoon.

12. The office manager answered the phone.

◇ **PRACTICE 6. Active vs. passive. (Charts 11-1 and 11-2)**
   Directions: Complete the sentences with the words in parentheses. Some of the sentences are active and some are passive. Use any appropriate tense.

1. You *(notify)* __will be notified__ by my secretary next week.

2. Last night I *(remember, not)* __didn't remember__ to lock my front door.

3. At the present time, the oldest house in town *(restore)* _____

   by the Historical Society. When the restoration is finished, the house is sure to be a popular

   tourist attraction.

4. A: What a beautiful old wooden chest!

   B: It *(build)* _____ by my grandfather over fifty years ago.

5. At one time, the entire world *(rule)* _____ by dinosaurs. Some

   dinosaurs *(walk)* _____ on their hind legs and *(stand)* _____

   as tall as palm trees.

6. Disneyland is a world famous amusement park in Southern California. It *(visit)* _____

   _____ by more than ten million people every year.

7. Many of us take water for granted in our daily lives, but people who live in the desert

   (use, not) _____ water carelessly. To them, each drop is precious.

8. I *(agree, not)* _____ with people who say space exploration is a waste of

   money. What do you think?

9. Do you really think that we *(invade)* _____ by creatures from

   outer space in the near future?

10. Most insects *(live)* _____ for less than a year. The common housefly *(live)*

    _____ from 19 to 30 days.

11. *(you, accept, already)* _____ by this university

    when you heard about the other scholarship?

12. I got into a taxi quickly because I *(follow)* _____ by two

    strange men. As soon as I got into the taxi, I *(feel)* _____ a little safer.

13. The impact of the earthquake yesterday *(feel)* _____ by people who lived

    hundreds of kilometers from the epicenter.

14. When Alex was only ten, his father *(die)* _____ .

15. Mark *(influence)* _____ a lot by his friends, isn't he? He should be more independent and think for himself.

16. A few days ago, my car *(steal)* _____ by one of the teenagers in my neighborhood. He *(catch)* _____ by the police a few blocks from my house. He just wanted to take it for a drive, but now he's in a lot of trouble.

◇ **PRACTICE 7. Using the *by*-phrase. (Chart 11-2)**
Directions: Change these active sentences to passive. Keep the same tense. Include the *by*-phrase only if necessary.

1. People grow rice in India. → *Rice is grown in India.* (no *by*-phrase)

2. My aunt made this rug. → *This rug was made by my aunt.*

3. They are fixing my car today. → *My car is being fixed today.* (no *by*-phrase)

4. They speak French in Quebec.

5. Mr. Eads designed that bridge in the 1870s.

6. Someone invented the wheel thousands of years ago.

7. Did Thomas Edison invent the telephone?

8. They are going to build a new hospital just outside of town.

9. How do people make candles?

10. Very few people watch that TV show.

11. Look! Someone is feeding the seals.

12. Sally made that pie.

13. Someone is considering Jack for that job.

14. Three continents surround the Mediterranean Sea.

15. I got upset when someone interrupted me in the middle of my story.

16. People didn't build Rome in a day.

17. Do they make those tractors in this country, or do they import them?

18. While I was walking down the street, a nice young man in a military uniform approached me.

◇ PRACTICE 8. Indirect objects as passive subjects. (Chart 11-3)
Directions: Identify the indirect object (I.O.). Change the sentences to the passive by using the indirect object as the subject of the sentence. Use the *by*-phrase only if necessary. Keep the same tense.

                              I.O.
1. Someone is going to serve Jack breakfast in bed on his birthday.
→ *Jack is going to be served breakfast in bed on his birthday.*

2. Someone has offered Mike the opportunity to study abroad.

3. People don't pay babysitters a lot of money.

4. When I was living in Kuwait, my neighbor taught me Arabic.

5. Someone awarded Jason a medal for distinguished service in the military.

6. The real estate office will send you a copy of the sales contract.

7. Someone handed me a telegram when I answered the door.

8. The director of the museum, Ms. Cynthia Hall, is going to give the schoolchildren a special tour of the modern art exhibit.

9. People gave Mr. French a gold watch upon his retirement from the company.

◇ PRACTICE 9. Active and passive. (Charts 11-1 → 11-3)
Directions: Complete the sentences with the given words. Some of the sentences are passive and some are active. Use any appropriate tense.

1. The examination papers are scored by machine. The students *(tell)* __will be told__ their results next week.

2. The project got finished early. The committee *(complete)* __completed__ its work three weeks ahead of schedule.

3. The teacher *(assist)* _____ by two graduate students during the exam yesterday.

4. Soon after I *(apply)* _____ for a job with the United Nations two years ago, I *(hire)* _____ .

5. The crocodiles at the zoo look like statues. They *(lie)* _____ perfectly still for hours at a time. They have no need to move because they don't have to hunt for their food. They *(feed)* _____ regularly by the zookeepers.

6. This lovely beach won't exist forever. Eventually, it *(erode, probably)* _____ _____ by the sea, and there will be nothing left but bedrock. The geologic forces of nature never stop.

7. Bananas originated in Asia. They *(introduce)* _____ to the Americas in 1516. Until the 1860s, bananas *(eat)* _____ principally by people of the tropics. Today, bananas *(export)* _____ to all parts of the world, and they *(enjoy)* _____ by people who live in all climates.

8. There's going to be a story in the local newspaper about my neighbor, Mrs. Morris. Tomorrow she *(interview)* _____ by one of the local reporters about her doll collection. Over the years, she *(collect)* _____ more than 400 dolls from all over the world.

9. Ali and Mustafa *(complain)* _____ to the landlord many times since they moved into their apartment, but to date nothing *(do)* _____ _____ about the leak in the roof and the broken window in the bedroom.

10. Yesterday I told my teenage daughter to clean her room before she *(go)* _____ to school. After she had left the house, I looked in her room. She *(pile)* _____ _____ all her clothes on a chair. Everything else *(shove)* _____ _____ under her bed.

11. Sometimes people *(intimidate)* _____ by salespeople. As a result, sometimes they *(buy)* _____ things they don't really want.

12. Two days ago I *(put)* _____ an ad in the classified section of the newspaper so I could find a buyer for my old car. Yesterday I *(sell)* _____ it. It *(buy)* _____ _____ by a teenager who *(look)* _____ for an old car to fix up himself. Today a friend of mine told me he wanted to buy my old car, but he was too late. By the time he talked to me, the car *(sell, already)* _____ _____ to the teenager.

13. The wheel *(invent)* _____ over 5,000 years ago. Throughout history, it *(assist)* _____ people in making better use of oxen, horses, and other animals in transporting goods.

14. The avalanche *(occur)* _____ around ten in the morning on October seventh. Six skiers *(cross)* _____ a steep slope when suddenly they *(sweep)* _____ off their feet by cascading snow. Back at the ski resort, an avalanche alert was sounded, and a rescue party *(leave)* _____ immediately. After several hours, all six skiers *(find)* _____ . Four of them *(injure, seriously)* _____ , but they were all alive. The rescue party *(take)* _____ the injured skiers down the mountain as quickly as they could.

◇ **PRACTICE 10. The present participle vs. the past participle.**
      (Charts 2-2, 2-5, and 11-1 → 11-3)

Directions: Use the present participle or the past participle of the given verbs to complete the sentences. Use each verb only once.

breed	finance	scrub	✔thread
broadcast	lean	shove	wind
drag	mine	smuggle	
expose	✔redecorate	stretch	

1. The Clarks' living room is being __redecorated__ in blue and white. They want it to look nice for their daughter's wedding reception.

2. Jack pricked his finger while he was __threading__ a needle.

3. The police talked to an informant. According to him, the illegal drugs had been _____ into the country in a private airplane.

4. The logging industry in that country still uses animal power. After the trees are cut down, the logs are _____ to the central camp by elephants.

5. On your trip to Tahiti, you will be _____ to many interesting customs, delicious food, and delightful people.

6. My hands and knees got sore while I was _____ the floor with soap and water.

7. The old clock wasn't ticking because it hadn't been _____ . Someone forgot to do it.

8. The news of the victory was _____ throughout the country over the radio and television. Everyone heard about it almost as soon as it happened.

9. The bus was extremely crowded. I was _____ this way and that by the other passengers every time the bus turned a corner.

10. Oil exploration costs a lot of money. The explorations in the southern part of the country are being _____ by the government.

11. Frank was resting. He had been _____ back on his chair for several minutes with his eyes closed when he heard a knock on the door.

12. Gold is _____ in several countries. The nugget that Elena is wearing came from Brazil.

13. We couldn't enter the street. A rope had been _____ across the street.

14. Arabian horses are _____ at the Bar X ranch. They are quite expensive.

◇ **PRACTICE 11. The present participle vs. the past participle.**
    (Charts 2-2, 2-5, and 11-1 → 11-3)
    Directions: Use the present participle or the past participle of the given verbs to complete the sentences. Use each verb only once.

bill	erase	✔photograph	rub
destroy	✔memorize	predict	vaccinate
equip	perform	rehearse	whisper

1. The vocabulary list had been ___memorized___ by all of the students, and each one scored over 90 percent on the exam.

2. Shhhh! Don't move. Don is ___photographing___ that deer, and we don't want to scare it off.

3. You'll want to buy this computer. It has been _____ with all of the latest accessories, including a built-in modem.

4. The earthquake that struck the village was terrible. About 75 percent of the buildings were completely _____ within two minutes.

5. Little Jackie was _____ her eyes because she was sleepy.

6. Anna and Susie didn't hear what the teacher said because they were _____ to each other in the back of the classroom about the new boy in fifth grade.

7. Paul drew a funny picture of the teacher on the board, but it had been _____ before she entered the classroom.

8. The dance company is having a successful tour of the United States. Their dances will have been _____ more than 500 times before they return to Senegal.

9. The National Weather Service is _____ another heat wave in the coming month. I hope they're wrong.

10. Robert and Julia had been _____ against cholera before they went abroad. They traveled without worrying about becoming infected.

11. When I went to the school auditorium, the children were _____ their musical play. The play is going to be presented this coming Friday at 7:00 P.M.

12. Carl spent two hours at the dentist's office today having some fillings put in. He will be _____ for the dental work at the end of the month.

◇ **PRACTICE 12. Passive modals. (Chart 11-4)**
    Directions: Change the active sentences to the passive.

1. People should save pandas from extinction. → *Pandas should be saved from extinction.*

2. People must obey all traffic laws.

3. Someone ought to repair this broken window.

4. Someone should have supplied the hotel guests with clean towels.

5. Someone had better take this garbage to the dump soon.

6. People can pick tomatoes before they are completely ripe.

7. Someone is supposed to divide the profits among the shareholders.

8. Someone must have hurt Bob's feelings.

9. Someone has to finish this work today.

10. Someone ought to have reported the accident to the police.

11. You shouldn't put fresh bananas in the freezer.

◇ **PRACTICE 13. Passive modals. (Chart 11-4)**
    Directions: Complete the sentences with the appropriate forms of the verbs in the list. Use each verb only once. Some of the sentences are active and some are passive.

consider	*pollute*	*sew*	*whisper*
cost	*read*	*sign*	*wrap*
discover	✓*repeat*	✓*tell*	
forget	*replace*	*wear*	

1. Jack has a right to know. He ought to ___be told___ the news immediately. If you don't do it, I will.

2. I have no patience with gossips. What I told Bill was a secret. He shouldn't have
   ___repeated___ it to you.

3. Use this brown paper and tape. A package has to _____ carefully before it is mailed. Otherwise, the post office won't send it.

4. I don't know why Jessica wasn't at the meeting. She must have _____ about it. Next time there's a meeting, I'll be sure to remind her about it.

5. The ancient ruins may have _____ as early as 1792. The historical record is difficult to interpret.

6. You should _____ this button back on right away — before you lose it.

7. This burnt out light bulb should have _____ days ago. There are some new bulbs in the green cabinet. Could you get one for me?

8. Did you know that Sylvia bought a new sports car? I don't know how much she paid for it, and of course it's none of my business, but it must have _____ her a lot of money.

9. Shhhh! Let's not talk so loudly. We don't want to awaken the baby. We'd better
   _____ .

10. You'd better not drink that river water. It could _____ .

11. We have no choice in the matter. I know Tommy wants to spend the night outside in a tent with his friends, but he's sick. His well-being must _____ above all else. We have to tell him he can't do it.

12. While you are working here, you are never to greet the public in your everyday clothes. When you are on duty, your uniform must _____ at all times.

13. Your passport is supposed to _____ . It is invalid without your signature.

14. I think everyone should _____ this paperback on the economic crisis. It contains information that everyone should have.

◇ **PRACTICE 14. Passive modals. (Chart 11-4)**
   Directions: Complete the sentences with the appropriate forms of the verbs in the list. Use each verb only once. Some of the sentences are active and some are passive.

distinguish	✓obtain	scrub	vaccinate
eat	participate	stop	win
establish	reply	teach	
kill	revise	trade	

1. A driver's license can __be obtained__ from the Licensing Bureau at the corner of Pine Street and 5th Avenue.

2. Sam Smith was awarded the prize, but it should have _____ by Jennifer Watson. Her drawing was much better than his in my opinion.

3. Surgeons must _____ their hands thoroughly with disinfectant soap and hot water before they enter the operating room.

4. A parrot can _____ to say words. I know a parrot that can say, "Me want food." Her grammar isn't very good, but she often manages to get something to eat.

HELLO, ME WANT FOOD.
HELLO, ME WANT FOOD.

5. What are you talking about? You can't have _____ against the common cold. Small pox, maybe — but not the common cold.

6. When Mr. Brown said "How do you do?" you should have _____ by saying "How do you do?" I know that's not an answer to a question, but that's the way people talk when they greet each other.

7. I shouldn't have _____ by the police. I'm sure I wasn't speeding, but I got a ticket anyway.

8. Maria's composition was quite good, but it still had to _____. Her introduction didn't clearly state her thesis, and some of the ideas she presented weren't supported by specifics.

9. If you don't want to work tonight, you ought to _____ work shifts with Emily. She can work for you tonight, and you can work for her tomorrow night. The boss doesn't mind as long as someone is there to serve the food.

10. The games are open to anyone who wants to join in. Everyone can _____ in them. You don't have to sign up first. We welcome all players.

11. A university may _____ in outer space before long. Ideas for such a university are presently in the planning stage.

12. Your body needs lots of vitamins and minerals. You should _____ more salads and less junk food in the future.

13. A bald eagle can _____ from other large birds by its white head and white tail.

14. Some ranchers still believe that bald eagles must _____ to protect their livestock. Research has shown, however, that eagles do little if any damage to a rancher's stock. Today eagles are a protected species. The sight of a bald eagle soaring over water and trees fills one with awe and wonder at the beauty of nature.

◇ **PRACTICE 15. Stative passive. (Chart 11-5)**

Directions: Complete the sentences with the verbs in the list. Use the SIMPLE PRESENT. Use each verb only once.

bury	cover	✔excite	insure
close	crack	exhaust	pollute
confuse	dress	finish	stick

1. The children ___*are excited*___ about going to the circus. They're looking forward to seeing the elephants, the clowns, and the acrobats.

2. Three of the children have the measles. Their bodies _____ with red spots. They also have fevers.

3. A: What happened to this mirror? It _____ .

   B: So it is. Someone must have dropped it.

4. The kids _____ from playing soccer all afternoon. They should rest for a while now.

5. _____ you _____ with that novel yet? I'd like to borrow it to read over the weekend.

6. A: I heard that a burglar broke into your house and stole all of your jewelry!

   B: Yes, and I feel terrible about it. Some of it was my grandmother's and can't be replaced. But at least all of it _____ , and I'll be reimbursed for its value. It's still not the same as having the jewelry, though.

7. You shouldn't eat any of the fish from that river. The river _____ with chemical wastes from the factory upstream.

8. A: I'm going over to the theater to get tickets for the next concert.

   B: The ticket booth _____ until 6:00 P.M. You'll have to go there after six to get the tickets.

9. What's wrong with this drawer? I can't pull it open. It _____ .

10. George _____ in his best suit today because he has an important interview this afternoon.

11. Douglas gave me one set of directions to their house, and Ann gave me a different set of directions. Needless to say, I _____ very _____ . I hope we don't get lost on the way.

12. I know the scissors are somewhere on this desk. I think they _____ somewhere under these piles of papers.

◇ **PRACTICE 16. Stative passive. (Chart 11-5)**
Directions: Complete the sentences with the appropriate form of the verbs in the list. Use the
SIMPLE PRESENT. Use each verb only once.

acquaint	*equip*	*locate*	*schedule*
cancel	*forbid*	*make*	*summarize*
clog	*list*	*overdraw*	*wrinkle*

1. Maria's family lives in New York City, and her husband's family lives in Philadelphia. They
   would like to live in a city which _____ between the two so that they
   can visit their relatives frequently.

2. Robert wrote a very good, well-organized composition. The introduction tells the reader
   what the composition is about, and the last paragraph reviews all of his main points. His
   conclusions _____ in the last paragraph.

3. I don't know how, but I've lost my brother's new telephone number. Unfortunately, it
   _____ , so I can't look it up in the directory. I'll have to call my
   mother and get it from her.

4. We can't climb over the fence to walk in that field. The sign says: "Trespassing
   _____ . Violators will be prosecuted."

5. I _____ not _____ with our new neighbors. They just
   moved in last week, and I haven't had the opportunity to introduce myself.

6. Your dental appointment _____ for 10:00 on Saturday. Please give
   us 24-hours notice if you need to cancel it.

7. I have to deposit some money in the bank immediately or I'm in big trouble. I've written
   too many checks, and there's not enough money to cover them. My bank account
   _____ .

8. Good news! Our meeting _____ . Now we can go to the beach
   after work instead of spending the evening at a meeting.

9. I can't wear this blouse because it _____ . I'd have to iron it, and I don't
   have time.

10. Some new automobiles _____ with air bags as well as seat belts.
    The air bags provide additional protection in case of an accident.

11. That table _____ of plastic, not wood. The manufacturer certainly did
    a good job of imitating the look of wood.

12. It takes a long time for the water to go down the drain in my kitchen sink. I think the drain
    _____ with grease and food particles. I'd better call the plumber tomorrow.

Directions: Complete the sentences with the appropriate prepositions.

1. This apartment comes furnished ___with___ only a stove and refrigerator.

2. My uncle is known _____ his generosity.

3. Alice is dressed _____ her warmest clothes today.

4. For the holiday meal, the bowls on the table were filled _____ specially prepared foods.

5. People who have been exposed _____ heavy doses of radiation may be more suspectible to certain diseases.

6. By the end of the long trip, the floor of the car was cluttered _____ junk.

7. Mr. Bellamy is discriminated _____ because of his age. When he applies for a job, he gets turned down as soon as they learn he is 61 years old.

8. The boss is so convinced _____ Jean's ability that he's paying her more money than he paid the previous employee.

9. Victor is blessed _____ a good sense of humor, which has helped him get out of some very difficult situations.

10. A: Are you disappointed _____ the color of this room? We could repaint it.

    B: I think I'm satisfied _____ it the way it is. What do you think?

11. George Washington, the first president of the United States, is remembered _____ his strong leadership during the Revolutionary War.

12. Zoology is more closely related _____ biology than it is to botany.

13. I'm annoyed _____ my boss. He scheduled a meeting for an hour beginning at ten o'clock, the same time I was planning to see a client.

14. As soon as you are done _____ the dictionary, I'd like to use it.

15. Last month, little Billy was bitten by a dog. Now he's scared _____ every dog he sees.

16. Carol is engaged _____ Larry. Their marriage is planned for May 3.

17. A: Why are you so upset _____ the children?

    B: They didn't call me when they missed their school bus, and I got very worried _____ them.

18. Each speaker was limited _____ three minutes.

19. Olga is exhausted. She's tired _____ working 19 straight hours at her computer, but she can't go home until the crisis is over.

20. I'm tired _____ living in a small apartment. I'd like to live in a house, or at least a larger apartment.

Directions: Complete the sentences with the verbs in the list. Use the present participle or the past participle. Include a PREPOSITION if necessary. Use each verb only once.

accompany	compose	✓explain	limit
annoy	✓concern	involve	provide
bless	connect	know	satisfy
blow	cross	laugh	

1. I am ___concerned about___ your health. You're not taking good care of yourself.

2. Shhh! The teacher is ___explaining___ the assignment, and I want to hear what he's saying.

3. Paris is famous for the Eiffel Tower. Bangkok is _____ its floating market, which is a favorite tourist attraction.

4. In elementary school, all of the children are _____ textbooks. They don't have to buy their own.

5. Everyone is _____ hard because Don is telling a very funny story.

6. Diane is a perfectionist when it comes to developing her photographs. She's been in the darkroom for hours and won't come out until she is completely _____ _____ the prints.

7. The Atlantic Ocean is _____ the Pacific Ocean by the Panama Canal. Ships can go from one ocean to the other without having to sail around the southern tip of South America.

8. While I was _____ the street, a car came out of nowhere and almost hit me.

9. Most teenagers are very busy after school. They are _____ many extracurricular activities, such as sports and special interest clubs.

10. An alloy is a metal compound that is _____ two or more metals.

11. Mrs. Hill doesn't have to travel alone. Her daughter is _____ her to Rome.

12. We are fortunate people. We are _____ a happy home and good health. We have many things to be thankful for.

13. The enrollment in that class is _____ 25 students. You'd better sign up for it early. Otherwise, you won't be able to get in.

14. My neighbors are quite inconsiderate. They make so much noise that I can't get to sleep at night. I am very _____ them.

15. The weather was awful. It was raining so hard that it was impossible to see across the valley, and the wind was _____ so hard that it was difficult to walk.

◇ **PRACTICE 19. The passive with *get*. (Chart 11-7)**
Directions: Complete the sentences by using an appropriate form of *get* and the PAST PARTICIPLE of the verbs in the list.

break	hurt	start	✓tear
bury	lose	stick	worry
hire	soak		

1. I had a terrible day. First the heel of my shoe broke off, then my dress ___got torn___ in the elevator door. I'm glad the day is over!

2. Oh! Look at that beautiful vase on the floor. How did it _____?

3. A: You're late. What happened?

   B: We _____. We took the wrong exit from the highway, and it took a long time to figure out where we were.

4. A: I really need a job.

   B: Why don't you apply for a job at the fast-food restaurant? They're looking for help. I'm sure you'll _____.

5. A: Did Susan _____ when she fell down the stairs?

   B: Not badly. Just a few bumps and bruises. She'll be fine.

6. A: You're here! I _____ about you. What happened to make you so late?

   B: I couldn't start my car. The battery was dead.

7. Maureen _____ thoroughly _____ when her canoe tipped over and she fell into the river. She looked like a drowned rat.

8. In two weeks the school term will be finished. I'd better _____ on my term paper before it's too late. I've been procrastinating too long.

9. It was a real tragedy. The rains were torrential, and the mudslide completely covered everything. Three houses _____ in the mud when it rolled down the hillside. We could barely see the rooftops.

10. A: I heard about your embarrassing situation last night.

 B: It was awful! I put my big toe in the faucet while I was taking a bath, and it _____! I couldn't pull it out no matter how hard I tried.

◇ **PRACTICE 20. The passive with get. (Chart 11-7)**
 Directions: Complete the sentences by using an appropriate form of **get** and the PAST PARTICIPLE of the verbs in the list.

accept	*dress*	*embarrass*	*invite*
catch	*elect*	*fire*	*mug*
cheat	*electrocute*	✓*hit*	*ruin*

1. I shouldn't have parked my car near the construction site. It ___got hit___ by falling rocks. Now it's covered with dents and scratches.

2. Tom has applied to three top universities. Since he's an excellent student, I'm sure he'll _____ by at least one of them. If he doesn't, there are other good schools he can attend.

3. Alex thought he had gotten a good deal when he bought a diamond ring from some guy on the street, but the "stone" turned out to be glass and was practically worthless. Alex _____ .

4. A: I can't believe Paul _____ from his job. I thought he was doing well.

 B: He was, but then he had a major disagreement with his boss, and tempers were flying. I hope he gets his job back.

5. A: Let's take the subway.

 B: Not me! The last time I was on the subway, I _____ . A man knocked me down and stole my wallet.

6. A: Did you _____ to the Saunders' dinner party tonight?

 B: Yes, but I can't go.

7. A: You're all out of breath!

 B: I was late getting home and had to _____ quickly. Then I ran all the way over here.

 A: Well, that explains why your collar is up and your tie is crooked.

8. The animal was running through the woods when it suddenly _____ in the hunter's trap.

9. It was a close election. The new president _____ by a very small margin.

10. What are you doing?!! Don't let the cord to your electric hair dryer fall into the sink. You'll _____!

11. We managed to save some of the furniture, but many of our things _____ _____ when the floodwaters poured into our house.

12. During the school play, little Annie _____ when she couldn't remember the lines she was supposed to say.

◇ **PRACTICE 21. Participial adjectives. (Chart 11-8)**
Directions: Complete the sentences by using an appropriate form (PRESENT or PAST PARTICIPLE) of the *italicized* word.

1. The book *interests* me. (a) It is an ___interesting___ book. (b) I am ___interested___ in it.

2. That chemical *irritates* your skin. (a) The chemical is _____. (b) Your skin is _____.

3. The trip *tired* everybody. (a) Everyone was _____. (b) The trip was _____.

4. Ann *boiled* an egg. (a) She took the egg out of the _____ water. (b) She had a _____ egg for breakfast.

5. The news *upset* us. (a) We were _____. (b) The news was _____.

6. The instructions on the box for assembling the tool *confuse* me. (a) They are _____. (b) I am thoroughly _____.

7. Bob's grades *disappointed* his parents. (a) His grades were _____. (b) His parents were _____.

8. My father often *reassured* me. (a) He was a very _____ person. (b) I always felt _____ when I was around him.

9. I waited for two hours to see the doctor, and it really *frustrated* me! (a) Long waits such as that can be very _____. (b) I was _____.

10. Anna has a noise in her car that *disturbs* her. (a) It is a _____ noise. (b) She is _____ when she hears it.

11. Jessica's arguments *convinced* us. (a) She presented _____ arguments. (b) We were _____.

12. The tender love story *moved* the audience. (a) It was a _____ story. (b) The audience felt _____.

13. Their behavior *shocked* us. (a) It was _____ behavior. (b) We were

    _____ .

14. The sad movie *depressed* me. (a) I was _____ . (b) It was a

    _____ movie.

15. The unkind teacher's harsh words *humiliated* the student. (a) The _____

    student hung his head in shame. (b) The student never forgot that _____

    experience.

16. The newspaper account of the new medical discovery *intrigued* me. (a) It was an

    _____ account. (b) Other _____ people wrote the

    newspaper to get more information.

◇ **PRACTICE 22. Participial adjectives. (Chart 11-8)**
    Directions: Complete each sentence with the correct form of the word in parentheses.

1. The poor people who live in shacks south of the city don't have *(run)* _____

    water.

2. No one may attend the lecture except *(invite)* _____ guests.

3. The *(suggest)* _____ remedy for the common cold is to rest and to drink

    plenty of fluids.

4. Because we have a *(write)* _____ agreement, our landlord won't be able

    to raise our rent for two years.

5. After an *(exhaust)* _____ trip of twelve hours, Jason fell asleep at the

    dinner table.

6. There are many *(stimulate)* _____ activities in a large city.

7. The anthropologist recorded the tribe's *(speak)* _____ language with a

    small tape recorder.

8. I like to hear the sound of gently *(fall)* _____ rain.

9. *(Freeze)* _____ fish is as nutritious as fresh fish, but it doesn't taste quite

    as good.

10. The *(invade)* _____ army plundered the villages of food and valuables.

11. Skydiving is a *(thrill)* _____ experience.

12. Ben's tasteless jokes didn't produce the *(intend)* _____ effect. Instead,

    his guests were offended.

13. The professor dispelled the tense atmosphere in the classroom by beginning her lecture with

    some *(amuse)* _____ anecdotes.

14. That country is highly industrialized but has very little arable land. Its economy depends upon the export of various *(manufacture)* _____ goods in exchange for imported agricultural products.

15. When I get home from work, I'm going to take a long, *(relax)* _____ bath.

16. The scientist reviewed all of his procedures for the experiment after the *(expect)* _____ results did not occur.

17. When Brenda heard the news of the *(approach)* _____ hurricane, she bought flashlight batteries, candles, and canned food to prepare for the storm.

18. Bright children have *(inquire)* _____ minds.

19. The game was played in our stadium. The *(visit)* _____ team scored the *(win)* _____ goal in the last seconds of the soccer game. Nevertheless, the *(disappoint)* _____ fans continued to cheer our team.

20. I heard some *(encourage)* _____ news.

21. Sally spends her vacations in the mountains. The fresh air invigorates her. She likes the cool, *(invigorate)* _____ air.

22. Waste from the factory poured into the river and contaminated it. Some of the villagers got sick from eating *(contaminate)* _____ fish.

◇ **PRACTICE 23. Verb form review: active and passive. (Chapters 1 › 5 and 11)**
Directions: Complete the sentences with the words in parentheses.

1. Only coffee and dessert *(serve)* __were served__ at the reception yesterday.

2. Kim wants very badly to make the Olympic team next year. She *(train)* __has been training__ hard for the last two years.

3. I've looked in my purse, on the dresser, in my coat pocket, and on all of the tables in the house, but I can't find my keys anywhere. They *(lose)* _____.

4. Some people in my country don't take politics seriously. In a recent parliamentary election, a cartoon character named Donald Duck *(receive)* _____ 291 votes.

5. According to present company policy, bonuses for the most sales *(give)* _____ _____ to the staff at the end of July every year.

6. According to our Constitution, everyone is equal. But in truth, some minorities *(discriminate)* _____ against in our country. In the last 20 years, new laws *(enact)* _____ to help ensure equality in housing and job opportunities.

7. Mark is a genius. By the time he graduated, he *(offer)* _____ jobs by a dozen computer companies.

8. When I *(finish)* _____ my work, I'm going to take a walk.

9. After the test papers *(return)* _____ to the students in class tomorrow, the students *(give)* _____ their next assignment.

10. The Olympic Games began in 776 B.C. in Olympia, a small town in Greece. At that time, only Greeks *(allow)* _____ to compete in them.

11. I *(fool, not)* _____ when Linda told us she'd won a million dollars at the racetrack. I knew she was only kidding.

12. There are certain *(establish)* _____ procedures that must *(follow)* _____ in conducting a scientific experiment.

13. Due to his abrasive, *(irritate)* _____ manner, Mr. Morrow has difficulty getting along with his co-workers. He *(replace)* _____ by Mr. Han next month as the coordinator of the production plans.

14. When Jake put a coin in the *(vend)* _____ machine for a can of soda pop, nothing came out. So in a fit of temper, he *(kick)* _____ it hard. Suddenly, it *(fall)* _____ over, right on top of Jake, who *(injure, seriously)* _____ _____ . Jake *(end)* _____ up in the hospital for three weeks, and today he *(wear, still)* _____ a cast on his arm. I bet that's the last time he ever kicks a *(vend)* _____ machine.

15. I have a serious problem with my *(propose)* _____ class schedule this semester. The chemistry class that I need for my science requirement *(offer, not)* _____ _____ this semester. I don't know what to do. I need that class in order to graduate in June.

16. A: Arthur *(jog)* _____ for a full hour. He must be tired.

    B: Why is he jogging so much these days?

    A: He *(plan)* _____ to run in the 10k race in Chicago next month, and he wants to be ready for it.

17. A census is a survey of the population of a country. In the United States, a population census *(conduct)* _____ by the government every ten years. Questionnaires *(send)* _____ to every household in the country. People *(ask)* _____ about such things as their employment, education, housing, and family size. After the information *(collect)* _____, it *(publish)* _____ by the Census Bureau. Many government agencies *(use)* _____ this information to make plans for the future about housing, agriculture, urban development, public transportation, and schools.

Directions: Choose the correct answer.

Example: Ms. Haugen ___D___ at the Ajax Company.
    A. is employing   B. employed   C. employing   D. is employed

1. I still can't believe it! My bicycle _____ last night.
    A. was stolen   B. was stealing   C. stolen   D. stole

2. The current constitutional problem is _____ by the top legal minds in the country.
    A. studying
    B. being studying
    C. being studied
    D. been studied

3. Something funny _____ in class yesterday.
    A. happened   B. was happened   C. happens   D. is happened

4. The child's arm was swollen because he _____ by a bee.
    A. stung
    B. had stung
    C. had been stung
    D. had being stung

5. Today, many serious childhood diseases _____ by early immunization.
    A. are preventing
    B. can prevent
    C. prevent
    D. can be prevented

6. I _____ with you on that subject.
    A. am agree   B. am agreed   C. agreeing   D. agree

7. Many U.S. automobiles _____ in Detroit, Michigan.
    A. manufacture
    B. have manufactured
    C. are manufactured
    D. are manufacturing

8. Let's go ahead and do it now. Nothing _____ by waiting.
    A. accomplishes
    B. accomplished
    C. has accomplished
    D. will be accomplished

9. "When _____?"
   "In 1928."
    A. penicillin was discovered
    B. did penicillin discovered
    C. was penicillin discovered
    D. did penicillin discover

10. In recent years, the government has imposed pollution controls on automobile manufacturers. Both domestic and imported automobiles must _____ anti-pollution devices.
    A. equip with
    B. be equipped with
    C. equip by
    D. be equipped by

11. A shortage of water is a problem in many parts of the world. In some areas, water _____ from the ground faster than nature can replenish the supply.
    A. is being taken   B. has been taking   C. is taking   D. has taken

12. Vitamin C _____ by the human body. It gets into the blood stream quickly.
    A. absorbs easily
    B. is easily absorbing
    C. is easily absorbed
    D. absorbed easily

13. "When can I have my car back?"
    "I think it'll _____ late this afternoon."
    A. finish   B. be finished   C. have finished   D. be finish

14. I didn't think my interview went very well, but I guess it must have. Despite all my anxiety,
    I _____ for the job I wanted. I'm really going to work hard to justify their confidence.
    A. was hiring   B. hired   C. got hiring   D. got hired

15. My country _____ the pursuit of world peace.
    A. is dedicating to   C. is dedicating by
    B. is dedicated to   D. is dedicated by

16. About 15,000 years ago, northern Wisconsin _____ under ice a mile deep.
    A. buried   B. was burying   C. was buried   D. had buried

17. Ed was new on the job, but he quickly fit himself into the _____ routine of the office.
    A. established   B. establishing   C. establishes   D. establish

18. The Mayan Indians _____ an accurate and sophisticated calendar more than seven
    centuries ago.
    A. were developed   B. developed   C. are developed   D. have been developed

19. George is _____ Lisa.
    A. marry with   B. marry to   C. married with   D. married to

20. The rescuers _____ for their bravery and fortitude in locating the lost mountain climbers.
    A. were praised   B. praised   C. were praising   D. praising

Directions: Choose the correct answer.

Example: Ms. Haugen ___D___ at the Ajax Company.
    A. is employing   B. employed   C. employing   D. is employed

1. "Can't we do something about the situation?"
   "Something _____ right now."
    A. is doing   B. is done   C. is being done   D. has been doing

2. "Are you interested in scuba diving?"
   "Very. Undersea life is _____."
    A. fascinated   B. fascinating   C. being fascinating   D. being fascinated

3. The university _____ by private funds as well as by tuition income and grants.
    A. is supported   B. supports   C. is supporting   D. has supported

4. My car made strange noises, sputtered to a stop, and then wouldn't start again. Fortunately, the mechanic at my garage _____ the source of the problem.
    A. was discover   C. was discovered
    B. discovered   D. has been discovered

5. "Ms. Jones, please type those letters before noon."
   "They've already _____, sir. They're on your desk."
    A. typed   B. been typed   C. being typed   D. been being typed

6. "Has the committee made its decision yet?"
   "Not yet. They are still _____ the proposal."
    A. considering   C. being considered
    B. been considered   D. considered

7. In some rural areas of the United States, health care _____ by only a small number of doctors, nurses, and other health professionals. It's often more than they can handle.
    A. is providing   C. provides
    B. is being provided   D. provided

8. "How did that window _____?"
   "I don't know."
    A. get broken   B. broke   C. got broken   D. broken

9. Renoir is one of the most popular French impressionist painters. His paintings _____ masterpieces all over the world.
    A. had considered   C. are considered
    B. are considering   D. consider

10. As the fairy tale goes, the prince _____ into a frog by an evil magician, and only a kiss from a beautiful princess could restore him to his original state.
    A. turned   C. was turned
    B. was turning   D. had been turning

11. When I woke up and looked outside, the landscape had changed. The ground had been lightly _____ with a dusting of snow during the night.
    A. covering   B. cover   C. covers   D. covered

12. We can't even walk in this storm. Let's wait in the hallway where we'll be _____ the strong winds until things quiet down.
    A. protected from   B. protected by   C. protecting from   D. protecting by

13. "_____ about the eight o'clock flight to Chicago?"
    "Not yet."
    A. Has been an announcement made   C. Has an announcement been made
    B. Has an announcement made   D. Has been made an announcement

14. Last night a tornado swept through Rockville. It _____ everything in its path.
    A. destroyed   C. was being destroyed
    B. was destroyed   D. had been destroyed

15. Be sure to wash these vegetables thoroughly. A lot of pesticide residue _____ on unwashed produce.
    A. can find   B. can found   C. can be found   D. can be finding

16. The building of the bridge had been delayed for three years because of political problems on both sides of the river. Finally, it _____ because the public demanded action, and now many hours of driving have been saved for daily commuters.
    A. was constructed   C. constructed
    B. gets constructed   D. has constructed

17. On Friday afternoon before a three-day holiday weekend, the highways _____ people on their way out of the city.
    A. are crowding by   C. are crowded with
    B. are being crowd with   D. crowd by

18. Fortunately, the hospital's new air-conditioning system _____ when the first heat wave of the summer arrived.
    A. had installed   C. had been installed
    B. installed   D. had been installing

19. It's hard to believe that my application for a scholarship _____. I was sure I'd get it. I don't know now if I'll go to school next year.
    A. was denied   B. denied   C. was denying   D. has denied

20. The man died because medical help was not summoned. A doctor should _____ immediately.
    A. have called   B. been called   C. called   D. have been called

9. Prof. Brown, who had had almost no teaching experience, was hired to teach the advanced physics courses. At first, some of us objected to that, but she has proven herself to be one of the best.

10. That automobile has the best safety record of any car manufactured this year. I am impressed by that and would definitely recommend that you buy that make.

◇ **PRACTICE 10. Quoted speech. (Chart 12-6)**
Directions: Add the necessary punctuation and capitalization to these sentences. Do not change the word order or add or delete any words.

1. The athlete said where is my uniform
   → *The athlete said, "Where is my uniform?"*

2. I can't remember Margaret said where I put my purse

3. Sandy asked her sister how can I help you get through this difficulty

4. I'll answer your question later he whispered I'm trying to hear what the speaker is saying

5. As the students entered the room, the teacher said please take your seats quickly

6. Why did I ever take this job Barry wondered aloud

7. After crashing into me and knocking all of my packages to the ground, the man stopped abruptly, turned to me and said softly excuse me

8. Do we want four more years of corruption and debt the candidate shouted into the microphone no the crowd screamed

9. The woman behind the fast-food counter shouted who's next

   I am three people replied at the same time

   Which one of you is really next she asked impatiently

   I was here first said a young woman elbowing here way up to the counter I want a hamburger

   You were not hollered an older man standing next to her I was here before you were give me a chicken sandwich and a cup of coffee

   Wait a minute I was in line first said a young man give me a cheeseburger and a chocolate shake

   The woman behind the restaurant counter spotted a little boy politely waiting his turn she turned to him and said hi, Sonny what can I get for you

◇ **PRACTICE 11. Reported speech. (Chart 12-7)**

Directions: Change the sentences by changing quoted to reported speech. Use formal sequence of tenses.

1. Tom said, "I am busy." → Tom said that he ___was___ busy.

2. Tom said, "I need some help." → Tom said that he _____ some help.

3. Tom said, "I am having a good time." → Tom said that he _____ a good time.

4. Tom said, "I have finished my work." → Tom said that he _____ his work.

5. Tom said, "I finished it an hour ago." → Tom said that he _____ it an hour ago.

6. Tom said, "I will arrive at noon." → Tom said that he _____ at noon.

7. Tom said, "I am going to be there at noon." → Tom said that he _____ there at noon.

8. Tom said, "I can solve that problem." → Tom said that he _____ that problem.

9. Tom said, "I may come early." → Tom said that he _____ early.

10. Tom said, "I might come early." → Tom said that he _____ early.

11. Tom said, "I must leave at eight." → Tom said that he _____ at eight.

12. Tom said, "I have to leave at eight." → Tom said that he _____ at eight.

13. Tom said, "I should go to the library." → Tom said that he _____ to the library.

14. Tom said, "I ought to go to the library." → Tom said that he _____ to the library.

15. Tom said, "Stay here." → Tom told me _____ here.

16. Tom said, "Don't move." → Tom told me _____ .

17. Tom said, "Are you comfortable?" → Tom asked me if I _____ comfortable.

18. Tom said, "When did you arrive?" → Tom asked me when I _____ .

◇ **PRACTICE 12. Reported speech. (Chart 12-7)**

Directions: Complete the sentences by changing the quoted speech to reported speech. Use formal sequence of tenses as appropriate. (Pay attention to whether the reporting verb is past or present.)

1. *I asked Martha, "Are you planning to enter law school?"*

   I asked Martha ___if/whether she was planning___ to enter law school.

2. *Ed just asked me, "What time does the movie begin?"*

   Ed wants to know ___what time the movie begins___ .

3. *Fred asked, "Can we still get tickets for the concert?"*

   Fred asked ___if/whether we could still get___ tickets for the concert.

4. *Thomas said to us, "How can I help you?"*

   Thomas wants to know ___how he can help___ us.

5. *Eva asked, "Can you help me, John?"*

   Eva asked John _____ her.

6. *Charles said, "When will the final decision be made?"*

   Charles wanted to know _____ .

7. *Frank asked Elizabeth, "Where have you been all afternoon?"*

   Frank asked Elizabeth _____ all afternoon.

8. *Bill just said, "What is Kim's native language?"*

   Bill wants to know _____ .

9. *Yesterday Ron said to Bob, "What's the problem?"*

   Ron asked Bob _____ .

10. *I asked myself, "Am I doing the right thing?"*

    I wondered _____ the right thing.

11. *All of the farmers are asking, "When is this terrible drought going to end?"*

    All of the farmers are wondering _____ to end.

12. *George asked me, "What time do I have to be at the laboratory in the morning?"*

    George asked me _____ to be at the laboratory in the morning.

13. *Beth asked, "Who should I give this message to?"*

    Beth asked me _____ .

14. *Our tour guide said, "We'll be leaving around 7:00 in the morning."*

    Our tour guide told us _____ around 7:00 in the morning.

15. *Nancy asked, "Why didn't you call me?"*

    Nancy wanted to know _____ her.

◇ **PRACTICE 13. Reported speech. (Chart 12-7)**

   Directions: Complete the sentences using the information in the dialogue. Use past verb forms in the noun clauses if appropriate and possible.

   1. *Joanne asked me, "Do you know Dave Clark?"*
      "Yes," I replied. "I've known him for many years. Why do you want to know?"

      Joanne asked me if I ___knew___ Dave Clark. I replied that I ___had known___ him

      for many years and asked her why she ___wanted___ to know.

   2. *I asked Mary, "Why do you still smoke?"*
      Mary replied, "I've tried to quit many times, but I just don't seem to be able to."

      When I asked Mary why she _____ , she replied that she _____

      _____ to quit many times, but she just _____ to be able to.

3. The teacher asked, "Bobby, what is the capital of Australia?"
   Bobby replied, "I'm not sure, but I think it's Sydney."

   Yesterday in class, Bobby's teacher asked him _____. He

   answered that he _____ sure, but that he _____

   Sydney.

4. The children inquired of their father, "Will we be able to visit the Air and Space Museum and the Natural History Museum, too?"
   Their father said, "We will if we leave the hotel before 10 o'clock tomorrow morning."

   The children asked their father whether they _____ able to visit the

   Air and Space Museum and the Natural History Museum, too. He told them they

   _____ if they _____ the hotel before 10 o'clock the next morning.

5. I told Jenny, "It's pouring outside. You'd better take an umbrella."
   Jenny said, "It'll stop soon. I don't need one."

   I told Jenny that it _____ outside and that she _____ an

   umbrella. However, Jenny said she thought the rain _____ soon and that she

   _____ one.

6. "Where are you going, Ann?" I asked.
   "I'm on my way to the market," she replied. "Do you want to come with me?"
   "I'd like to, but I have to stay home. I have a lot of work to do."
   "Okay," Ann said. "Is there anything I can pick up for you at the market?"
   "How about a few bananas? And some apples if they're fresh?"
   "Sure. I'd be happy to."

   When I asked Ann where she _____, she said she _____ on

   her way to the market and _____ me to come with her. I said I

   _____ to, but that I _____ to stay home because I _____ a lot of

   work to do. Ann kindly asked me if there _____ anything she _____

   pick up for me at the market. I asked her to pick up a few bananas and some apples if they

   _____ fresh. She said she'd be happy to.

7. "Where are you from?" asked the passenger sitting next to me on the plane.
   "Chicago," I said.
   "That's nice. I'm from Mapleton. It's a small town in northern Michigan. Have you heard of it?"
   "Oh yes, I have," I said. "Michigan is a beautiful state. I've been there on vacation many times."
   "Were you in Michigan on vacation this year?"
   "No. I went far away from home this year. I went to India," I replied.
   "Oh, that's nice. Is it a long drive from Chicago to India?" she asked me. My mouth fell open.
   I didn't know how to respond. Some people certainly need to study geography.

The passenger sitting next to me on the plane _____ me where I _____ from. I _____ her I _____ from Chicago. She _____ that she _____ from Mapleton, a small town in northern Michigan. She wondered if I _____ _____ of it, and I told her that I _____. I went on to say that I thought Michigan _____ a beautiful state and explained that I _____ there on vacation many times. She _____ me if I _____ in Michigan on vacation this year. I replied that I _____ and _____ her that I _____ far away, to India. Then she asked me if it _____ a long drive from Chicago to India! My mouth fell open. I didn't know how to respond. Some people certainly need to study geography.

◇ **PRACTICE 14. Using the subjunctive. (Chart 12-8)**
   Directions: Complete the sentences, using the idea of the words in parentheses.

1. *(You should organize a camping trip.)*
   The girls proposed that their scout leader __organize__ a camping trip.

2. *(Ms. Hanson thinks that the director should divide our class into two sections.)*
   Ms. Hanson recommended that our class __be divided__ into two sections.

3. *(You must call home every week.)*
   Dan's parents insisted that he _____ home every week.

4. *(Someone must tell her the truth about her illness.)*
   It is essential that she _____ the truth about her illness.

5. *(Open your suitcases for inspection.)*
   The customs official demanded that all passengers _____ their suitcases.

6. *(Ann, you should take some art courses.)*
   The counselor recommended that Ann _____ some art courses.

7. *(All parts of the motor must work correctly.)*
   It is vital that all parts of the motor _____ in proper working order.

8. *(Please mail all packages at the central office.)*
   The director requests that all packages _____ at the central office.

9. *(Soldiers must obey their officers.*
   It is imperative that soldiers _____ their officers.

10. *(We must remember to give the babysitter certain phone numbers to call in case of emergency.)*
    It is important that the babysitter _____ phone numbers to call in case of emergency.

◇ **PRACTICE 15. Using -ever words. (Chart 12-9)**
   Directions: Complete these sentences by using **-ever** words.

1. As vice-president of international sales, Robert has complete control over his travel schedule.
   He can travel __whenever__ he wants.

2. Robert is free to decide which countries he will visit during his overseas trips. He can travel
   __wherever__ he wants.

3. The English professor told us that we could write our papers on _____
   subject we wanted as long as it related to the topics we discussed in class this semester.

4. There are only two appointment time slots remaining. You may select _____
   one you prefer.

5. To Ellen, the end justifies the means. She will do _____ she has to do
   in order to accomplish her objective.

6. Linda is very amiable and gregarious. She makes friends with _____
   she meets.

7. It doesn't matter which class you take to fulfill this requirement. Just take _____
   one fits best into your schedule.

8. _____ is the last to leave the room should turn off the lights and lock
   the door.

9. I know that Norman will succeed. He'll do _____ is required to succeed.

10. My wife and I are going to ride our bicycles across the country. We will ride for six to seven
    hours every day, then stop _____ we happen to be at the end of the day.

◇ **PRACTICE 16. TEST A: Noun clauses. (Chapter 12)**

Directions: In each sentence, select the ONE correct answer.

Example: He asked me where ___B___ .
    A. did I live   B. I lived   C. do you live   D. that I lived

1. I talked to Bob two weeks ago. I thought he wanted to know about my cat, but I misunderstood him. He asked me where _____, not my cat.
    A. is my hat   B. my hat was   C. my hat is   D. was my hat

2. "The people in the apartment upstairs must have a lot of children."
"I don't know how many _____, but it sounds like they have a dozen."
    A. children do they have   C. children they have
    B. do they have children   D. they have children

3. Do you know _____? I myself have no idea.
    A. how many years the earth is   C. how long is the earth
    B. how old the earth is   D. how much time has been the earth

4. "There's too much noise in this room. I can't understand what _____."
    A. is the professor saying   C. that the professor is saying
    B. is saying the professor   D. the professor is saying

5. When I was little, my father gave me some advice. He said _____ talk to strangers.
    A. I shouldn't   B. that shouldn't   C. don't   D. that I don't

6. "I didn't expect Ann's husband to be here at the opera with her."
"I'm surprised, too. Ann must have insisted that _____ with her."
    A. he come   B. he comes   C. he came   D. he had come

7. "Ms. Wright, can you give me a little extra help typing some letters today?"
"Sorry, I can't. The boss has an urgent report for me to write. She demanded that it _____ on her desk by 5 P.M. today."
    A. was   B. will be   C. is   D. be

8. "Did you tell Carol where _____ us this evening?"
"Yes, I did. I can't understand why she is late."
    A. should she meet   C. she meets
    B. she to meet   D. to meet

9. A fortune-teller predicted _____ inherit a lot of money before the end of the year.
    A. that I would   B. that I   C. what I will   D. what I

10. "Bill Frazer seems like a good person for the job, but we don't know why he left his last job."
"I know why. He told me _____ a serious policy disagreement with his boss last January."
    A. if he'd had   B. he'd had   C. what he'd had   D. that what he had

11. "Is it true that you fell asleep in class yesterday and began to snore?"
"Unfortunately, yes. _____ is unbelievable! I'm very embarrassed."
    A. That I could do such a thing it   C. I could do such a thing it
    B. That I could do such a thing   D. I could do such a thing

12. "Officer, can you tell me how to get to Springfield?"
    "Sure. What part of Springfield _____ to go to?"
    A. do you want   B. you want   C. that you want   D. where you want

13. "Is it true _____ the law says there is no smoking in restaurants in this city?"
    A. that what   B. what   C. if   D. that

14. _____ prompt is important to our boss.
    A. A person is   C. If a person is
    B. Is a person   D. Whether or not a person is

15. A scientific observer of wildlife must note every detail of how _____ in their environment:
    their eating and sleeping habits, their social relationships, and their methods of self-
    protection.
    A. do animals live   B. live animals   C. do live animals   D. animals live

16. The mystery movie was clever and suspenseful. The audience couldn't guess _____
    committed the murder until the surprise ending.
    A. who he   B. who had   C. that who   D. that

17. How do you like your new school? Tell me _____.
    A. who in your class is   C. who is in your class
    B. who your class is in   D. your class who is in it

18. "What do you recommend _____ about this tax problem?"
    "I strongly suggest that we consult an expert as soon as possible."
    A. do we do   B. we will do   C. we do   D. should we do

19. The college does not grant degrees simply to _____ pays the cost of tuition; the student
    must satisfy the academic requirements.
    A. whoever   B. who   C. whomever   D. whoever that

20. "What are you going to buy in this store?"
    "Nothing. _____ want is much too expensive."
    A. That I   B. What I   C. That what I   D. What do I

Directions: In each sentence, select the ONE correct answer.

Example: He asked me where ___B___ .
    A. did I live   B. I lived   C. do you live   D. that I lived

1. "Does anybody know _____ on the ground?"
   "Your guess is as good as mine."
    A. how long this plane will be   C. how long will this plane be
    B. how long will be this plane   D. that how long this plane will be

2. "This restaurant is very expensive!"
   "It is, but order _____ want. Your birthday is a very special occasion."
    A. what is it you   C. whatever you
    B. what do you   D. whatever you do

3. Why did Beth ask you _____ a bicycle?
    A. that if you had   B. do you have   C. that you had   D. if you had

4. "What did your grammar teacher want to talk to you about?"
   "I did badly on the last test. She _____ studied for it."
    A. said why hadn't I   C. said why I hadn't
    B. asked why hadn't I   D. asked why I hadn't

5. "Why are you staring out the window? What _____ about?"
   "Nothing."
    A. you are thinking   C. are you thinking
    B. you think   D. do you are thinking

6. "I can't decide what color I want for my bedroom. What do you think?"
   "You should choose _____ color you want. You're the one who will have to live with it."
    A. whichever that   B. whatever   C. however   D. that what

7. "Did you remember to tell Marge _____ she should bring to the meeting tomorrow?"
   "Oh, my gosh! I completely forgot! I'm sorry."
    A. that   B. what   C. if   D. that what

8. "My aunt has been feeling bad since Uncle George died. Is it because she's depressed?"
   "I think so. _____ can cause debilitating physical symptoms is a medical fact."
    A. Depression   C. That depression
    B. That depression it   D. It is that depression

9. There was an earthquake on the coast yesterday. Fortunately, there was no loss of life. However, because of the danger of collapsing sea walls, it was essential that the area _____ evacuated quickly.
    A. to be   B. will be   C. be   D. is

10. _____ saying was so important that I asked everyone to stop talking and listen.
    A. What the woman was   C. That the woman was
    B. The woman was   D. What was the woman

11. "This cake is terrible. What happened?"
"It's my grandmother's recipe, but she forgot to tell me how long _____ it."
   A. did I bake   B. should I bake   C. do I bake   D. to bake

12. "Let's go to to Riverton this weekend."
"Sounds like fun. _____ from here?"
   A. How far is   B. How far it is   C. It how far is   D. How far is it

13. "Somebody forgot this hat. I wonder _____."
   A. whose is this hat   C. whose hat is
   B. whose hat this is   D. is this whose hat

14. Edward's interview was very intense. The interviewer wanted to know many facts about his personal life, and even asked him _____ had ever used any illegal drugs of any kind.
   A. that if he   B. that he   C. if or not he   D. whether or not he

15. It is hoped that all present-day communicable diseases will be conquered. However, _____ about certain diseases is still not sufficient to prevent them from spreading easily among the population.
   A. what we know   C. what we know that
   B. what do we know   D. that we know what

16. "Why didn't Henry attend the meeting this morning?"
"He's been very sick. His doctor insisted that he _____ in bed this week."
   A. will stay   B. stayed   C. stays   D. stay

17. Nobody yet knew what _____ to cause the dam to burst, but the residents of the area organized quickly to protect life and property against the rising floods.
   A. happens   B. had happened   C. happen   D. did it happen

18. Did the teacher explain how _____ this problem?"
   A. do we solve   B. can we solve   C. to solve   D. solve

19. _____ the National Weather Bureau predicted severe storms did not deter the fishing boats from going out into the open seas.
   A. The fact that   B. That fact is that   C. Is fact that   D. The fact is that

20. Tom walked into the huge hall to register for classes. At first, he simply looked around and wondered what _____ supposed to do.
   A. was he   B. am I   C. he was   D. I am

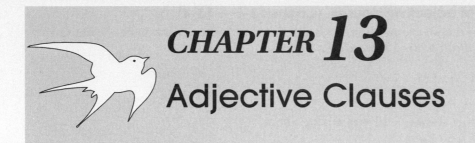

CHAPTER *13*
Adjective Clauses

◇ **PRACTICE 1. Basic patterns of adjective clauses. (Charts 13-1 → 13-4)**
Directions: <u>Underline</u> the adjective clauses in these sentences.

1. a. The paintings <u>that are marked with a small red dot</u> have already been sold.
   b. The paintings <u>which are marked with a small red dot</u> have already been sold.

2. a. The secretary who sits at the first desk on the right can give you the information.
   b. The secretary that sits at the first desk on the right can give you the information.

3. a. The shoes that I bought were made in Italy.
   b. The shoes which I bought were made in Italy.
   c. The shoes I bought were made in Italy.

4. a. I wrote a letter to the woman that I met at the meeting.
   b. I wrote a letter to the woman who(m) I met at the meeting.
   c. I wrote a letter to the woman I met at the meeting.

5. a. The speech we listened to last night was informative.
   b. The speech that we listened to last night was informative.
   c. The speech which we listened to last night was informative.
   d. The speech to which we listened last night was informative.

6. a. Dr. Jones is the professor I told you about.
   b. Dr. Jones is the professor who(m) I told you about.
   c. Dr. Jones is the professor that I told you about.
   d. Dr. Jones is the professor about whom I told you.

7. The student whose parents you just met is in one of my classes.

8. The pianist who played at the concert last night is internationally famous.

9. Some of the people a waiter has to serve at a restaurant are rude.

10. The restaurant Bob recommended was too expensive.

11. Thomas Raven is a physicist whose book on time and space has been translated into a dozen languages.

12. The woman who lives next door to us is a weathercaster on a local TV station.

◇ **PRACTICE 2. Basic patterns of adjective clauses. (Charts 13-1 → 13-4)**
    Directions: In the spaces, write all the pronouns possible to complete each sentence. Write Ø if the sentence is correct without adding a pronoun.

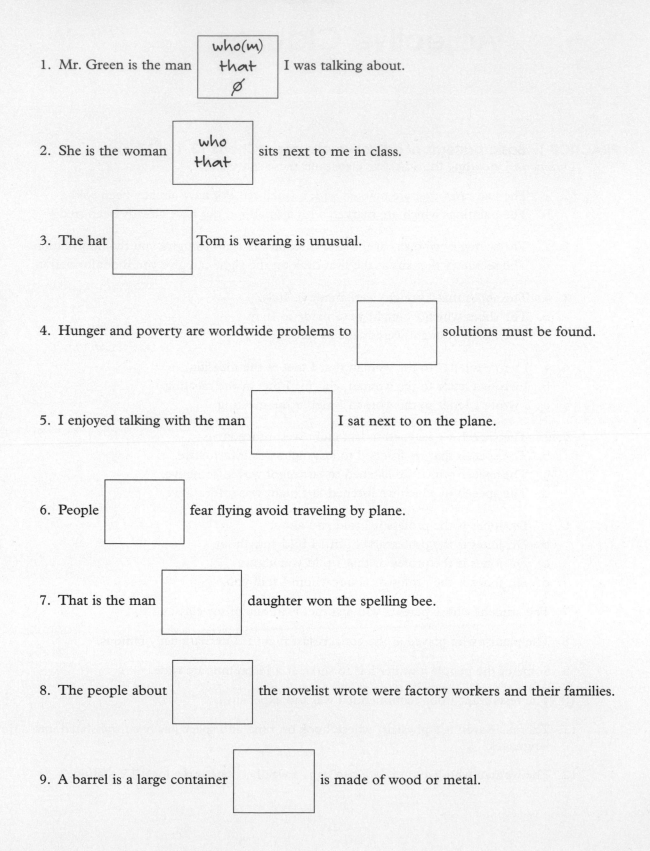

1. Mr. Green is the man [who(m) / that / Ø] I was talking about.

2. She is the woman [who / that] sits next to me in class.

3. The hat [ ] Tom is wearing is unusual.

4. Hunger and poverty are worldwide problems to [ ] solutions must be found.

5. I enjoyed talking with the man [ ] I sat next to on the plane.

6. People [ ] fear flying avoid traveling by plane.

7. That is the man [ ] daughter won the spelling bee.

8. The people about [ ] the novelist wrote were factory workers and their families.

9. A barrel is a large container [ ] is made of wood or metal.

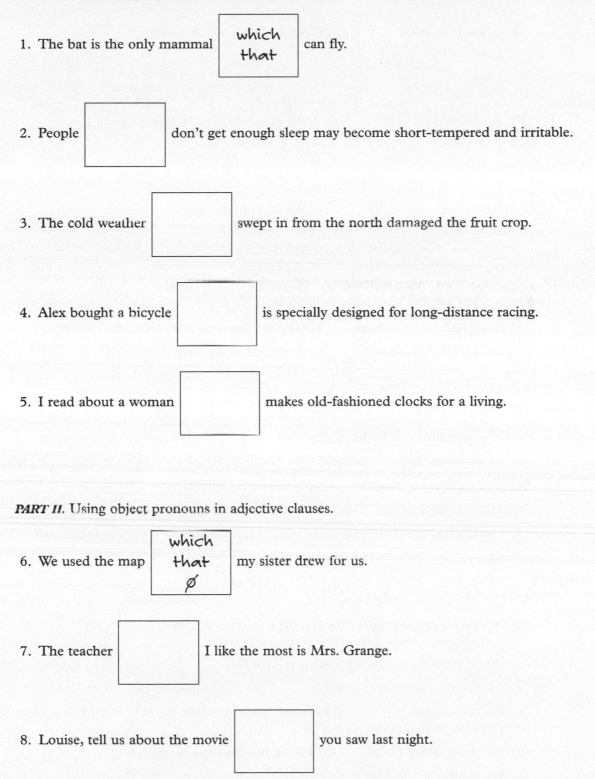

◇ **PRACTICE 3. Basic patterns of adjective clauses. (Charts 13-1 → 13-4)**
Directions: Write all the pronouns possible to complete each sentence. Write Ø if the sentence is correct without adding a pronoun.

PART I. Using subject pronouns in adjective clauses.

1. The bat is the only mammal [which / that] can fly.

2. People [   ] don't get enough sleep may become short-tempered and irritable.

3. The cold weather [   ] swept in from the north damaged the fruit crop.

4. Alex bought a bicycle [   ] is specially designed for long-distance racing.

5. I read about a woman [   ] makes old-fashioned clocks for a living.

PART II. Using object pronouns in adjective clauses.

6. We used the map [which / that / Ø] my sister drew for us.

7. The teacher [   ] I like the most is Mrs. Grange.

8. Louise, tell us about the movie [   ] you saw last night.

9. The subject about ☐ Dr. Gold spoke was interesting.

10. The subjects ☐ we talk about in class are interesting.

11. The person to ☐ Ann spoke could not answer her question.

12. I enjoyed the people ☐ I talked to at the party.

◇ **PRACTICE 4. Adjective clause patterns. (Charts 13-1 → 13-4)**
Directions: Combine the sentences, using all possible forms. Use (b) as an adjective clause.

1. (a) Louis knows the woman.   (b) The woman is meeting us at the airport.
   → *Louis knows the woman* $\begin{Bmatrix} \textbf{\textit{who}} \\ \textbf{\textit{that}} \end{Bmatrix}$ *is meeting us at the airport.*

2. (a) The chair is an antique.   (b) Sally inherited it from her grandmother.

3. (a) The bench was wet.   (b) I sat on it.

4. (a) The man finished the job in four days.   (b) I hired him to paint my house.

5. (a) I miss seeing the old woman.   (b) She used to sell flowers on that street corner.

6. (a) The architect is brilliant.   (b) Mario works with him.

7. (a) Mary tutors students.   (b) They need extra help in geometry.

8. (a) I took a picture of the rainbow.   (b) It appeared in the sky after the shower.

◇ **PRACTICE 5. Adjective clauses: using *whose*. (Chart 13-6)**
Directions: Combine the sentences, using *whose* in an adjective clause.

1. (a) Do you know the man?   (b) His car is parked over there.
   → *Do you know the man whose car is parked over there?*

2. (a) I know a woman.   (b) Her name is May Day.

3. (a) The people were very hospitable.   (b) We visited their home.

4. (a) The school principal walked down the hallway to find the boy.   (b) His parents had been injured in an automobile accident.

5. (a) Mrs. Lake is the teacher.   (b) I enjoy her class the most.

6. (a) Any company is stifling the creativity of its workforce.   (b) Their employees are in constant fear of losing their jobs.

◇ **PRACTICE 6. Adjective clauses: using *where* and *when*. (Charts 13-7 and 13-8)**

Directions: Begin your response with "That is . . . . " Use ***where*** or ***when*** in an adjective clause.

Example: You were born in *that* city.
Response: That is *the* city **where** I was born.

1. We have class in that room.
2. We ate dinner at that restaurant.
3. Anna works in that building
4. I was born in that year.
5. You eat lunch at that cafeteria.
6. The monsoons arrive in that month.
7. Alex lives on that street.
8. You spent your vacation on that island.
9. You went swimming in that lake.
10. You grew up in that town.
11. The space flight to Mars is scheduled to leave on that day.
12. The earthquake occurred in that country.
13. The examination will be given in that room.
14. You lived in that city until you were ten years old.
15. You felt the happiest at that time.

◇ **PRACTICE 7. Adjective clauses. (Charts 13-1 → 13-4)**

Directions: Choose the correct answer or answers.

1. Yoko told me about students __A, D__ have taken the entrance exam 13 times.
   A. who   B. whom   C. which   D. that

2. The secretary __B, C, D__ I talked to didn't know where the meeting was.
   A. which   B. whom   C. that   D. Ø

3. You need to talk to a person _____ you can trust. You will feel better if you do.
   A. whose   B. which   C. whom   D. Ø

4. Bob is the kind of person to _____ one can talk about anything.
   A. who   B. whom   C. that   D. him

5. He is a person _____ friends trust him.
   A. who   B. his   C. that   D. whose

6. I'm looking for an electric can opener _____ also can sharpen knives.
   A. who   B. which   C. that   D. Ø

7. People _____ live in glass houses shouldn't throw stones.*
   A. who   B. whom   C. which   D. Ø

8. The problems _____ Tony has seem insurmountable.
   A. what   B. he   C. that   D. Ø

---

*This is an idiom that means people shouldn't criticize others for faults they themselves have. For example, a lazy person shouldn't criticize another person for being lazy.

9. The man _____ I introduced you to last night may be the next president of the university.
   A. which   B. whom   C. that   D. Ø

10. Cathy is trustworthy. She's a person upon _____ you can always depend.
    A. who   B. whom   C. that   D. Ø

11. Your career should focus on a field in _____ you are genuinely interested.
    A. which   B. what   C. that   D. Ø

12. People _____ outlook on life is optimistic are usually happy people.
    A. whose   B. whom   C. that   D. which

◇ **PRACTICE 8. Adjective clauses: subject–verb agreement.**
             (Charts 13-1 and 13-2; Chapter 6)
   Directions: Choose the correct verb in *italics*.

   1. There are three students in my class who   *speaks,* *(speak)*   French.

   2. There is one student in my class who   *speaks, speak*   Greek.

   3. The patients who   *is, are*   treated at City Hospital   *doesn't, don't*   need to have private physicians.

   4. The courses this school   *offers, offer*   *is, are*   listed in the catalog.

   5. A pedometer is an instrument that   *measures, measure*   the distance a person *walks, walk.*

   6. People who   *suffers, suffer*   from extreme shyness can sometimes overcome their problem by taking a public speaking class.

   7. In the months that   *has, have*   passed since the accident, Robert has regained the use of his legs.

   8. Malnutrition and illiteracy are among the problems in the world that   *has, have*   no simple solutions.

   9. Most advertisements are directed toward adults and teenagers, but you can see commercials on television that   *is, are*   aimed at prompting children to persuade their parents to buy certain products.

   10. The requirements of the school as written in the catalog   *states, state*   that all students who   *wishes, wish*   to attend must take an entrance exam.

◇ **PRACTICE 9. Punctuating adjective clauses. (Chart 13-10)**
   Directions: Circle YES if the adjective clause requires commas and add them in the appropriate places. Circle NO if the adjective clause does not require commas.

   1. YES (NO) I made an appointment with a doctor who is considered an expert on eye disorders.
   2. (YES) NO I made an appointment with Dr. Raven, who is considered an expert on eye disorders.
   3. YES NO   The car that Al bought had had three previous owners, but it was in excellent condition.
   4. YES NO   We thoroughly enjoyed the music which we heard at the concert last Sunday.

5. YES NO Bogota which is the capital of Colombia is a cosmopolitan city.

6. YES NO They climbed Mount Rainier which is in the State of Washington twice last year.

7. YES NO Emeralds which are valuable gemstones are mined in Colombia.

8. YES NO The company offered the position to John whose department performed best this year.

9. YES NO On our trip to Africa we visited Nairobi which is near several fascinating game reserves and then traveled to Egypt to see the pyramids.

10. YES NO I think the waiter who took our order used to work at Captain Bob's Restaurant.

11. YES NO Someone who understands physics better than I do is going to have to help you.

12. YES NO Larry was very close to his only brother who was a famous social historian.

13. YES NO Violent tropical storms that occur in western Asia are called typhoons.

14. YES NO Similar storms that occur on the Atlantic side of the Americas are called hurricanes rather than typhoons.

15. YES NO A typhoon which is a violent tropical storm can cause great destruction.

16. YES NO According to the news report, the typhoon that threatened to strike the Indonesian coast has moved away from land and toward open water.

◇ **PRACTICE 10. Punctuating adjective clauses. (Chart 13-10)**
Directions: Choose the correct answer or answers.

1. Ms. Donaldson, ____A____ teaches linguistics at the university, recently received recognition for her research on the use of gestures in communication.
   A. who   B. whom   C. which   D. that   E. Ø

2. A woman ___A, D___ teaches linguistics at the university received an award for outstanding research.
   A. who   B. whom   C. which   D. that   E. Ø

3. The earth, _____ is the fifth largest planet in the solar system, is the third planet from the sun.
   A. who   B. whom   C. which   D. that   E. Ø

4. A grant of $1.5 million was awarded to Dr. Sato, _____ has impressed the scientific community with his research on the common cold.
   A. who   B. whom   C. which   D. that   E. Ø

5. The award for the Most Valuable Player was won by a player _____ the coaches and the entire team respect.
   A. who   B. whom   C. which   D. that   E. Ø

6. The award was won by Dennis Johnson, _____ the coach highly respects.
   A. who   B. whom   C. which   D. that   E. Ø

7. My accountant, _____ understands the complexities of the tax system, is doing my taxes this year.
   A. who   B. whom   C. which   D. that   E. Ø

8. The school board voted to close a neighborhood elementary school. The decision, _____ affected over 200 students, was not warmly received in the community.
   A. who   B. whom   C. which   D. that   E. Ø

9. Our office needs a secretary _____ knows how to use various word processing programs.
   A. who   B. whom   C. which   D. that   E. Ø

10. The winner of the Nobel Prize in physics dedicated the honor to his high school physics teacher, _____ had been an inspiration during his early years.
    A. who   B. whom   C. which   D. that   E. Ø

11. The consultant _____ was hired to advise us never really understood our situation.
    A. who   B. whom   C. which   D. that   E. Ø

12. I gave the check to Oliver, _____ promptly cashed it and spent all the money before the day was out.
    A. who   B. whom   C. which   D. that   E. Ø

13. The check _____ I gave Oliver was for work he'd done for me.
    A. who   B. whom   C. which   D. that   E. Ø

◇ **PRACTICE 11. Punctuating adjective clauses. (Chart 13-10)**
   Directions: Choose the correct explanation of the meaning of each sentence.

   1. The students, who attend class five hours per day, have become quite proficient in their new language.
      (a.) *All* of the students attend class for five hours per day.
      b. *Only some* of the students attend class for five hours per day.

   2. The students who attend class five hours per day have become quite proficient in their new language.
      a. *All* of the students attend class for five hours per day.
      (b.) *Only some* of the students attend class for five hours per day.

   3. The orchestra conductor signaled the violinists, who were to begin playing.
      a. *All* of the violinists were to begin playing.
      b. *Only some* of the violinists were to begin playing.

   4. The orchestra conductor signaled the violinists who were to begin playing.
      a. *All* of the violinists were to begin playing.
      b. *Only some* of the violinists were to begin playing.

   5. I put the vase on top of the TV set, which is in the living room.
      a. I have *more than one* TV set.
      b. I have *only one* TV set.

   6. I put the vase on top of the TV set that is in the living room.
      a. I have *more than one* TV set.
      b. I have *only one* TV set.

   7. Trees which lose their leaves in winter are called deciduous trees.
      a. *All* trees lose their leaves in winter.
      b. *Only some* trees lose their leaves in winter.

   8. Pine trees, which are evergreen, grow well in a cold climate.
      a. *All* pine trees are evergreen.
      b. *Only some* pine trees are evergreen.

◇ **PRACTICE 12. Punctuating adjective clauses. (Charts 13-10 → 13-13)**

Directions: Circle YES if the adjective clause requires commas and add the commas in the appropriate places. Circle NO if the adjective clause does not require commas.

1. (YES) NO Thirty people**,** two of whom were members of the crew**,** were killed in the ferry accident.

2. YES (NO) I'm trying to convince my mother to buy a small car which has front-wheel drive instead of a large car with rear-wheel drive.

3. YES NO Over 500 students took the entrance examination the results of which will be posted in the administration building at the end of the month.

4. YES NO The newspapers carried the story of an accident in which four pedestrians were injured.

5. YES NO The newly married couple that lives next door just moved here from California.

6. YES NO The new supervisor was not happy with his work crew none of whom seemed interested in doing quality work.

7. YES NO My oldest brother in whose house I lived for six months when I was ten has been a father to me in many ways.

8. YES NO Tom is always interrupting me which makes me mad.

9. YES NO To express the uselessness of worrying, Mark Twain once said, "I've had a lot of problems in my life most of which never happened."

◇ **PRACTICE 13. Expressions of quantity in adjective clauses. (Chart 13-11)**

Directions: Combine the sentences. Use the second sentence as an adjective clause.

1. I received two job offers. I accepted neither of them.
   → *I received two job offers, neither of which I accepted.*

2. I have three brothers. Two of them are professional athletes.

3. Jerry is engaged in several business ventures. Only one of them is profitable.

4. The United States of America is a union of fifty states. The majority of them are located east of the Mississippi River.

5. The two women have already dissolved their business partnership. Both of them are changing careers.

6. Tom is proud of his success. Much of it has been due to hard work, but some of it has been due to good luck.

◇ **PRACTICE 14. Adjective phrases. (Charts 13-14 and 13-15)**

Directions: Change the adjective clauses to adjective phrases.

1. Only a few of the movies that are shown at the Gray Theater are suitable for children.
   → *Only a few of the movies shown at the Gray Theater are suitable for children.*

2. We visited Madrid, which is the capital of Spain..
   → *We visited Madrid, the capital of Spain.*

3. The couple who live in the house next door are both college professors.

4. Astronomy, which is the study of planets and stars, is one of the world's oldest sciences.

5. Only a small fraction of the eggs that are laid by a fish actually hatch and survive to adulthood.

6. Jasmine, which is a viny plant with fragrant flowers, grows only in warm places.

7. Arizona, which was once thought to be a useless desert, is today a rapidly growing industrial and agricultural state.

8. Simon Bolivar, who was a great South American general, led the fight for independence early in the 19th century.

9. In hot weather, many people enjoy lemonade, which is a drink that is made from lemon juice, water, and sugar.

10. I was awakened by the sound of laughter which came from the room which was next to mine at the motel.

11. Few tourists ever see a jaguar, which is a spotted wild cat that is native to tropical America.

◇ **PRACTICE 15. Punctuating adjective phrases. (Charts 13-14 and 13-15)**
Directions: Add commas where necessary.

1. A national holiday has been established in memory of Martin Luther King, Jr. the leader of the civil rights movement in the United States in the 1950s and 1960s.

2. Neil Armstrong the first person to set foot on the moon reported that the surface was fine and powdery.

3. Mark Twain is an author known far and wide as one of the greatest American humorists.

4. Susan B. Anthony one of the first leaders of the campaign for women's rights worked tirelessly during her lifetime to gain the right to vote for women.

◇ **PRACTICE 16. Adjective phrases. (Charts 13-14 and 13-15)**
Directions: Combine the sentences. Use the second sentence as an adjective phrase.

1. Louisville was founded in 1778. It is the largest city in Kentucky.
   → *Louisville, the largest city in Kentucky, was founded in 1778.*

2. John Quincy Adams was born on July 11, 1767. He was the sixth president of the United States.

3. Two languages, Finnish and Swedish, are used in Helsinki. It is the capital of Finland.

4. The Washington National Monument is a famous landmark in the nation's capital. It is a towering obelisk made of white marble.

5. Honolulu has consistently pleasant weather. It is best known to the traveler for Waikiki Beach.

6. Libya is a leading producer of oil. It is a country in North Africa.

◇ **PRACTICE 17. Adjective phrases. (Charts 13-14 and 13-15)**
Directions: Change all of the adjective clauses to adjective phrases.

1. None of the pedestrians who were walking up and down the busy street stopped to help or even inquire about the elderly man who was slumped in the doorway of an apparently unoccupied building.
   → *None of the pedestrians walking up and down the busy street stopped to help or even inquire about the elderly man slumped in the doorway of an apparently unoccupied building.*

2. Food that passes from the mouth to the stomach goes through a tube which is called the esophagus.

3. Animals that are born in a zoo generally adjust to captivity better than those that are captured in the wild.

4. The children attended a special movie program that consisted of cartoons that featured Donald Duck and Mickey Mouse.

5. One of the most important foodstuffs in the world is flour, which is a fine powder that is made by grinding wheat or other grains.

6. Nero, who was Emperor of Rome from A.D. 54 to 68, is believed to have murdered both his mother and his wife.

7. The conclusion which is presented in that book states that most of the automobiles which are produced by American industry in the 1960s and '70s had some defect.

8. Pictures that showed the brutality of war entered the living rooms of millions of TV watchers on the nightly news.

9. The Indians who lived in Peru before the discovery of the New World by Europeans belonged to the Incan culture.

10. My uncle Elias, who is a restaurant owner, often buys fish and shellfish from boats that are docked at the local pier. Customers come from miles around to dine on a seafood feast that is considered to be the best in all of the northeastern United States.

11. Hundreds of volunteers went to a northern village yesterday to reinforce firefighters who are trying to save a settlement which is threatened by a forest fire. The fire started when a cigarette ignited oil which was leaking from a machine which is used to cut timber.

12. Researchers have developed a way to mark genes so that they glow in the dark, which is a technique that scientists can use to follow specific genetic activity of cells which are within plants and animals. This development, which was announced by the National Science Foundation, which is the sponsor of the research, should prove useful to scientists who study the basic functions of organisms.

Directions: All of the following sentences contain errors in adjective clauses, adjective phrases, or punctuation. Find the errors and correct them, using any appropriate form.

1. When we walked past the theater, there were a lot of people waited in a long line outside the box office.

2. Students who living on campus are close to their classrooms and the library.

3. If you need any information, see the librarian sits at the central desk on the second floor.

4. My oldest sister is Anna is 21 years old.

5. Hiroko was born in Sapporo that is a city in Japan.

6. Patrick who is my oldest brother. He is married and has one child.

7. The person sits next to me is someone I've never met him.

8. My favorite place in the world is a small city is located on the southern coast of Brazil.

9. Last Saturday I attended a party giving by one of my friends. My friend, who his apartment is in another town, was very glad I could come.

10. Dr. Darnell was the only person to whom I wanted to see.

11. There are eighty students, are from all over the world, study English at this school.

12. The people who we met them on our trip last May are going to visit us in October.

13. Dianne Jones that used to teach Spanish has organized a tour of Central America for senior citizens.

14. I've met many people since I came here who some of them are from my country.

15. People can speak English can be understood in many countries.

Directions: Choose the correct answer.

Example: Friends are people ___B___ close to us.
    A. who is   B. who are   C. which is   D. which are

1. "Who is eligible for the scholarship?"
   "Anyone _____ scholastic record is above average can apply for the scholarship."
    A. who has a   B. has a   C. who's a   D. whose

2. Dr. Sales is a person _____.
    A. in whom I don't have much confidence   C. whom I don't have much confidence in him
    B. in that I don't have much confidence   D. I don't have much confidence

3. "Is April twenty-first the day _____?"
   "No, the twenty-second."
    A. you'll arrive then   C. on that you'll arrive
    B. when you'll arrive   D. when you'll arrive on

4. The severe drought _____ occurred last summer ruined the corn crop.
    A. that it   B. which it   C. it   D. that

5. Florida, _____ the Sunshine State, attracts many tourists every year.
    A. is   B. known as   C. is known as   D. that is known as

6. The new shopping mall is gigantic. It's advertised as a place _____ you can find just about anything you might want to buy.
    A. where   B. which   C. in where   D. in that

7. Lola's marriage has been arranged by her family. She is marrying a man _____.
    A. that she hardly knows him   C. she hardly knows
    B. whom she hardly knows him   D. she hardly knows him

8. People who exercise frequently have greater physical endurance than those _____.
    A. who doesn't   B. that doesn't   C. which don't   D. who don't

9. "Is this the address to _____ you want the package sent?"
    A. where   B. that   C. which   D. whom

10. Ann quit her job at the advertising agency, _____ surprised everyone.
    A. which   B. that   C. who   D. that it

11. That book is by a famous anthropologist. It's about the people in Samoa _____ for two years.
    A. that she lived   C. among whom she lived
    B. that she lived among them   D. where she lived among them

12. The missing man's family is desperately seeking anyone _____ information about his activities.
    A. has   B. having   C. who have   D. have

13. The publishers expect that the new biography of Simon Bolivar will be bought by people _____ in Latin American history.
    A. who are interested   C. interested
    B. are interested   D. they are interested

14. I have always wanted to visit Paris, _____ of France.
    A. is the capital   C. that is the capital
    B. which the capital is   D. the capital

15. The chemistry book _____ was a little expensive.
    A. that I bought it   B. I bought that   C. what I bought   D. I bought

16. "Have you ever met the man _____ over there?"
    "No. Who is he?"
    A. stands   C. is standing
    B. standing   D. who he is standing

17. "Do you have the book _____ the teacher?"
    "Yes, I do."
    A. that it belongs to   C. to which belongs
    B. to which belongs to   D. that belongs to

18. The voters were overwhelmingly against the candidate _____ proposals called for higher taxes.
    A. who his   B. whose   C. whom he had   D. that his

19. "Do you remember Mrs. Goddard, _____ taught us English composition?"
    "I certainly do."
    A. who   B. whom   C. that   D. which

20. I have three brothers, _____ are businessmen.
    A. that all of them   C. all of whom
    B. who they all   D. who all of them

Directions: Choose the correct answer.

Example: Friends are people ___B___ close to us.
    A. who is   B. who are   C. which is   D. which are

1. "Were you able to locate the person _____ wallet you found?"
"Luckily, yes."
    A. which   B. that his   C. whose   D. that's

2. Some fish is frozen, but _____ is best.
    A. fish is fresh   C. fish fresh
    B. fresh fish   D. fresh fish is caught

3. "Why do you get up at 4:00 A.M.?"
"Because it's the only time _____ without being interrupted."
    A. when I can work on my book   C. when I can work on my book then
    B. when I can work on my book at   D. at when I can work on my book

4. "You seem so happy today."
"I am. You are looking at a person _____ has just been accepted into medical school!"
    A. who   B. who she   C. whom she   D. whom

5. "The movie _____ last night was terrific."
"What's it about?"
    A. I went   B. I went to it   C. I went to   D. that I went

6. Many people lost their homes in the earthquake. The government needs to establish more shelters to care for those _____ have homes.
    A. who doesn't   B. who don't   C. which doesn't   D. which don't

7. The problem _____ never occurred.
    A. I hadn't expected it   C. that I had expected it
    B. who I had expected   D. I had expected

8. I had to drive to the factory to pick up my brother, _____ car wouldn't start.
    A. who his   B. who   C. who's   D. whose

9. I read a book about Picasso, _____.
    A. is a Spanish painter   C. who a Spanish painter is
    B. a Spanish painter   D. that is a Spanish painter

10. The people _____ the acrobat turn circles in the air were horrified when he missed the outstretched hands of his partner and fell to his death.
    A. watched   B. watch   C. watching   D. were watching

11. "My writing has improved a lot in this class."
"Mine has, too. All the students _____ do well in writing."
    A. whom Mr. Davis teaches them   C. that Mr. Davis teaches them
    B. which Mr. Davis teaches   D. Mr. Davis teaches

12. "Have you seen the place _____ the graduation ceremony will be held?"
    "Yes. It's big enough to hold 5,000 people."
    A. in that   B. where   C. is where that   D. which

13. "How's your class this term?"
    "Great. I have seventeen students, most of _____ speak English very well."
    A. who   B. those   C. whom   D. which

14. "Will everyone like the book?"
    "No. Only people _____ interested in anthropology."
    A. are   B. who are   C. in whom are   D. that is

15. "How did you enjoy your dinner with Mr. Jackson?"
    "It was boring. He talked only about himself, _____ almost put us to sleep."
    A. which   B. that   C. who   D. that he

16. My grandfather, _____ a wise man, has greatly influenced my life.
    A. is   B. that is   C. who is   D. who he is

17. "Is Dr. Brown the person _____ you wish to speak?"
    "Yes, please."
    A. that   B. whom   C. to that   D. to whom

18. In the movie, a teenager _____ to pursue a singing career meets resistance from his strong-willed father.
    A. wants   B. wanted   C. wanting   D. who want

19. "Excuse me, but there is something about _____ immediately."
    "Certainly."
    A. which I must speak to you   C. that I must speak to you about
    B. which I must speak to you about it   D. that I must speak to you

20. *Little Women,* _____ in 1868, is my sister's favorite book.
    A. is a novel published   C. a novel was published
    B. a novel published   D. was a novel published

CHAPTER 14
Gerunds and Infinitives, Part 1

◇ **PRACTICE 1. Gerunds as objects of prepositions. (Chart 14-2)**
Directions: Complete the sentences with prepositions followed by gerunds. Use the verbs in the given list. Use each verb only once.

✓ask	have	make	see
break	kill	open	talk
finish	lock	practice	wash

1. Instead _of asking_ for help on each arithmetic problem, you should use your book and try to figure out the answers yourself

2. I look forward _____ you next time I'm in town. I'll be sure to let you know ahead of time so that we can plan to get together.

3. Alice told us that she was tired _____ the dishes every night.

4. The four-year-old was blamed _____ the glass candy dish.

5. Because of the bomb scare, no one was allowed in the building. People were prevented _____ the front door by a guard who was stationed there.

6. You should listen to other people instead _____ about yourself all the time.

7. What do you feel _____ for dinner? Does chicken and rice sound good?

8. Frank is an environmentalist who believes animals should be protected from hunters. He objects _____ wild animals for sport.

9. Please don't argue _____ your homework. Just do it.

10. Marie is responsible _____ all the doors and windows and _____ sure all the lights are turned off before she leaves work in the evening.

11. Mario spent all month preparing for the tennis match, but in spite _____ for many hours each day, he lost the match to Ivan.

◇ **PRACTICE 2. Gerunds as objects of prepositions. (Charts 14-2 and 14-3)**
Directions: Complete the sentences in column A with the ideas in column B. Be sure to link them with an appropriate preposition.

Example: I thanked my classmate . . . .
→ *I thanked my classmate for helping me with my homework.*

Column A	**Column B**
1. I thanked my classmate	A. answer students' questions
2. The treasurer is responsible	B. get a new doll for her birthday
3. The students complained	✔C. help me with my homework
4. I apologized	D. lift heavy weights
5. A bodybuilder is capable	E. get me a pillow
6. A teacher is used★	F. step on my friend's toe
7. The rainy weather prevented us	G. enter a military base
8. All of the children participated	H. balance the checkbook
9. Unauthorized persons are prohibited	I. be forced to work overtime
10. The little girl was excited	J. go on a picnic
11. I thanked the flight attendant	K. have too many tests
12. The employees objected	L. make decorations for their classroom

◇ **PRACTICE 3. Verbs followed by gerunds. (Charts 14-4 and 14-5)**
Directions: Make sentences using the given verbs.

Examples: enjoy + watch → *Do you enjoy watching old movies on television?*
mind + have to be → *I don't mind having to be in class at 8:00 A.M.*
put off + pack → *Dan usually puts off packing his suitcase until the very last minute.*

1. enjoy + take
2. avoid + eat
3. go + jog
4. finish + do
5. suggest + change
6. consider + go + swim
7. stop + cry
8. discuss + go + shop
9. mention + have to go
10. delay + put
11. mind + take
12. keep + ask
13. quit + worry about
14. postpone + take

★COMPARE:
   Used + to + -ing means "accustomed to doing something."
      *Mary is **used to living** in a cold climate. = Mary is accustomed to living in a cold climate.*
   Used + to + simple form (infinitive) expresses habitual past activities.
      *Jack **used to live** in Chicago. = Jack lived in Chicago in the past, but now he doesn't.*

◇ **PRACTICE 4. Special expressions followed by -ing. (Chart 14-6)**
   Directions: Combine the given ideas into one sentence.

   1. play soccer . . . spend . . . all yesterday afternoon . . . we
      → *We spent all yesterday afternoon playing soccer.*

   2. a really good time . . . all of us . . . have . . . play soccer in the park . . . yesterday

   3. find . . . have trouble . . . Omar . . . my house . . . last night

   4. my bicycle . . . my mother . . . try to steal . . . catch . . . some neighborhood kids . . . yesterday

   5. at the window . . . stand . . . when the boss walked into the office . . . all of the employees . . . watch the parade on the street below

   6. my father always said, ". . . read novels . . . your time . . . from other kinds of books . . . when you could be learning something worthwhile . . . don't waste"

   7. when Mrs. Smith checked on the children last night . . . play a game . . . find . . . instead of sleeping . . . them . . . she

   8. Susan . . . find . . . when I opened the door . . . I . . . on her bed . . . cry . . . lie

◇ **PRACTICE 5. Gerund vs. infinitive. (Charts 14-1 → 14-7)**
   Directions: Select the correct answer for each sentence.

   1. Whenever we met, Jack avoided ___B___ at me.
      A. to look   B. looking

   2. Most people enjoy _____ to different parts of the world.
      A. to travel   B. traveling

   3. Marjorie needs _____ another job. Her present company is going out of business.
      A. to find   B. finding

   4. May I change the TV channel, or do you want _____ more of this program?
      A. to watch   B. watching

   5. Joan is considering _____ her major from pre-med studies to psychology.
      A. to change   B. changing

   6. Although Joe slammed on his brakes, he couldn't avoid _____ the small dog that suddenly darted out in front of his car.
      A. to hit   B. hitting

   7. I hope _____ my autobiography before I die. Do you think anyone would read it?
      A. to write   B. writing

   8. Joyce thanked us for _____ them to dinner and said that they wanted to have us over for dinner next week.
      A. to invite   B. inviting

   9. If you delay _____ your bills, you will only incur more and more interest charges.
      A. to pay   B. paying

   10. My lawyer advised me not _____ anything further about the accident.
       A. to say   B. saying

11. A procrastinator is one who habitually postpones _____ things — especially tasks that are unpleasant.
    A. to do   B. doing

12. You should plan _____ at the stadium early or you won't be able to get good seats.
    A. to arrive   B. arriving

13. My mom asked me _____ up some eggs at the supermarket on my way home from work.
    A. to pick   B. picking

14. Nobody has offered _____ the house next door, so I think they're going to lower the price.
    A. to buy   B. buying

15. The highway patrol advises _____ the old route through the city because the interstate highway is under major repairs.
    A. to take   B. taking

16. Would you mind _____ that apple for me? My arthritis is acting up in my right hand.
    A. to peel   B. peeling

17. Stop _____ me! I'll get everything finished before I go to bed.
    A. to nag   B. nagging

18. When the university suggested _____ the tuition again, the student senate protested vigorously.
    A. to raise   B. raising

19. Are we permitted _____ guests to the ceremony? I'd like to invite my friend to join us.
    A. to bring   B. bringing

20. The city council agreed _____ the architect's proposed design for a new parking garage.
    A. to accept   B. accepting

◇ **PRACTICE 6. Verbs followed by infinitives. (Chart 14-7)**
Directions: Restate the given sentences. Choose the most appropriate reporting verb in parentheses. Make it active or passive as appropriate. Include an infinitive in the completion and any other necessary words.

1. The teacher said to Jim, "Would you give your book to Mary, please?"
   (ask, tell, order)
   → The teacher ___asked Jim to give___ his book to Mary.

2. The sign said, "No parking in this area. Violators will be towed away."
   (invite, warn, force)
   → Drivers ___were warned not to park___ in the area.

3. Before Bobby went to bed, his father said, "Don't forget to brush your teeth."
   (invite, allow, remind)
   → Before Bobby went to bed, his father _____ his teeth.

4. Under the law, drivers and all passengers must wear seat belts while in a moving vehicle.
   (encourage, require, permit)
   → Drivers and passengers _____ seat belts while in a moving vehicle.

5. When I asked the nurse about my skin rash, she said, "You should consult a dermatologist."
   (ask, permit, advise)
   → The nurse _____ a dermatologist.

6. The fire chief said, "Everyone must leave the building immediately."
   (order, remind, allow)
   → Everyone _____ the building immediately.

7. The instructor said to the students, "You will have exactly one hour to complete the exam."
   (order, expect, warn)
   → The students _____ the exam in one hour.

8. Because he forgot last year, I told my husband several times that he should buy some flowers for his mother on Mother's Day.
   (remind, require, allow)
   → I _____ some flowers for his mother on Mother's Day.

9. My garage mechanic said, "You should get a tune-up every 5,000 miles."
   (ask, order, advise)
   → My garage mechanic _____ a tune-up every 5,000 miles.

10. The factory manager said to the employees, "Do not come late. If you do, you will lose your jobs."
    (ask, warn, encourage)
    → The employees _____ late.

11. The sign on the side door says, "Do not enter," so we have to use a different door.
    (ask, permit, force)
    → Nobody _____ the side door.

12. The little girl said to her father, "Daddy, I really like this tricycle. Can we buy it?"
    (require, ask, advise)
    → The little girl _____ the tricycle for her.

13. We often told our grandfather, "Your experiences as a sailor in the navy were fascinating. You should write a book about them."
    (remind, encourage, require)
    → We _____ a book about his experiences in the navy.

14. The judge said to the defendant, "You must not shout in the courtroom again."
    (ask, order, encourage)
    → The defendant _____ in the courtroom again.

◇ **PRACTICE 7. Verbs followed by infinitives. (Chart 14-7)**
   Directions: Report what the speakers say by using a verb from the following list and an infinitive phrase. Use each verb in the list only once. Make your sentence passive if the speaker is not specifically identified.

advise	✓ask	invite	remind
allow	encourage	order	warn

   1. During the water shortage, someone in authority said to the public, "Curtail your use of water as much as possible."
      → *During the water shortage, the public was asked to curtail its use of water as much as possible.*

   2. Laura said to her roommate, "Don't forget to set your alarm clock for 6:00."

3. Mrs. Jones said to the children, "Each of you may have one piece of candy."

4. The doctor said to my father, "It would be best if you limited your sugar consumption."

5. My parents often said to me, "Good for you! It's good to be independent!"

6. Someone said to the children, "Don't swim in the lake without an adult present."

7. The police officer shouted to the reckless driver, "Pull over!"

8. Rose said to Jerry, "I'd like you to come to my house Sunday night to meet my parents."

◇ **PRACTICE 8. Gerund vs. infinitive. (Chart 14-8)**
Directions: Choose the best answer or answers. In some cases, BOTH answers are correct.

1. John was trying ——*B*—— the door with the wrong key.
   A. unlocking   B. to unlock

2. The audience began ——*A, B*—— before the curtains closed.
   A. clapping   B. to clap

3. The soccer teams continued _____ even though it began to snow.
   A. playing   B. to play

4. We like _____ outside when the weather is warm and sunny.
   A. eating   B. to eat

5. We began _____ to the news when we heard the Olympics mentioned.
   A. listening   B. to listen

6. I was just beginning _____ asleep when the phone rang.
   A. falling   B. to fall

7. I really hate _____ late for appointments.
   A. being   B. to be

8. The cake was starting _____ when I took it out of the oven.
   A. burning   B. to burn

9. She's so impatient! She can't stand _____ in line for anything.
   A. waiting   B. to wait

10. I prefer _____ my bicycle to work because the automobile traffic is too heavy.
    A. riding   B. to ride

11. Lillian prefers _____ to taking the bus.
    A. walking   B. to walk

12. Tim prefers _____ than to jog for exercise.
    A. walking   B. to walk

13. The baby loves _____ in the car.
    A. riding   B. to ride

14. Near the end of the performance, the audience began _____ their feet on the floor.
    A. stamping   B. to stamp

15. The audience began to clap and _____ their feet on the floor.
    A. stamping   B. (to) stamp

16. The audience began clapping and _____ their feet on the floor.
    A. stamping   B. (to) stamp

17. My son sometimes forgets _____ the stove when he is finished cooking.
    A. turning off   B. to turn off

18. Alex will never forget _____ his first helicopter ride.
    A. taking   B. to take

19. Would you please remember _____ away all the tapes when you're finished listening to them?
    A. putting   B. to put

20. I remember _____ them away when I finished with them last night.
    A. putting   B. to put

21. I remember _____ Bolivia for the first time. It's a beautiful country.
    A. visiting   B. to visit

22. What am I going to do? I forgot _____ my calculus text, and I need it for the review today.
    A. bringing   B. to bring

23. My boss regrets _____ his secretary now that she is gone.
    A. firing   B. to fire

24. The letter said, "I regret _____ you that your application has been denied."
    A. informing   B. to inform

25. I haven't been able to get in touch with Shannon. I tried _____ her. Then I tried _____ her a letter. I tried _____ a message with her brother when I talked to him. Nothing worked.
    A. calling . . . writing . . . leaving   B. to call . . . to write . . . to leave

26. I always try _____ my bills on time, but sometimes I'm a little late.
    A. paying   B. to pay

◇ **PRACTICE 9. Gerund vs. Infinitive. (Charts 14-9 and 14-10)**
    Directions: Work with another person. One of you should read the beginning of the sentence, and the other, without looking at the book, should supply the correct response: ***to do it*** or ***doing it***. (If you are studying alone, cover up the answers in parentheses and check yourself as you go.)

    Example: A: I enjoy . . . .
              B: . . . doing it.

    1. I dislike .... (doing it.)
    2. She was ordered .... (to do it.)
    3. I urged my friend .... (to do it.)
    4. Can he afford .... (to do it?)

5. We all discussed .... (doing it.)
6. The institute requires us .... (to do it.)
7. We will eventually complete .... (doing it.)
8. The whole class practiced .... (doing it.)
9. I really don't care .... (to do it.)
10. My friend recommended not .... (doing it.)
11. She was expected .... (to do it.)
12. Bill resented his roommate .... (doing it.)
13. Did the criminal admit .... (doing it?)
14. Please allow us .... (to do it.)
15. The whole family anticipated .... (doing it.)
16. No one recollected .... (doing it.)
17. Did you risk .... (doing it?)
18. Did they recall .... (doing it?)
19. My friend challenged me .... (to do it.)
20. The teacher postponed .... (doing it.)
21. Do you mind .... (doing it?)
22. Why did he pretend .... (to do it?)
23. The teacher arranged .... (to do it.)
24. The regulations permit us .... (to do it.)
25. The dentist wanted to delay .... (doing it.)
26. Can anyone learn .... (to do it?)
27. Did your roommate offer .... (to do it?)
28. He doesn't deny .... (doing it.)
29. Somehow, the dog managed .... (to do it.)
30. Everyone avoided .... (doing it.)
31. The boy dared Al .... (to do it.)
32. Our teacher threatened .... (to do it.)
33. The contestant practiced .... (doing it.)
34. My friend consented .... (to do it.)
35. I miss .... (doing it.)

◇ **PRACTICE 10. Gerund vs. infinitive. (Charts 14-2 → 14-10)**
Directions: Complete the sentences with the correct form, gerund or infinitive, using the words in parentheses.

1. The store offered __to refund__ the money I paid for the book I returned. *(refund)*

2. Don't pretend __to be__ what you aren't. *(be)*

3. I persuaded my brother-in-law not _____ that old car. *(buy)*

4. Annie denied _____ the brick through the window. *(throw)*

5. My father expects me _____ high marks in school. *(get)*

6. According to the sign on the restaurant door, all diners are required _____

   shirts and shoes. *(wear)*

7. We are planning _____ several historical sites in Moscow. *(visit)*

8. There appears _____ no way to change our reservation for the play at this late date. *(be)*

9. For some strange reason, I keep _____ today is Saturday. *(think)*

10. All of the members agreed _____ the emergency meeting. *(attend)*

11. I've arranged _____ work early tomorrow. *(leave)*

12. Even though Anna had never cut anyone's hair before, she readily consented _____ her husband's hair. *(cut)*

13. Mary decided _____ her friend's critical remarks. *(ignore)*

14. My roommate says I have a terrible voice, so I stopped _____ in the shower. *(sing)*

15. Did the doctor mention _____ any foods in particular? *(avoid)*

16. The cashier always remembers _____ the money in her cash register each day before she leaves work. *(count)*

17. Let's hurry! We must finish _____ the office before 3:00 today. *(paint)*

18. The student with the highest average deserves _____ an "A." *(get)*

19. I appreciate your _____ for my dinner. I'll buy next time. *(pay)*

20. The physically handicapped child struggled _____ up with the other children on the playground, but she couldn't. *(keep)*

21. Janice misses _____ walks with her father in the evening now that she has moved away from home. *(take)*

22. The customs official demanded _____ what was inside the gift-wrapped box. *(know)*

23. We've discussed _____ to New York in the fall, but I'm worried about our children having to adjust to a new school system and new friends. *(move)*

24. Children shouldn't be allowed _____ violent programs on TV. *(watch)*

25. In a fit of anger, I ordered my neighbor _____ his mule off my property. *(keep)*

◇ **PRACTICE 11. Gerund vs. infinitive. (Charts 14-2 → 14-10)**
   Directions: Complete the sentences with the correct form, gerund or infinitive, using the words in parentheses.

1. The doctor was forced ___to operate___ immediately to save the patient's life. *(operate)*

2. The newspaper hired Bill _____ pictures of the championship match between the two boxers. *(shoot)*

3. Most passengers dislike _____ to sit in small, uncomfortable seats on transoceanic flights. *(have)*

4. I choose _____ to Stanford University for my undergraduate studies. *(go)*

5. I must drive more carefully. I can't risk _____ another speeding ticket. *(get)*

6. All of the members agreed _____ the emergency meeting. *(attend)*

7. Jack promised _____ to the meeting. *(come)*

8. The sign warns you not _____ right on a red light. *(turn)*

9. Did Dick mean _____ Sue about the surprise party, or did it slip out accidentally? *(tell)*

10. You must keep _____ on the computer until you understand how to use all of the programs. *(practice)*

11. Our class volunteered _____ the classroom during the maintenance workers' strike. *(clean)*

12. When you get through _____ the newspaper, I could use your help in the kitchen. *(read)*

13. I think we should delay _____ these reports to the main office. *(send)*

14. The judge demanded _____ the original document, not the photocopy. *(see)*

15. After hearing the weather report, I advise you not _____ skiing this afternoon. *(go)*

16. George is interested in _____ an art class. *(take)*

17. I was furious. I threatened never _____ to him again. *(speak)*

18. My parents appreciated _____ the thank-you note you sent them. *(receive)*

19. The committee is planning _____ next Friday. *(meet)*

20. If I don't leave on the 15th, I will miss _____ home in time for my mother's birthday party. *(get)*

21. I know you're anxious to get out of here and get back home, but you should seriously consider _____ in the hospital a few more days. *(stay)*

22. Alex refused _____ for his rude behavior. *(apologize)*

23. When I was in the army, I had to swear _____ my senior officers' orders. *(obey)*

24. I don't recall _____ your dictionary anywhere in the apartment. Maybe you left it in the classroom. *(see)*

25. Mrs. Lind required the children _____ off their muddy boots before they came into the house. *(take)*

◇ **PRACTICE 12. Gerund vs. infinitive. (Charts 14-9 and 14-10)**
   Directions: Choose the correct answer.

1. The groom anticipated ___A___ the wedding ceremony.
   A. enjoying   B. to enjoy

2. The department store agreed _____ back the damaged radio.
   A. taking   B. to take

3. Would the doctor mind _____ some time talking to me after the examination?
   A. spending   B. to spend

4. We miss _____ Professor Sanders in Asian history this quarter.
   A. having   B. to have

5. Dan failed _____ the firefighter's examination and was quite upset.
   A. passing   B. to pass

6. The travelers anticipated _____ safely at their destination.
   A. arriving   B. to arrive

7. She expects _____ her baby at the new hospital.
   A. delivering   B. to deliver

8. The bad weather caused us _____ our connecting flight to Rome.
   A. missing   B. to miss

9. We dislike _____ dinner at 9:00 P.M.
   A. eating   B. to eat

10. Most of the students completed _____ their research papers on time.
    A. writing   B. to write

11. My niece hopes _____ with me to Disneyland next April.
    A. traveling   B. to travel

12. This note will remind me _____ the chicken for dinner tomorrow night.
    A. defrosting   B. to defrost

13. Willy denied _____ a whole bag of chocolate chip cookies before lunch.
    A. eating   B. to eat

14. You must swear _____ the truth in a court of law.
    A. telling   B. to tell

15. I didn't mean _____ him.
    A. interrupting   B. to interrupt

◇ **PRACTICE 13. Gerund vs. infinitive. (Charts 14-9 and 14-10)**

Directions: Create sentences from the following verb combinations. Select any tense for the first verb, but use a gerund or infinitive for the second verb. Include a (PRO)NOUN OBJECT if necessary.

Examples: can't afford + buy → *I can't afford to buy a new car for at least another year.*
         dare + dive → *My friends dared me to dive into the pool.*

1. keep + play
2. direct + save
3. regret + tell
4. manage + get
5. remind + take
6. be used to + stay
7. persuade + not buy
8. mention + give
9. suggest + go
10. can't imagine + travel
11. recommend + take
12. convince + go + swim
13. miss + be
14. not appreciate + hear
15. fail + tell
16. resent + be
17. resist + eat
18. claim + know
19. deserve + get
20. not recall + say
21. look forward to + see
22. beg + give
23. agree + hire + work
24. remember + tell + be
25. urge + practice + speak
26. tell + keep + try + call

◇ **PRACTICE 14. Using *it* + infinitive. (Chart 14-11)**
  Directions: Restate the sentences by changing a sentence with a gerund as the subject to a
  sentence with *it* + *an infinitive phrase,* and vice-versa.

  1. Teasing animals is cruel. → *It is cruel to tease animals.*

  2. It wasn't difficult to find their house. → *Finding their house wasn't difficult.*

  3. Voting in every election is important.

  4. It was exciting to meet the king and queen.

  5. Hearing the other side of the story would be interesting.

  6. It is unusual to see Joan awake early in the morning.

  7. If you know how, it is easy to float in the water for a long time.

  8. Mastering a second language takes time and patience.

  9. Driving to Atlanta will take us ten hours.

  10. It takes courage to dive into the sea from a high cliff.

CHAPTER 15
Gerunds and Infinitives, Part 2

◇ **PRACTICE 1. *In order to.* (Chart 15-1)**
  Directions: Add **in order** if possible. If nothing should be added, write Ø.

1. Emily likes ___Ø___ to go ice skating every weekend.

2. Please open the door ___in order___ to let some fresh air in.

3. Elizabeth has to practice at least four hours every day _____ to be ready for her piano recital next month.

4. Shelley sent me an e-mail _____ to inform me that the meeting had been canceled.

5. We've decided _____ not to take a vacation this year.

6. Did you remember _____ to call Mr. Johnson?

7. After dinner we drove to the top of a hill outside the city _____ to watch the sunset.

8. The children were making so much noise that I had to shout at them _____ to get their attention.

9. Jane is so disgusted by politics and politicians these days that she refuses _____ to vote in either local or national elections.

10. We waded across the mountain stream _____ to continue our hike to Wall's Meadow.

11. We stopped briefly on the other side of the stream _____ to rest before beginning one of the steepest parts of the climb.

12. One of the climbers hesitated _____ to continue because of a painful blister on his right heel. He tried _____ to keep up with the rest of us, but finally stopped climbing with us because of the pain.

◇ **PRACTICE 2. Adjectives followed by infinitives. (Chart 15-2)**
   Directions: Complete the sentences with infinitives.

   1. I was glad ___to get___ a letter from you.

   2. I was relieved ___to find out___ that I had passed the exam.

   3. Sue is lucky _____ alive after the accident.

   4. The soldiers were prepared _____ .

   5. The children are anxious _____ to the circus.

   6. Dick didn't feel like going anywhere. He was content _____ home and
      _____ a book.

   7. The teacher is always willing _____ us.

   8. The students are motivated _____ English.

   9. Be careful not _____ on the icy sidewalks!

   10. Tom was hesitant _____ home alone on the dark street.

   11. Sally is afraid _____ home alone.

   12. Ann is proud _____ the top student in her class.

   13. I was surprised _____ Mr. Yamamoto at the meeting.

   14. We were sorry _____ the bad news.

◇ **PRACTICE 3. *Too* vs. *very*. (Chart 15-3)**
   Directions: Add *too* or *very* to the sentences as appropriate.

   1. The box is ___very___ heavy, but I can lift it.

   2. John dropped his physics course because it was ___too___ difficult for him.

   3. I think it's _____ late to get tickets to the concert. I heard they were all sold.

   4. It's _____ cold today, but I'm still going to take my daily walk.

   5. Our cat is fourteen years old. Now he's _____ old to catch mice in the field across the
      street.

   6. It's _____ dark to see in here. Please turn on the lights.

   7. She was _____ ill. Nevertheless, she came to the family reunion.

   8. The boys were _____ busy to help me clean out the garage, so I did it myself.

   9. Learning a second language is _____ difficult, but most of the students are doing well.

   10. We enjoyed our dinner at the restaurant last night. It was _____ good.

11. Professor Andrews is always _____ interesting, but I'm _____ tired to go to the lecture tonight.

12. He's _____ young to understand. He'll understand when he's older.

13. The meal was _____ good. I enjoyed every morsel.

14. I'm _____ sleepy to watch the rest of the TV movie. Let me know how it turns out.

15. Sally was running _____ fast for me to keep up with her, so I lagged behind.

◇ **PRACTICE 4. Using *too* and *enough*. (Chart 15-3)**
Directions: Combine the given ideas into one sentence. Add *to* when an infinitive is required.

1. my work . . . yesterday . . . finish . . . enough . . . not . . . time . . . have
   → *I didn't have enough time* **to** finish my work yesterday.*

2. enough . . . not . . . well . . . go back to work . . . is . . . Linda

3. use . . . scissors . . . too . . . are . . . for . . . sharp . . . very young children

4. narrow . . . are . . . two-way traffic . . . the streets in the old part of the city . . . too . . . for

5. old . . . Jimmy . . . enough . . . not . . . ride on the bus by himself . . . is

6. many . . . in grammar and spelling in the first one . . . careless mistakes . . . Jules . . . because he had made . . . had to rewrite his composition . . . too

7. everyone assigned to this class . . . there . . . seats in the classroom . . . are . . . enough . . . not . . . for

8. we couldn't go . . . too . . . call the box office for tickets . . . because we waited . . . long . . . to the musical

◇ **PRACTICE 5. Passive infinitives. (Chart 15-4)**
Directions: Choose the correct answer.

1. When I told Tim the news, he seemed _____.
   A. to surprise   B. to be surprised

2. The children agreed _____ the candy equally.
   A. to divide   B. to be divided

3. Janice is going to fill out an application. She wants _____ for the job.
   A. to consider   B. to be considered

4. The mail is supposed _____ at noon.
   A. to deliver   B. to be delivered

5. I expect _____ at the airport by my uncle.
   A. to meet   B. to be met

---

*Also possible: *time enough*. In everyday English, **enough** usually precedes the noun.

6. Mr. Steinberg offered _____ us to the train station.
   A. to drive   B. to be driven

7. The children appear _____ about the trip.
   A. to excite   B. to be excited

◇ **PRACTICE 6. Passive gerunds. (Chart 15-4)**
   Directions: Choose the correct answer.

   1. I don't appreciate _____ when I'm speaking.
      A. interrupting   B. being interrupted

   2. Avoid _____ your houseplants too much water.
      A. giving   B. being given

   3. The mountain climbers are in danger of _____ by an avalanche.
      A. killing   B. being killed

   4. Does Dr. Johnson mind _____ at home if his patients need his help?
      A. calling   B. being called

   5. I'm interested in _____ my communication skills.
      A. improving   B. being improved

   6. Mrs. Gates appreciated _____ breakfast in bed when she wasn't feeling well.
      A. serving   B. being served

   7. Sally's low test scores kept her from _____ to the university.
      A. admitting   B. being admitted

   8. Mr. Miller gave no indication of _____ his mind.
      A. changing   B. being changed

◇ **PRACTICE 7. Passive infinitives and gerunds. (Chart 15-4)**
   Directions: Choose the correct answer.

   1. Instead of _____ about the good news, Tom seemed to be indifferent.
      A. exciting   C. to excite
      B. being excited   D. to be excited

   2. The new students hope _____ in many of the school's social activities.
      A. including   C. to include
      B. being included   D. to be included

   3. The owner of the building supply store doesn't mind _____ his customers discounts when they buy in large quantities.
      A. giving   C. to give
      B. being given   D. to be given

   4. Jack got into trouble when he refused _____ his briefcase for the customs officer.
      A. opening   C. to open
      B. being opened   D. to be opened

5. Barbara didn't mention _____ about her progress report at work, but I'm sure she is.
   A. concerning
   B. being concerned
   C. to concern
   D. to be concerned

6. The City Parks Department is putting in several miles of new trails because so many people have said that they enjoy _____ on them.
   A. walking
   B. being walked
   C. to walk
   D. to be walked

7. You'd better save some money for a rainy day. You can't count on _____ by your parents every time you get into financial difficulty.
   A. rescuing
   B. being rescued
   C. to rescue
   D. to be rescued

8. Please forgive me. I didn't mean _____ you.
   A. upsetting
   B. being upset
   C. to upset
   D. to be upset

9. I don't remember _____ of the decision to change the company policy on vacations. When was it decided?
   A. telling
   B. being told
   C. to tell
   D. to be told

10. Ms. Drake expects _____ about any revisions to her manuscript before it is printed.
    A. consulting
    B. being consulted
    C. to consult
    D. to be consulted

11. Sally gave such a good speech that I couldn't resist _____ loudly when she finished.
    A. applauding
    B. being applauded
    C. to applaud
    D. to be applauded

12. Tommy admitted _____ the rock through the window.
    A. throwing
    B. being thrown
    C. to throw
    D. to be thrown

13. If you want to develop inner tranquility, you have to stop _____ by every little thing that happens.
    A. bothering
    B. being bothered
    C. to bother
    D. to be bothered

14. Paul really didn't mind _____ by the party to celebrate his fortieth birthday, although he told his friends that they shouldn't have done it.
    A. surprising
    B. being surprised
    C. to surprise
    D. to be surprised

15. Anne hopes _____ to join the private club. She could make important business contacts there.
    A. inviting
    B. being invited
    C. to invite
    D. to be invited

◇ **PRACTICE 8. Past and past-passive infinitives and gerunds. (Chart 15-4)**
Directions: Choose the correct answer.

1. Are you sure you told me? I don't recall _____ about it.
   A. having told
   B. having been told
   C. to have told
   D. to have been told

2. Tom made a bad mistake at work, but his boss didn't fire him. He's lucky _____ a second chance.
   A. having given
   B. having been given
   C. to have given
   D. to have been given

3. Dr. Wilson is a brilliant and dedicated scientist who had expected to be selected as the director of the institute. She was very surprised not _____ the position.
   A. having offered
   B. having been offered
   C. to have offered
   D. to have been offered

4. By the time their baby arrives, the Johnsons hope _____ painting and decorating the new nursery.
   A. having finished
   B. having been finished
   C. to have finished
   D. to have been finished

5. The stockbroker denied _____ of the secret business deal.
   A. having informed
   B. having been informed
   C. to have informed
   D. to have been informed

6. The Smiths wanted to give their son every advantage. However, they now regret _____ him by providing too many material possessions.
   A. having spoiled
   B. having been spoiled
   C. to have spoiled
   D. to have been spoiled

7. The spy admitted _____ some highly secret information to enemy agents.
   A. having given
   B. having been given
   C. to have given
   D. to have been given

◇ **PRACTICE 9. Past and past-passive infinitives and gerunds. (Chart 15-4)**
Directions: Supply an appropriate form for each verb in parentheses.

1. Sharon wants us to tell her the news as soon as we hear anything. If we find out anything about the problem, she wants *(tell)* _____ about it immediately.

2. Yesterday Anna wrote a check for fifty dollars, but when she wrote it she knew she didn't have enough money in the bank to cover it. Today she is very worried about *(write)* _____ that check. She has to find a way to put some money in her account right away.

3. A: What's the difference between "burn up" and "burn down"?
   B: Hmmm. That's an interesting question. I don't recall ever *(ask)* _____ _____ that question before.

4. Living in a foreign country has been a good experience for me. I am glad that my company sent me to another country to study. I am very pleased *(give)* _____ the opportunity to learn about another culture.

5. Martha doesn't like to have her picture taken. She avoids *(photograph)* _____
   _____ .

6. A: It's been nice talking to you. I really have enjoyed our conversation, but I have to leave now. I'm very happy *(have)* _____ this opportunity to meet you and talk with you. Let's try to get together again soon.

   B: I'd like that.

7. A: This letter needs *(send)* _____ immediately. Will you take care of it?

   B: Right away.

8. Sally is very quick. You have to tell her how to do something only once. She doesn't need *(tell)* _____ twice.

9. A: I thought Sam was sick.

   B: So did I. But he seems *(recover)* _____ very quickly. He certainly doesn't seem *(be)* _____ sick now.

10. Last year I studied abroad. I appreciate *(have)* _____ the opportunity to live and study in a foreign country.

◇ **PRACTICE 10. Using a possessive to modify a gerund. (Chart 15-6)**
   Directions: Combine the following. Change ***that fact*** to a gerund phrase. Use formal English.

   Example: We answered all of the exam questions correctly. The teacher was pleased with that fact.
   → *The teacher was pleased with our answering* (OR: *having answered*) *all of the exam questions correctly.*

   1. I lost my new watch. My mother was angry about that fact.
   2. They are going to spend their vacation with us. We look forward to that fact.
   3. Tony failed the economics test even though he studied hard. No one can understand that fact.
   4. The students are required to pay an extra fee to use the laboratory. I am upset about that fact.
   5. Mary worked late to finish the project. The supervisor appreciated that fact.

◇ **PRACTICE 11. Review: gerunds and infinitives. (Charts 14-1 → 15-6)**
   Directions: Choose the correct answer.

   1. Alice didn't expect _____ to Bill's party.
      A. asking   B. being asked   C. to ask   D. to be asked

   2. I finally finished _____ at 7:00 P.M. and served dinner.
      A. cooking   B. being cooked   C. to cook   D. to be cooked

   3. Sam always remembers _____ in the garage so that the driveway is free for other cars.
      A. parking   B. being parked   C. to park   D. to be parked

4. The nurse suggested _____ two aspirin.
   A. taking   B. being taken   C. to take   D. to be taken

5. Would you mind not _____ the radio until I've finished with this phone call?
   A. turning on   C. to turn on
   B. being turned on   D. to be turned on

6. They were fortunate _____ from the fire before the building collapsed.
   A. rescuing   B. to have rescued   C. to rescue   D. to have been rescued

7. The mouse family avoided _____ by coming out only when the house was empty and the
   two cats were outside.
   A. catching   C. to have been caught
   B. being caught   D. to be caught

8. The baby continued _____ even after she was picked up.
   A. being crying   B. having cried   C. to cry   D. having been crying

9. Arthur pretended not _____ hurt when his younger sister bit him.
   A. having   B. be   C. to have   D. to have been

10. We were shocked to hear the news of your _____.
    A. having fired   C. to be fired
    B. having been fired   D. to have been fired

11. Even though she was much younger than the other children, Alexis demanded _____ in
    the game they were playing.
    A. including   B. being including   C. to include   D. to be included

12. Our mechanic said that he expects _____ the brakes on the car before we pick it up.
    A. fixing   B. being fixed   C. to have fixed   D. to have been fixed

13. Marge's children are used to _____ after school every day. They don't have to walk home.
    A. picking up   B. being picked up   C. be picked up   D. pick up

14. The bus driver was so tired of _____ the same route every day that he asked for a transfer.
    A. to drive   B. being driven   C. driving   D. drive

15. I'm sure it's not my fault that Peter found out what we were planning. I don't remember
    _____ anyone about it.
    A. having told   B. being told   C. to tell   D. to be told

◇ **PRACTICE 12. Using verbs of perception. (Chart 15-7)**
   Directions: Complete the sentences with the words in the list. Use each word only once. Use the
   SMALL form or the **-ing** form, whichever seems better to you.

arrive	emerge	perform	prevent
chirp	explain	✔practice	win
climb	melt		

1. Whenever I have free time, I like to watch the basketball team __practice__ .

2. A few years ago, I saw a dog _____ a child from wandering into a busy
   street by standing in front of her and not letting her get by.

3. It was a thrill to see my brother _____ the chess tournament last year.

4. I was amazed to see the firefighters _____ so soon after my call.

5. The boy watched the butterfly _____ from its cocoon.

6. It is educational for children to observe adults _____ their daily tasks.

7. When I look at my gym teacher _____ the rope, it looks easy, but when
   I try it, it is hard.

8. Hearing the birds _____ tells us that spring has indeed arrived.

9. I listened to the teacher _____ how to solve the math problem.

10. I held out my hand and watched each snowflake _____ as soon as it
    touched my skin.

◇ **PRACTICE 13.** *Let, help,* and causative verbs. (Charts 15-8 and 15-9)
Directions: Choose the correct answer(s).

1. Instead of buying a new pair of shoes, I had my old ones ___C___.
   A. repair   B. to repair   C. repaired

2. I helped my daughter __A, B__ her homework.
   A. finish   B. to finish   C. finished

3. I made my son _____ the windows before he could go outside to play with his friends.
   A. wash   B. to wash   C. washed

4. Maria had her landlord _____ the broken window before winter.
   A. fix   B. to fix   C. fixed

5. To please my daughter, I had her old bicycle _____ bright red.
   A. paint   B. to paint   C. painted

6. Sam was reluctant, but we finally got him _____ his guitar for us.
   A. play   B. to play   C. played

7. When I had to make an emergency phone call, the secretary let me _____ her phone.
   A. use   B. to use   C. used

8. Jack, could you help me _____ a place in the garden to plant some tomatoes?
   A. dig   B. to dig   C. dug

9. Before we leave, let's have Shelley _____ a map for us so we won't get lost.
   A. draw   B. to draw   C. drawn

10. Are you going to let me _____ that last piece of blueberry pie?
    A. eat   B. to eat   C. eaten

◇ **PRACTICE 14. Verb form review.** (Charts 14-1 → 15-9)
Directions: Choose the correct answer.

1. I enjoy _____ to the park on summer evenings.
   A. to go   B. going   C. being gone   D. go

2. Don't forget _____ home as soon as you arrive at your destination.
   A. to call   B. calling   C. having called   D. to be called

3. When I kept getting unwanted calls, I called the phone company and had my phone number _____. The process was easier than I expected it to be.
   A. change   B. changed   C. to change   D. changing

4. Jean should seriously consider _____ an actress. She is a very talented performer.
   A. to become B. become   C. becoming   D. will become

5. _____ television to the exclusion of all other activities is not a healthy habit for a growing child.
   A. To be watched   B. Being watched   C. Watching   D. Watch

6. After their children had grown up, Mr. and Mrs. Sills decided _____ to a condominium in the city. They've never been sorry.
   A. to have moved   B. moving   C. move   D. to move

7. I truly appreciated _____ to give the commencement address, but I wasn't able to accept the honor because of a previous commitment.
   A. asking   B. to have asked   C. to ask   D. having been asked

8. The store manager caught the cashier _____ money from the cash register and promptly called the police. They discovered that it had been going on for a long time.
   A. to sneak   B. sneaking   C. to have sneaked   D. being sneaked

9. My roommate's handwriting is very bad, so he had me _____ his paper for him last night.
   A. to type   B. type   C. to have typed   D. typed

10. The municipal authorities advised _____ all drinking water during the emergency.
    A. to boil   B. to be boiled   C. boiling   D. boil

11. If we leave now for our trip, we can drive half the distance before we stop _____ lunch.
    A. having   B. to have   C. having had   D. for having

12. Our schedule is not working out. We should discuss _____ our daily routine. I don't feel as though we're getting enough accomplished.
    A. changing   B. to change   C. to have changed   D. being changed

13. I can't recall _____ that old movie, but maybe I did many years ago.
    A. having seen   B. to have seen   C. to see   D. having been seen

14. Our school basketball team won the championship game by _____ two points in the last five seconds. It was the most exciting game I have ever attended.
    A. being scored   B. to score   C. scoring   D. score

15. The flight attendants made all the passengers _____ their seat belts during the turbulence.
    A. to buckle   C. buckling
    B. to have buckled   D. buckle

16. It has become necessary _____ water in the metropolitan area because of the severe drought.
    A. rationing   B. ration   C. to have rationed D. to ration

17. You can't blame Ralph for _____ to eat that dessert. It looked delicious.
    A. to be tempted B. tempted   C. be tempted   D. having been tempted

18. Let's leave early so we'll be ahead of the rush of commuters. We can't risk _____ in heavy traffic during rush hour.
    A. holding up   B. being held up   C. having held up   D. to hold up

19. It is always interesting _____ people in airports while you're waiting for a flight.
    A. being observed   C. to have observed
    B. observe   D. to observe

20. I got everyone in the family _____ Jane's birthday card before I sent it to her.
    A. sign   B. signed   C. to sign   D. having signed

◇ **PRACTICE 15. Verb form review. (Charts 14-1 → 15-9)**
    Directions: Complete each sentence with an appropriate form of the verb in parentheses.

1. Bill decided *(buy)* ___to buy___ a new car rather than a used one.

2. We delayed *(open)* _____ the doors of the examination room until exactly 9:00.

3. I really dislike *(ask)* _____ to answer questions in class when I haven't prepared my lesson.

4. I certainly didn't anticipate *(have)* _____ to wait in line for three hours for tickets to the baseball game!

5. When I was younger, I used *(wear)* _____ mini-skirts and bright colors. Now I am accustomed to *(dress)* _____ more conservatively.

6. Skydivers must have nerves of steel. I can't imagine *(jump)* _____ out of a plane and *(fall)* _____ to the earth. What if the parachute didn't open?

7. We are looking forward to *(take)* _____ on a tour of Athens by our Greek friends.

8. I told the mail carrier that we would be away for two weeks on vacation. I asked her *(stop)*

_____ *(deliver)* _____ our mail until the 21st. She told

me *(fill)* _____ out a form at the post office so that the post office would

hold our mail until we returned.

9. The elderly man next door is just sitting in his rocking chair *(gaze)* _____ out

the window. I wish there were something I could do *(cheer)* _____

him up.

10. I resent *(have)* _____ to work on this project with Fred. I know I'll end up

with most of the work falling on my shoulders.

11. Rick moved from a big city to a small town. He appreciates *(be)* _____

able to drive to work in five minutes with very little traffic congestion.

12. The power lines outside my house were dangerous. I finally got the power company *(move)*

_____ them to a safer place.

13. I wanted *(help)* _____ them *(resolve)* _____ their differences,

but Sally persuaded me *(interfere, not)* _____ .

14. Sara was encouraged by her teachers *(apply)* _____ for study at the Art

Institute.

15. I was happy *(learn)* _____ of your new position in the company, but I was

disappointed *(discover)* _____ that you had recommended *(promote)*

_____ Carl to your old position instead of me.

16. I don't mind *(remind)* _____ you every day *(lock)* _____ the

door when you leave the apartment, but I would appreciate your *(try)* _____

(remember) _____ on your own.

17. Now I remember your *(ask)* _____ me to bring sandwiches to the picnic. Your

complaints about my *(forget)* _____ things seem justified. I'm sorry.

18. After our automobile accident, the insurance company had a stack of papers for us to sign,

but our lawyer advised us *(sign, not)* _____ them until she had a chance

to study them very carefully.

19. John was responsible for *(notify)* _____ everyone about the meeting, but

he apparently failed *(call)* _____ several people. As a result, not enough

people showed up, and we have to try to get everybody together again soon.

20. You shouldn't let children *(play)* _____ with matches.

21. Art smelled something *(burn)* _____ . When he ran into the kitchen, he saw
fire *(come)* _____ out of the oven and panicked. If Barbara hadn't come
running in with the fire extinguisher, I don't know what would have happened.

22. I finally told him *(be)* _____ quiet for a minute and *(listen)* _____ to
what I had to say.

23. Irene was lying in bed *(think)* _____ about what a wonderful time she'd had.

24. The illogic of his statements made me *(tear)* _____ my hair out.

25. Recently Jo has been spending most of her time *(do)* _____ research for a book on
pioneer women.

26. Mary Beth suggested *(go)* _____ on a picnic.

27. Isabel expected *(admit)* _____ to the university, but she wasn't.

28. Jason wouldn't let them *(take)* _____ his picture.

29. I couldn't understand what the passage said, so I had my friend *(translate)* _____
it for me.

30. No, that's not what I meant *(say)* _____ . How can I make you *(understand)*
_____ ?

31. I have finally assembled enough information *(begin)* _____ writing my thesis.

32. It's a serious problem. Something needs *(do)* _____ about it soon.

33. I was terribly disappointed *(discover)* _____ that he had lied to me.

34. I had the operator *(put)* _____ the call through for me.

35. No one could make Ted *(feel)* _____ afraid. He refused *(intimidate)* _____ _____ by anyone.

36. I don't see how she can possibly avoid *(fail)* _____ the course.

37. Do something! Don't just sit there *(twiddle)* _____ your thumbs.

38. I don't know how to get to Harry's house, so I had him *(draw)* _____ a map for me.

39. Barbara has a wonderful sense of humor. She can always make me *(laugh)* _____.

40. The teacher had the class *(open)* _____ their books to page 185.

41. I found my roommate in the other room *(sleep)* _____ on the floor in the middle of the day.

42. They refused *(pay)* _____ their taxes, so they were sent to jail.

43. I admit *(be)* _____ a little nervous about the job interview. I don't know what *(expect)* _____.

44. I found a coin *(lie)* _____ on the sidewalk.

◇ **PRACTICE 16. Verb form review. (Charts 14-1 → 15-9)**
Directions: Complete each sentence with an appropriate form of the verb in parentheses.

1. After I decided *(have)* _____ a garage *(build)* _____ next to the house, I hired a carpenter *(do)* _____ the work.

2. The coach didn't let anyone *(watch)* _____ the team *(practice)* _____ before the championship game. He wanted to keep the opposing team from *(find)* _____ out about the new plays he had devised.

3. My son is playing in his first piano recital this evening. I'm looking forward to *(hear)* _____ him *(play)* _____, but I know he's worried about *(forget)* _____ the right notes and *(make)* _____ a fool of himself. I told him just *(relax)* _____ and *(enjoy)* _____ himself.

4. There's not much point in *(waste)* _____ a lot of time and energy on that project. It's likely *(fail)* _____ no matter what we do. Spend your time *(do)* _____ something more worthwhile.

5. (Attend) _____ the dance proved to be an (embarrass) _____ experience for me, especially since I don't know how to dance. I felt like a fish out of water. I wanted (hide) _____ someplace or (get) _____ out of there, but my friend wouldn't let me (leave) _____ .

6. I'm over sixty now, but I enjoy (recall) _____ my high-school days. I remember (choose) _____ by my classmates as "Most Likely to Succeed" when I was a senior. My best friend was chosen as "Least Likely to Succeed," and he is now the president of an electronics company. Once in a while when we get together, we have a good time (look) _____ through the high-school yearbook and (laugh) _____ at the way we looked then. We reminisce about (act) _____ in school dramas and (play) _____ on the basketball team. We remember (be) _____ serious young men who knew how to have fun. We congratulate ourselves for (achieve) _____ more than we had thought we could when we were eighteen.

7. Our house needs (clean) _____ . The floors need (sweep) _____ . The dishes need (wash) _____ . The furniture needs (dust) _____ . However, I think I'll read a book. (Read) _____ is a lot more interesting than (do) _____ housework.

8. As an adult, I very much appreciate (give) _____ the opportunity to travel extensively with my parents when I was a child. Those experiences were important in (form) _____ my view of the world. I learned (accept) _____ different customs and beliefs. At times, I would resist (go) _____ away on another trip, especially when I was a teenager. In the end, I always accompanied my parents, and I am grateful that I did. I didn't understand at that time how those trips would influence my later life. My (be) _____ a compassionate and caring adult is due in large part to my (expose) _____ to many different ways of life as a child.

9. (Find) _____ a cure for the common cold does not appear (be) _____ imminent. Colds are caused by hundreds of different viruses. You can possibly avoid (expose) _____ to the viruses by (stay) _____ away from those with colds, but it's almost impossible (avoid) _____ the viruses

completely. If you want *(minimize)* _____ the risk of *(get)* _____ a cold, it is prudent *(get)* _____ enough rest and *(eat)* _____ properly. Some people believe in *(take)* _____ large amounts of Vitamin C. In the long run, it is probably easier *(prevent)* _____ *(catch)* _____ a cold than it is to cure one.

10. Modern cars have systems that protect us from *(inconvenience)* _____ _____ or *(hurt)* _____ by our own carelessness. In most cars, when the keys are left in the ignition, a buzz sounds in order *(remind)* _____ the driver *(remove)* _____ them. In some models, if the driver does not remember *(turn)* _____ off the lights, it does not matter because the lights go off automatically. In some cases, when the seat belts are not buckled, the ignition does not start, and then the driver is actually forced *(buckle)* _____ up. Often when the driver has failed *(shut)* _____ a door properly, another signal noise may be given. A few cars emit sounds to warn us *(fill)* _____ the tank before it is completely empty.

It is easy *(forget)* _____ *(do)* _____ many routine tasks in *(drive)* _____ a car. The automatic warning systems help drivers *(avoid)* _____ *(make)* _____ some common mistakes. While some people may resent *(instruct)* _____ by their own automobiles *(perform)* _____ certain procedures, many others do not mind at all *(remind)* _____ *(carry)* _____ out these easily overlooked procedures.

Directions: Choose the correct answer.

Example: The office staff decided ___C___ a retirement party for Dolores.
A. having had   B. to have had   C. to have   D. having

1. I don't blame you for not _____ outside in this awful weather.
   A. wanting to go   B. wanting go   C. want to go   D. to want go

2. I think I hear someone _____ the back window. Do you hear it, too?
   A. trying open   B. trying to open   C. try opening   D. try to open

3. When Alan was questioned by the police, he admitted knowing about the embezzlement of funds from his company, but denied _____ in any way.
   A. to be involved   B. involving   C. having involved   D. being involved

4. Mr. Lee was upset by _____ him the truth.
   A. our not having told   C. we didn't tell
   B. us not tell   D. not to tell

5. We considered _____ after work.
   A. to go shop   B. going shopping   C. going to shop   D. to go to shop

6. Jack offered _____ care of my garden while I was out of town.
   A. take   B. taking   C. to have taken   D. to take

7. Could you please come over? I need you _____ the refrigerator.
   A. help me moving   C. to help me move
   B. helping me to move   D. help me to move

8. I just heard that there's been a major accident that has all of the traffic tied up. If we want to get to the play on time, we'd better avoid _____ the highway.
   A. having taken   B. take   C. to take   D. taking

9. The painting was beautiful. I stood there _____ it for a long time.
   A. for admiring   B. being admired   C. admire   D. admiring

10. Jim should have asked for help instead _____ to do it himself.
    A. of trying   B. to try   C. try   D. from trying

11. A plane with an engine on fire approached the runway. _____ was frightening. There could have been a terrible accident.
    A. Watch it landing   C. To watch it land
    B. Watching it land   D. Watching to land it

12. The customs officer opened the suitcase _____ if anything illegal was being brought into the country.
    A. seeing   B. for seeing   C. see   D. to see

13. Sometimes very young children have trouble _____ fact from fiction and may believe that dragons actually exist.
    A. to separate   B. separating   C. to be separated   D. for separating

14. Do you have an excuse _____ late to class two days in a row?
     A. for to be   B. for being   C. to be   D. being

15. Jack made me _____ him next week.
     A. to promise to call   C. promise to call
     B. to promise calling   D. promise calling

16. I got Barbara _____ her car for the weekend.
     A. to let me to borrow   C. to let me borrow
     B. let me borrow   D. let me to borrow

17. I'll never forget _____ that race. What a thrill!
     A. to win   B. win   C. being won   D. winning

18. No one has better qualifications. Carol is certain _____ for the job.
     A. to choose   B. having chosen   C. to be chosen   D. being chosen

19. I was enjoying my book, but I stopped _____ a program on TV.
     A. reading to watch   C. to read for watching
     B. to read to watch   D. reading for to watch

20. Who is the woman talking to Mr. Quinn? I don't recall _____ her around the office before.
     A. to have seen   B. seeing   C. to see   D. being seen

◇ **PRACTICE 18. TEST B: Gerunds and infinitives. (Chapters 14 and 15)**
   Directions: Choose the correct answer.

Example: The office staff decided __C__ a retirement party for Dolores.
   A. having had   B. to have had   C. to have   D. having

1. Roger proved that the accident wasn't his fault by _____ two witnesses who testified in his favor.
   A. produce   B. produced   C. to produce   D. producing

2. The front door is warped from the humidity. We have a difficult time _____ it.
   A. open   B. to open   C. having opened   D. opening

3. I stood up at the meeting and demanded _____. At last, I got the chance to express my opinion.
   A. to be heard   C. having been heard
   B. to hear   D. to have heard

4. Did you ever finish _____ the office for that new client of yours?
   A. to design   B. designing   C. designed   D. having designed

5. It's a beautiful day, and I have my brother's boat. Would you like to go _____?
   A. to sail   B. sailing   C. to sailing   D. for sailing

6. I called a plumber _____ the kitchen sink.
   A. for repairing   B. for to repair   C. to repair   D. to be repaired

7. I'm angry because you didn't tell me the truth. I don't like _____.
   A. deceiving   B. to deceive   C. being deceived   D. having deceived

8. A good teacher makes her students _____ the world from new perspectives.
   A. to view   B. viewing   C. view   D. to be viewed

9. Please remember _____ your hand during the test if you have a question.
   A. raising   B. to raise   C. having raised   D. to have raised

10. It is important _____ care of your health.
    A. to take   B. to be taken   C. take   D. taken

11. _____ in restaurants as often as they do is very expensive.
    A. Being eaten   C. Having been eating
    B. Having eaten   D. Eating

12. I expect Mary _____ here early tonight. She should arrive in the next half hour.
    A. to come   B. coming   C. having come   D. to have come

13. I advised my niece not _____ at an early age.
    A. marrying   C. to marry
    B. being married   D. to have been married

14. Shhh! I hear someone _____ in the distance. Do you hear it, too?
    A. shout   B. shouted   C. to shout   D. shouting

15. I don't understand _____ your job so suddenly. Why did you do that?
   A. your quitting
   B. you to have quit
   C. to quit
   D. you quit

16. Last night, we saw a meteor _____ through the sky.
   A. streaked   B. to streak   C. streak   D. to have streaked

17. My parents wouldn't let me _____ up late when I was a child.
   A. to be stay   B. staying   C. to stay   D. stay

18. Children should be encouraged _____ their individual interests.
   A. develop   B. to be developed   C. to develop   D. developing

19. This room is too dark. We need _____ a lighter shade.
   A. to have it painted
   B. to be painted
   C. painting it
   D. to have it paint

20. I'm sorry I never graduated. I've always regretted not _____ college.
   A. to finish   B. finish   C. finished   D. having finished

CHAPTER 16

Coordinating Conjunctions

◇ **PRACTICE 1. Parallel structure. (Chart 16-1)**

Directions: Write the words that are parallel in each of the sentences.

1. These apples are fresh and sweet.

1. <u>   fresh   </u> and <u>   sweet   </u>
    (adjective)   +   (adjective)

2. These apples and pears are fresh.

2. <u>   </u> and <u>   </u>
    (noun)   +   (noun)

3. I washed and dried the apples.

3. <u>   </u> and <u>   </u>
    (verb)   +   (verb)

4. I am washing and drying the apples.

4. <u>   </u> and <u>   </u>
    (verb)   +   (verb)

5. We ate the fruit happily and quickly.

5. <u>   </u> and <u>   </u>
    (adverb)   +   (adverb)

6. I enjoy biting into a fresh apple and tasting the juicy sweetness.

6. <u>   </u> and <u>   </u>
    (gerund)   +   (gerund)

7. I like to bite into a fresh apple and taste the juicy sweetness.

7. <u>   </u> and <u>   </u>
    (infinitive)   +   (infinitive)

8. Those imported apples are delicious but expensive.

8. <u>   </u> but <u>   </u>
    (adjective)   +   (adjective)

9. Apples, pears, and bananas are kinds of fruit.

9. <u>   </u>, <u>   </u>, and <u>   </u>
  (noun) (noun) + (noun)

10. Those apples are red, ripe, and juicy.

10. <u>   </u>, <u>   </u>, and <u>   </u>
  (adjective) (adjective) + (adjective)

◇ **PRACTICE 2. Parallel structure: use of commas. (Chart 16-1)**

Directions: Add commas as appropriate.

1. Jack was calm and quiet. *(no commas)*

2. Jack was calm quiet and serene.

   → *Jack was calm**,** quiet**,*** and serene.*

---

*The comma before *and* in a series is optional. See Chart 16-1.

3. The children sang and danced.

4. The children sang danced and played games.

5. Tom and Tariq joined the soccer game.

6. Tom Tariq and Francisco joined the soccer game.

7. I told the children to sit down be quiet and open their reading books.

8. I told the children to sit down and be quiet.

9. Did you know that the pupil* of your eye expands and contracts slightly with each heartbeat?

10. Our waitress's tray held two cups of coffee three glasses of water and one glass of orange juice.

11. My parents were strict but fair with their children.

12. Is a newborn blue whale smaller or larger than an adult elephant?

◇ **PRACTICE 3. Parallel structure. (Charts 16-1 and 16-2)**
Directions: Write "C" if the parallel structure is CORRECT. Write "I" if the parallel structure is INCORRECT, and make any necessary corrections. <u>Underline</u> the parallel elements of the sentences.

1. ___I___ I admire him for his <u>intelligence</u>, cheerful <u>disposition</u>, and ~~he is honest~~ honesty.

2. ___C___ Abraham Lincoln was a <u>lawyer</u> and a <u>politician</u>.

3. _____ The boat sailed across the lake smoothly and quiet.

4. _____ Barb studies each problem carefully and works out a solution.

5. _____ Aluminum is plentiful and relatively inexpensive.

6. _____ Many visitors to Los Angeles enjoy visiting Disneyland and to tour movie studios.

7. _____ Children are usually interested in but a little frightened by snakes.

8. _____ Either fainting can result from a lack of oxygen or a loss of blood.

9. _____ So far this term, the students in the writing class have learned how to write thesis statements, organize their material, and summarizing their conclusions.

10. _____ When I looked more closely, I saw that it was not coffee but chocolate on my necktie.

11. _____ Not only universities support medical research but also many government agencies.

12. _____ Physics explains why water freezes and how the sun produces heat.

13. _____ All plants need light, a suitable climate, and an ample supply of water and minerals from the soil.

14. _____ With their keen sight, fine hearing, and refined sense of smell, wolves hunt day or night in quest of elk, deer, moose, or caribou.

---

*The pupil of one's eye is the dark center of the eye.

15. _____ The comedian made people laugh by telling jokes and make funny faces.

16. _____ Tina is always understanding, patient, and sensitive when helping her friends with their problems.

17. _____ Not only the post office but also all banks close on national holidays.

18. _____ Walking briskly for 30 minutes or to run for 15 minutes will burn an approximately equal number of calories.

◇ **PRACTICE 4. Parallel structure. (Chart 16-1)**
Directions: Choose the letter of the phrase from the list that best completes each sentence. Use each phrase in the list only once.

A. reliable health care	E. provide quality education
B. carefully	F. responsible
C. excellence in	G. seeking practical solutions
✔ D. in agriculture	H. who finds a way to get the important jobs done

1. Mr. Turner has had wide experience. He has worked in business, in the news media, and ___D___.

2. People want safe homes, good schools, and _____ .

3. As a taxpayer, I want my money used wisely and _____ .

4. Mrs. Adams is respected for researching issues and _____ .

5. Ms. Hunter has established a record of effective and _____ leadership in government.

6. She has worked hard to control excess government spending, protect our environment, and

7. Carol is a hard-working personnel manager who welcomes challenges and _____ .

8. I will continue to fight for adequate funding of and _____ education.

◇ **PRACTICE 5. Paired conjunctions: subject–verb agreement. (Chart 16-2)**
Directions: Supply the correct present tense form of the verb in parentheses.

1. *(know)* Neither the students nor the teacher ___knows___ the answer.

2. *(know)* Neither the teacher nor the students ___know___ the answer.

3. *(know)* Not only the students but also the teacher _____ the answer.

4. *(know)* Not only the teacher but also the students _____ the answer.

5. *(know)* Both the teacher and the students _____ the answer.

6. *(want)* Neither Alan nor Carol _____ to go skiing this weekend.

7. *(like)* Both John and Ted _____ to go cross-country skiing.

8. *(have)* Either Jack or Alice _____ the information you need.

9. *(agree)* Neither my parents nor my brother _____ with my decision.

10. *(be)*   Both intelligence and skill _____ essential to good teaching.

11. *(realize)*   Neither my classmates nor my teacher _____ that I have no idea what's going on in class.

12. *(think)*   Not only Laura's husband but also her children _____ she should return to school and finish her graduate degree.

◇ **PRACTICE 6. Paired conjunctions. (Chart 16-2)**
Directions: Combine the following into sentences which contain parallel structure. Use the paired conjunctions in parentheses. Pay special attention to the exact place you put the paired conjunctions in the combined sentence.

1. Many people don't drink coffee. Many people don't drink alcohol. *(neither . . . nor)*
   → *Many people drink neither coffee nor alcohol.*

2. Barbara is fluent in Chinese. She is also fluent in Japanese. *(not only . . . but also)*

3. I'm sorry to say that Paul has no patience. He has no sensitivity to others. *(neither . . . nor)*

4. She can sing. She can dance. *(both . . . and)*

5. If you want to change your class schedule, you should talk to your teacher, or you should talk to your academic counselor. *(either . . . or)*

6. Diana is intelligent. She is very creative. *(both . . . and)*

7. You may begin working tomorrow or you may begin next week. *(either . . . or)*

8. Michael didn't tell his mother about the trouble he had gotten into. He didn't tell his father about the trouble he had gotten into. *(neither . . . nor)*

9. Success in karate requires balance and skill. Success in karate requires concentration and mental alertness. *(not only . . . but also)*

Directions: Punctuate these sentences by adding periods (.) or commas (,) as necessary. Do not add any words. Capitalize letters where necessary. Some sentences need no changes.

1. I like French cooking my wife prefers Italian cooking.
   → *I like French cooking. My wife prefers Italian cooking.*

2. I like French cooking but my wife prefers Italian cooking.
   → *I like French cooking, but my wife prefers Italian cooking. (optional comma)*

3. I've read that book it's very good.

4. I've read that book but I didn't like it.

5. I opened the door and asked my friend to come in.

6. I opened the door my sister answered the phone.

7. I opened the door and my sister answered the phone.

8. Minerals are common materials they are found in rocks and soil.

9. The most common solid materials on earth are minerals they are found in rocks soil and water.

10. You can travel to England by plane or you can go by ship if you prefer.

11. You can travel to England by plane or by ship.

12. Jason was going to study all night so he declined our invitation to dinner.

13. Jason declined our invitation to dinner he needed to stay home and study.

14. The wind was howling outside yet it was warm and comfortable indoors.

15. I hurried to answer the phone for I didn't want the children to wake up.

16. Last weekend we went camping it rained the entire time.

17. The highway was under construction so we had to take a different route to work.

18. No one thought we would win the championship yet our team won by a large margin.

19. We arrived at the theater late but the play had not yet begun we were quite surprised.

20. A central heating system provides heat for an entire building from one central place most central heating systems service only one building but some systems heat a group of buildings, such as those at a military base a campus or an apartment complex.

◇ **PRACTICE 8. Combining independent clauses: periods and commas. (Charts 16-1 and 16-3)**

Directions: Find and correct the errors in punctuation and capitalization.

I spent yesterday with my brother. **W**we had a really good time he's visiting me for a couple of days so I decided not to go to work yesterday we spent the day in the city first I took him to the waterfront we went to the aquarium, where we saw fearsome sharks some wonderfully funny marine mammals and all kinds of tropical fish after the aquarium, we went downtown to a big mall and went shopping my brother doesn't like to shop as much as I do so we didn't stay there long.

I had trouble thinking of a place to take him for lunch for he's a strict vegetarian luckily I finally remembered a restaurant that has vegan food so we went there and had a wonderful lunch of fresh vegetables and whole grains I'm not a vegetarian yet I must say that I really enjoyed the meal.

In the afternoon it started raining so we went to a movie it was pretty good but had too much violence for me I felt tense when we left the theater I prefer comedies or dramas my brother loved the movie.

We ended the day with a good home-cooked meal and some good talk in my living room it was a good day I like spending time with my brother.

◇ **PRACTICE 9. Combining independent clauses: periods and commas. (Charts 16-1 and 16-3)**

Directions: Find and correct the errors in punctuation and capitalization.

Some of the most interesting working women of the American West in the nineteenth century were African-American women Mary Fields was one of them she had been born a slave in the mid-1800s in the South but moved west to the Rocky Mountains as a free woman in 1884 her first job was hauling freight she drove a wagon and delivered freight in the valleys and mountains of Montana she was tall strong and fast on the draw* she didn't hesitate to protect her wagon of goods with her gun.

She drove a freight wagon for many years then in her late fifties she opened a restaurant but her business failed so in her sixties she became a stagecoach driver carrying the U.S. mail because of outlaws, driving a mailcoach was dangerous yet her mailcoach always arrived safely in her seventies she opened her own laundry business she continued successfully in that business until her death in 1914.

Mary Fields deserves our respect and can be seen as a role model by young women everywhere for she rose above unfortunate circumstances and became a determined hardworking and successful businesswoman

---

*"Fast on the draw" means that she could pull her gun out of her belt or holster and shoot fast.

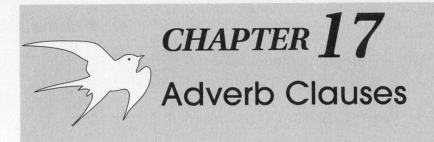

CHAPTER 17
Adverb Clauses

◇ **PRACTICE 1. Adverb Clauses. (Chart 17-1)**
Directions: Change the position of the adverb clause in the sentence. <u>Underline</u> the adverb clause in the given sentence, and <u>underline</u> the adverb clause in the new sentence. Punctuate carefully.

Example: Sue dropped a carton of eggs <u>as she was leaving the store</u>.
→ <u>*As Sue was leaving the store*</u>, *she dropped a carton of eggs.*★

1. We'll all take a walk in the park after Dad finishes working on the car.

2. Since Douglas fell off his bicycle last week, he has had to use crutches to walk.

3. Because I already had my boarding pass, I didn't have to stand in line at the airline counter.

4. Productivity in a factory increases if the workplace is made pleasant.

5. After Ceylon had been independent for 24 years, the country's name was changed to Sri Lanka.

6. Ms. Johnson regularly returns her e-mail messages as soon as she has some free time from her principal duties.

7. Tarik will be able to work more efficiently once he becomes familiar with the new computer program.

8. When the flooding river raced down the valley, it destroyed everything in its path.

◇ **PRACTICE 2. Periods and commas. (Charts 16-1, 16-3, and 17-1)**
Directions: Add periods and commas as necessary. Do not change, add, or omit any words. Capitalize as necessary.

1. The lake was calm Tom went fishing.
→ *The lake was calm. Tom went fishing.*

2. Because the lake was calm Tom went fishing.
→ *Because the lake was calm, Tom went fishing.*

★Also possible: ***As she was leaving the store,*** *Sue dropped a carton of eggs.*

3. Tom went fishing because the lake was calm he caught two fish.

4. Tom went fishing because the lake was calm and caught two fish.

5. When Tom went fishing the lake was calm he caught two fish.

6. The lake was calm so Tom went fishing he caught two fish.

7. Because the lake was calm and quiet Tom went fishing.

8. The lake was calm quiet and clear when Tom went fishing.

9. Mr. Hood is admired because he dedicated his life to helping the poor he is well known for his work on behalf of homeless people.

10. Microscopes automobile dashboards and cameras are awkward for left-handed people to use they are designed for right-handed people when "lefties" use these items they have to use their right hand to do the things that they would normally do with their left hand.

◇ **PRACTICE 3. Verb tenses in adverb clauses of time. (Chapter 5 and Chart 17-1)**
Directions: Choose the letter of the correct answer.

1. After Marco ___C___ his degree, he plans to seek employment in an engineering firm.
   A. will finish   C. finishes
   B. will have finished   D. is finishing

2. By the time Colette leaves work today, she _____ the budget report.
   A. will finish   B. has finished   C. will have finished   D. finishes

3. When my aunt _____ into the airport tomorrow, I'll be at work, so I can't pick her up.
   A. will get   B. got   C. will have gotten   D. gets

4. Natasha heard a small "meow" and looked down to discover a kitten at her feet. When she saw it, she _____.
   A. was smiling   B. had smiled   C. smiled   D. smiles

5. Ahmed has trouble keeping a job. By the time Ahmed was thirty, he _____ eight different jobs.
   A. had   B. was having   C. had had   D. had been having

6. Maria waits until her husband Al _____ to work before she calls her friends on the phone.
   A. will go   B. went   C. will have gone   D. goes

7. I went to an opera at Lincoln Center the last time I _____ to New York City.
   A. go   B. went   C. had gone   D. have gone

8. When the police arrived, the building was empty. The thieves _____ and escaped through an unlocked window.
   A. will have entered   C. have entered
   B. had entered   D. entered

9. It seems that whenever I try to take some quiet time for myself, the phone _____.
   A. has been ringing   C. rings
   B. is ringing   D. has rung

10. I'll invite the Thompsons to the potluck the next time I _____ them.
   A. see   B. will see   C. will have seen   D. have seen

11. I _____ hard to help support my family ever since I was a child.
   A. worked   B. work   C. am working   D. have worked

12. A small animal ran across the path in front of me as I _____ through the woods.
   A. was walking   B. had walked   C. am walking   D. had been walking

◇ **PRACTICE 4. Using adverb clauses to show cause-and-effect relationships. (Chart 17-2)**
   Directions: Combine the sentences, using the word or phrase in parentheses. Add commas where necessary. Make two sentences for each, showing the two possible positions of the adverb clause. Underline the adverb clause.

   Example: Our flight was delayed. We decided to take a long walk around the terminal. *(since)*
      → *Since our flight was delayed, we decided to take a long walk around the terminal.*
      → *We decided to take a long walk around the terminal since our flight was delayed.*

   1. My registration was canceled. I didn't pay my fees on time. *(because)*

   2. Erica has qualified for the Olympics in speedskating. She must train even more vigorously. *(now that)*

   3. We decided not to buy the house on Fourth Street. It's directly below flight patterns from the nearby international airport. *(since)*

◇ **PRACTICE 5. Using *even though* vs. *because*. (Charts 17-2 and 17-3)**
   Directions: Complete the sentences with *even though* or *because*.

   1. I put on my raincoat ___even though___ it was a bright, sunny day.

   2. I put on my raincoat ___because___ it was raining.

   3. _____ Sue is a good student, she received a scholarship.

   4. _____ Ann is a good student, she didn't receive a scholarship.

   5. _____ it was raining, we went for a walk.

   6. _____ it was raining, we didn't go for a walk.

   7. This letter was delivered _____ it didn't have enough postage.

   8. That letter was returned to the sender _____ it didn't have enough postage.

   9. I'm going horseback riding with Judy this afternoon _____ I'm afraid of horses.

   10. I'm going horseback riding with Judy this afternoon _____ I enjoy it.

   11. _____ you've made it clear that you don't want any help, I have to at least offer to help you.

12. I knew that I should get some sleep, but I just couldn't put my book down _____ I was really enjoying it.

13. _____ Tom didn't know how to dance, he wanted to go to the school dance _____ he felt lonely sitting at home and staring blankly at the TV while all of his friends were having fun together.

14. My hair stylist subscribes to three different fashion magazines _____ she's not interested in clothes. She subscribes to them _____ her customers like them.

◇ **PRACTICE 6. Direct contrast: *while* and *whereas*. (Chart 17-4)**
Directions: Write "**C**" if the sentence (including punctuation) is CORRECT. Write "**I**" if the sentence is INCORRECT.

1. __*C*__ While some chairs are soft, others are hard.

2. _____ While some chairs are hard, others are soft.

3. _____ Some chairs are soft, while others are hard.

4. _____ Some chairs are hard, while others are soft.

5. _____ Whereas some chairs are soft, others are hard.

6. _____ Some chairs are hard, whereas others are soft.

7. _____ Some chairs are soft, whereas others are hard.

8. _____ Whereas some chairs are hard, others are soft.

9. _____ While some chairs are soft, others are comfortable.

◇ **PRACTICE 7. *If*-clauses. (Chart 17-5)**
Directions: Underline the *if*-clause. Correct any errors in verb forms.

1. Let's not go to the park <u>if it ~~will rain~~ tomorrow</u>. *(rains — written above "will rain")*

2. <u>If my car doesn't start tomorrow morning</u>, I'll take the bus to work. *(no change)*

3. If I have free time during my work day, I send e-mail messages to friends.

4. I'll send you an e-mail if I will have some free time tomorrow.

5. If we don't leave within the next ten minutes, we are late to the theater.

6. If we will leave within the next two minutes, we will make it to the theater on time.

◇ **PRACTICE 8. Using *whether or not* and *even if*. (Chart 17-6)**
Directions: Complete the sentences, using the given information.

1. Tom is going to go to the horse races no matter what. He doesn't care if his wife approves.

In other words, Tom is going to go to the horse races even if his wife __*doesn't approve*__.

He's going to go whether his wife __*approves*__ or not.

2. Fatima is determined to buy an expensive car. It doesn't matter to her if she can't afford it. In other words, Fatima is going to buy an expensive car whether she _____ _____ it or not. She's going to buy one even if she _____ it.

3. William wears his raincoat every day. He wears it when it's raining. He wears it when it's not raining. In other words, William wears his raincoat whether it _____ or not. He wears it even if it _____ .

4. Some students don't understand what the teacher is saying, but still they smile and nod. In other words, even if they _____ what the teacher is saying, they smile and nod. They smile and nod whether they _____ what the teacher is saying or not.

◇ **PRACTICE 9. Using *in case* and *in the event that*. (Chart 17-7)**
    Directions: Complete the sentences by using *in case*. Decide if it goes in the first blank or in the second blank. Add necessary punctuation and capitalization.

PART I.

1. __In case__ you need to get in touch with me, I'll be in my office until late this evening.

2. __W__ we'll be at the Swan Hotel __in case__ you need to call us.

3. Mary is willing to work with you on your design project. _____ you find that you need help with it _____ she'll be back in town next Monday and can meet with you then.

4. _____ my boss has to stay near a phone all weekend _____ the company wants him to go to London to close the deal they've been working on all month.

5. _____ I'm not back in time to make dinner _____ I put the phone number for carry-out Chinese food on the refrigerator. You can call and order the food for yourself.

PART II. Complete the sentences using *in the event that*.

6. __In the event that__ Janet is late for work again tomorrow, she will be fired.

7. Are you sure you're taking enough money with you? _____ you'd better take a credit card with you _____ you run out of cash.

8. The political situation is getting more unstable and dangerous. _____ my family plans to leave the country _____ there is civil war.

9. Just to be on the safe side, _____ I always take a change of clothes in my carry-on bag _____ the airline loses my luggage.

10. Ann is one of five people nominated for an award to be given at the banquet this evening. _____ she has already prepared an acceptance speech _____ she wins it tonight.

◇ **PRACTICE 10. Using *unless* vs. *if* and *only if*. (Charts 17-8 and 17-9)**
   Directions: Choose the correct answer.

   1. I'll give you a hand ___B___ you need it, but I hope I don't hurt my back.
      A. unless   B. if

   2. I can't buy a car _____ I save enough money.
      A. unless   B. only if

   3. Our kids are allowed to watch television after dinner _____ they have finished their homework. Homework must come first.
      A. unless   B. only if

   4. There can be peace in the world _____ all nations sincerely lend their energy to that effort.
      A. unless   B. only if

   5. I'm afraid the battery is dead. _____ I buy a new one, the car won't start.
      A. Unless   B. If

   6. Let's plan on an old-fashioned sit-down dinner with the whole family at the table at once. I'll prepare a really special dinner _____ you all promise to be home on time this evening.
      A. unless   B. only if

◇ **PRACTICE 11. Adverb clauses of condition. (Charts 17-5 → 17-9)**
   Directions: Choose the correct words in *italics* so that the sentences make sense.

   1. I'll pass the course only if I *(pass,)* *don't pass* the final examination.

   2. I'm *going to go, not going to go* to the park unless the weather is nice.

   3. I'm going to the park unless it *rains, doesn't rain*.

   4. Tom doesn't like to work. He'll get a job *unless, only if* he has to.

   5. I *always eat, never eat* breakfast unless I get up late and don't have enough time.

   6. I always finish my homework *even if, only if* I'm sleepy and want to go to bed.

   7. You *will, won't* learn to play the violin well unless you practice every day.

   8. Even if the president calls, *wake, don't wake* me up. I don't want to talk to anyone. I want to sleep.

   9. Jack is going to come to the game with us today *if, unless* his boss gives him the afternoon off.

   10. *Borrow, Don't borrow* money from your friends unless you absolutely must.

Directions: Change the position of the adverb clause to the front of the sentence. Make any necessary changes in the verb of the main clause.

   1. I can finish this work on time only if you help me.

     → ***Only if*** *you help me* **can I finish** *this work on time.*

   2. I can finish this work on time if you help me.

     → ***If*** *you help me,* **I can finish** *this work on time.*

   3. I will go only if I am invited.

   4. I will go if I am invited.

   5. I eat only if I am hungry.

   6. I usually eat some fruit if I am hungry during the morning.

   7. You will be considered for that job only if you know both Arabic and Spanish.

   8. John goes to the market only if the refrigerator is empty.

   9. I will tell you the truth about what happened only if you promise not to get angry.

  10. I won't marry you if you can't learn to communicate your feelings.

◇ **PRACTICE 13. Summary: abverb clauses. (Chapter 17)**

Directions: Choose the best completion.

   1. Alice will tutor you in math _____ you promise to do everything she says.

     A. unless   B. only if   C. whereas   D. even though

   2. Oscar won't pass his math course _____ he gets a tutor.

     A. because   B. in the event that   C. unless   D. only if

   3. Most people you meet will be polite to you _____ you are polite to them.

     A. in case   B. only if   C. unless   D. if

   4. I'm glad that my mother made me take piano lessons when I was a child _____ I hated it at the time. Now, I play the piano every day.

     A. even though   B. because   C. unless   D. if

   5. Chicken eggs will not hatch _____ they are kept at the proper temperature.

     A. because   B. unless   C. only if   D. even though

   6. You'd better take your raincoat with you _____ the weather changes. It could rain before you get home again.

     A. now that   B. even if   C. in case   D. only if

7. Ms. Jackson was assigned the fifth-grade science class _____ she has the best qualifications among the available faculty.

    A. although   B. whereas   C. if   D. since

8. My sister can fall asleep under any conditions, but I can't get to sleep _____ the light is off and the room is perfectly quiet.

    A. if   B. unless   C. in case   D. now that

9. The majority will of the people rules in a democracy, _____ in a dictatorship, power is in the hands of a single person.

    A. because   B. even though   C. while   D. unless

10. The cheapest way to get from an airport to a hotel is to take an airport bus, but I'm not sure if River City has one. _____ there is no airport bus, you can always take a taxi.

    A. Unless   B. Now that   C. In the event that   D. Even though

11. _____ my country has a new democractic government, the people at last have more freedom.

    A. Even though   B. Even if   C. In the event that   D. Now that

12. Parents love and support their children _____ the children misbehave or do foolish things.

    A. even if   B. since   C. if   D. only if

CHAPTER 18
Reduction of Adverb Clauses to Modifying Adverbial Phrases

◇ **PRACTICE 1. Reduction of adverb clauses to modifying phrases. (Charts 18-1 → 18-3)**
Directions: Change the adverb clause to a modifying phrase.

               opening
1. Since ~~he opened~~ his new business, Bob has been working 16 hours a day.

2. I shut off the lights before I left the room

3. While he was herding his goats in the mountains, an Ethiopian named Kaldi discovered the coffee plant more than 1200 years ago.

4. Before they marched into battle, ancient Ethiopian soldiers ate a mixture of raw coffee beans and fat for extra energy.

5. After I had met the movie star in person, I understood why she was so popular.

6. I found my keys after I searched through all my pockets.

7. When it was first brought to Europe, the tomato was thought to be poisonous.

8. Since it was first imported into Australia many years ago, the rabbit has become a serious pest because it has no natural enemies there.

◇ **PRACTICE 2. Modifying phrases. (Charts 18-1 › 18-3)**
Directions: Underline the subject of the adverb clause and the subject of the main clause. Change the adverb clauses to modifying phrases, if possible.

1. While <u>Sam</u> was driving to work in the rain, his car got a flat tire. → *(no change)*

2. While <u>Sam</u> was driving to work, <u>he</u> had a flat tire.
   → *While driving to work, Sam had a flat tire.*

3. Before Nick left on his trip, his son gave him a big hug and a kiss.

4. Before Nick left on his trip, he gave his itinerary to his secretary.

5. After Tom had worked hard in the garden all afternoon, he took a shower and then went to the movies with his friends.

6. After Sunita had made a delicious chicken curry for her friends, they wanted the recipe.

7. Before a friend tries to do something hard, an American may say "Break a leg!" to wish him or her good luck.

8. Emily always straightens her desk before she leaves the office at the end of the day.

◇ PRACTICE 3. Verb forms in adverb clauses and modifying phrases. (Charts 18-1 → 18-3)
   Directions: Complete the sentences with the correct forms of the verbs in parentheses.

1. a. Before *(leave)* _____leaving_____ on his trip, Tom renewed his passport.

   b. Before Tom *(leave)* _____left_____ on his trip, he renewed his passport.

2. a. After Thomas Edison *(invent)* _____invented/had invented_____ the light bulb, he
      went on to create many other useful inventions.

   b. After *(invent)* _____inventing/having invented_____ the light bulb, Thomas Edison went
      on to create many other useful inventions.

3. a. While *(work)* _____ with uranium ore, Marie Curie discovered
      two new elements, radium and polonium.

   b. While she *(work)* _____ with uranium ore, Marie Curie
      discovered two new elements, radium and polonium.

4. a. Before an astronaut *(fly)* _____ on a space mission, s/he will
      have undergone thousands of hours of training.

   b. Before *(fly)* _____ on a space mission, an astronaut will have
      undergone thousands of hours of training.

5. a. After they *(study)* _____ the stars, the ancient Mayans in
      Central America developed a very accurate solar calendar.

   b. After *(study)* _____ the stars, the ancient Mayans in Central
      America developed a very accurate solar calendar.

6. a. Since *(learn)* _____ that cigarettes cause cancer, many people
      have stopped smoking.

   b. Since they *(learn)* _____ that cigarettes cause cancer, many
      people have stopped smoking.

7. a. Aspirin can be poisonous when it *(take)* _____ in excessive
      amounts.

   b. Aspirin can be poisonous when *(take)* _____ in excessive
      amounts.

8. a. When *(take)* _____ aspirin, you should be sure to follow the
      directions on the bottle.

   b. When you *(take)* _____ aspirin, you should be sure to follow
      the directions on the bottle.

9. a. I took a wrong turn while I *(drive)* _____ to my uncle's house
      and ended up back where I started.

   b. I took a wrong turn while *(drive)* _____ to my uncle's house
      and ended up back where I started.

◇ **PRACTICE 4. Modifying phrases. (Charts 18-3 and 18-4)**
Directions: Combine the two sentences, making a modifying phrase out of the first sentence, if possible.

1. Larry didn't want to disturb his sleeping wife. He tiptoed out of the room.
   → *Not wanting to disturb his sleeping wife, Larry tiptoed out of the room.*

2. Larry didn't want to disturb his sleeping wife. She needed to catch up on her sleep.
   → *(no change)*

3. I misunderstood the directions to the hotel. I arrived one hour late for the dinner party.

4. I misunderstood the directions to the hotel. The taxi driver didn't know how to get there either.

5. The taxi driver misunderstood my directions to the hotel. He took me to the wrong place.

6. Ann remembered that she hadn't turned off the oven. She went directly home.

7. I met Gina after work. She suggested playing tennis.

8. My family and I live in the Pacific Northwest, where it rains a great deal. We are accustomed to cool, damp weather.

◇ **PRACTICE 5. Modifying phrases. (Charts 18-1 → 18-5)**
Directions: Make sentences that combine a modifying phrase with a main clause. Write the capital letter of the most logical main clause to complete the sentence. Use each capital letter only once.

Modifying phrases	**Main clauses**
1. Trying to understand the physics problem, __E__	A. the desperate woman grasped a floating log after the boat capsized.
2. Since injuring my arm, _____	B. I collapsed in my chair for a rest.
3. Fighting for her life, _____	C. the taxi driver caused a multiple-car accident.
4. Wanting to ask a question, _____	D. carefully proofread all your answers.
5. Exhausted after washing the windows, _____	E. the students repeated the experiment.
6. Not wanting to disturb the manager, _____	F. the athletes waved to the cheering crowd.
7. Upon hearing the announcement that their plane was delayed, _____	G. the little girl raised her hand.
8. Talking with the employees after work, _____	H. the manager learned of their dissatisfaction with their jobs.
9. Attempting to enter the freeway, _____	I. the passengers angrily walked back to the ticket counter.
10. Currently selling at record-low prices, _____	J. I haven't been able to play tennis.
11. Stepping onto the platform to receive their medals, _____	K. gold is considered a good investment.
12. Before turning in your exam paper, _____	L. the worker in charge of Section B of the assembly line told the assistant manager about the problem.

◇ **PRACTICE 6. Modifying phrases with _upon_. (Chart 18-5)**
  Directions: Write completions using the ideas in the given list.

> _She learned the problem was not at all serious._
> _She was told she got it._
> _He heard these words._
> _He investigated the cause._
> ✓ _I arrived at the airport._
> _I reached the other side of the lake._

1. It had been a long, uncomfortable trip. Upon ___arriving at the airport___, I quickly unfastened my seat belt and stood in the aisle waiting my turn to disembark.

2. I rented a small fishing boat last weekend, but I ended up doing more rowing than fishing. The motor died halfway across the lake, so I had to row to shore. It was a long distance away. Upon _____, I was exhausted.

3. At first, we thought the fire had been caused by lightning. However, upon _____ _____, the fire chief determined it had been caused by faulty electrical wiring.

4. Amy felt terrible. She was sure she had some dread disease, so she went to the doctor for some tests. Upon _____, she was extremely relieved.

5. Janet wanted that scholarship with all her heart and soul. Upon _____ _____, she jumped straight up in the air and let out a scream of happiness.

◇ **PRACTICE 7. Modifying phrases. (Charts 18-1 → 18-5)**
  Directions: Write "**I**" if the sentence is INCORRECT. Write "**C**" if the sentence is CORRECT.
  Reminder: A modifying phrase must modify the subject of the sentence.

1. ___I___ While taking a trip across Europe this summer, Jane's camera suddenly quit working.

2. ___C___ When using a microwave oven for the first time, read the instructions carefully about the kind of dish you can use.

3. _____ Having been given their instructions, the teacher told her students to begin working on the test.

4. _____ After receiving the Nobel Peace Prize in 1979, Mother Teresa returned to Calcutta, India, to work and live among the poor, the sick, and the dying.

5. _____ Having studied Greek for several years, Sarah's pronunciation was easy to understand.

6. _____ Since returning to her country after graduation, Maria's parents have enjoyed having all their children home again.

7. _____ While bicycling across the United States, the wheels on my bike had to be replaced several times.

8. _____ When told he would have to have surgery, the doctor reassured Bob that he wouldn't have to miss more than a week of work.

9. _____ Upon hearing the bad news, tears began to flow from her eyes.

10. _____ Before driving across a desert, be sure that your car has good tires as well as enough oil, water, and gas to last the trip.

Directions: Choose the correct answer.

Example: __B__ I get angry and upset, I try to take ten deep breaths.
 A. Until B. Whenever C. Whereas D. For

1. _____ Paul brings the money for our lunch, we'll go right down to the cafeteria.
 A. Since B. As soon as C. Now that D. Until

2. The first time I went swimming in deep water, I sank to the bottom like a rock. _____
 I've learned to stay afloat, I feel better about the water, but I still can't swim well.
 A. As soon as B. The first time C. When D. Now that

3. It's obvious that neither the workers _____ to fight the new rules.
 A. nor the manager intend C. nor the manager intends
 B. intend nor the manager D. intend nor the manager intends

4. _____ I heard the telephone ring, I didn't answer it.
 A. Because B. Only if C. Even though D. So

5. After _____ to 45 minutes of an extremely boring speech, I found myself nodding off.
 A. was listening B. listen C. listening D. having listen

6. Why did I stay until the end? I am never going to stay and watch a bad movie again!
 _____ I am in that situation, I'm going to leave the theater immediately.
 A. The next time B. Now that C. After D. Until

7. "Why aren't you ready to go?"
 "I am ready."
 "How can that be? It's freezing outside, _____ you're wearing shorts and a T-shirt!"
 A. for B. so C. because D. yet

8. Erin likes to swim, jog, and _____ tennis.
 A. plays B. play C. to play D. playing

9. Since _____ to a warmer and less humid climate, I've had no trouble with my asthma.
 A. upon moving B. I moving C. moving D. I move

10. While _____ to help Tim with his math, I got impatient because he wouldn't pay attention
 to what I was saying.
 A. I am trying B. having tried C. I try D. trying

11. We're going to lose this game _____ our team doesn't start playing better soon.
 A. if B. unless C. although D. whereas

12. Some fish can survive only in salt water, _____ other species can live only in fresh water.
 A. since B. unless C. if D. whereas

13. Joe seemed to be in a good mood, _____ he snapped at me angrily when I asked him to
 join us.
 A. for B. so C. yet D. and

14. _____ Jan arrives, we will have finished this group project.
 A. By the time B. Until C. Now that D. Since

15. For the most part, young children spend their time playing, eating, and _____ a lot.
    A. they sleep   B. sleeping   C. sleep   D. they are sleeping

16. _____ I get back from my next business trip, I'm taking a few days off. I'm worn out!
    A. Every time   B. Since   C. Now that   D. Once

17. _____ unprepared for the exam, I felt sure I would get a low score.
    A. Having   B. Being   C. Because   D. Upon

18. Ever since _____ Ted the bad news, he's been avoiding me.
    A. I told   B. told   C. telling   D. having told

19. _____ my daughter reaches the age of sixteen, she will be able to drive.
    A. Having   B. Since   C. Once   D. Because

20. Matt will enjoy skiing more the next time he goes to the Alps _____ he has had skiing lessons.
    A. unless   B. before   C. now that   D. and

Directions: Choose the correct answer.

Example: ___B___ I get angry and upset, I try to take ten deep breaths.
   A. Until   B. Whenever   C. whereas   D. For

1. Before _____ a promotion and transfer to another city, I will discuss it at length with my whole family to be sure that everyone will be able to adjust to the change.
   A. accept   C. having been accepted
   B. accepted   D. accepting

2. The flowers will soon start to bloom _____ winter is gone and the weather is beginning to get warmer.
   A. even if   B. now that   C. so   D. even though

3. Only if you promise to study hard _____ to tutor you.
   A. will I agree   B. agree I   C. I agree   D. I will agree

4. Great white sharks are dangerous to _____ will attack without warning.
   A. humans, they   C. humans. Because they
   B. humans   D. humans. They

5. _____ the need to finish this project soon, I want you to work on this overtime for the next few days.
   A. Because   B. Despite   C. Because of   D. Even though

6. _____ the secret of how to make silk remained inside Asia, Europeans were forced to pay incredibly high sums of money for this mysterious material to be brought overland to Europe.
   A. Although   B. Only if   C. Since   D. Until

7. Jack insisted that he didn't need any help, _____ I helped him anyway.
   A. and   B. so   C. for   D. but

8. _____ by the swimming pool, I realized I was getting sunburned.
   A. Because   C. While I am lying
   B. Lying   D. Even though I was lying

9. _____ it was a formal dinner party, James wore his blue jeans.
   A. Since   C. In the event that
   B. Even though   D. Until

10. Ancient Egyptians mummified their dead through the use of chemicals, _____ ancient Peruvians mummified their dead through natural processes by putting dead bodies in extremely dry desert caves.
   A. whereas   B. because   C. even though   D. whether or not

11. Mr. Jackson hopes to avoid surgery. He will not agree to the operation _____ he is convinced that it is absolutely necessary.
   A. in the event that   C. if
   B. unless   D. only if

12. Some English words have the same pronunciation _____ they are spelled differently, for example, *dear* and *deer*.
    A. unless   B. since   C. even though   D. only if

13. Both my books _____ from my room last night.
    A. were stolen and my wallet   C. and my wallet stolen
    B. and my wallet were stolen   D. and my wallet was stolen

14. When _____ a dictionary, you need to be able to understand the symbols and abbreviations it contains.
    A. having used   B. use   C. to use   D. using

15. You must obey the speed limits on public roads. They are designed to keep you safe. You shouldn't exceed the speed limit _____ you are an experienced race car driver.
    A. even if   B. only if   C. if   D. in the event that

16. My nose got sunburned _____ I wore a hat with a wide brim to shade my face.
    A. if   B. since   C. because   D. even though

17. Do you like jazz? You should go to the jazz festival _____ you like that kind of music.
    A. if   B. unless   C. although   D. while

18. Only if you get to the theater early _____ a chance to get a ticket for tonight's performance.
    A. you will have   B. have   C. will you have   D. you have

19. The bread was old and stale, _____ Martha ate it anyway.
    A. and   B. so   C. for   D. but

20. _____ you're better at numbers than I am, why don't you take over as treasurer of the organization?
    A. Since   B. Only if   C. For that   D. Unless

CHAPTER 19

Connectives That Express Cause and Effect, Contrast, and Condition

◇ **PRACTICE 1. *Because* vs. *because of*.** (Charts 17-2 and 19-1)
   Directions: Complete the sentences with either *because* or *because of*.

1. We delayed our trip ___because of___ the bad weather.

2. Sue's eyes were red ___because___ she had been crying.

3. The water in most rivers is unsafe to drink _____ pollution.

4. The water in most rivers is unsafe to drink _____ it is polluted.

5. Some people think Harry succeeded in business _____ his charming personality rather than his business skills.

6. You can't enter this secured area _____ you don't have an official permit.

7. My lecture notes were incomplete _____ the instructor talked too fast.

8. It's unsafe to travel in that country _____ the ongoing civil war.

◇ **PRACTICE 2. *Because* vs. *therefore*.** (Charts 17-2, 19-1, and 19-2)
   Directions: Complete the sentences with either *because* or *therefore*.

1. Matt didn't go to work yesterday ___because___ he didn't feel well.

2. Matt didn't feel well. ___Therefore___, he didn't go to work yesterday.

3. Sharon hid her feelings from everyone. _____, no one suspected the deep emotional pain she was suffering.

4. No one ever knows what's going on inside of Sharon _____ she hides her feelings behind a mask of smiles.

5. _____ young Joseph was an inquisitive student, he was always liked by his teachers.

6. The television broadcast was interrupted in the middle of the eighth inning; _____, most of the audience missed the conclusion of the baseball game.

◇ **PRACTICE 3. Showing cause and effect. (Charts 17-2, 19-1, and 19-2)**

PART I. Complete the sentences with *because of, because,* or *therefore*. Add any necessary punctuation and capitalization.

1. ___Because___ it rained, we stayed home.

2. It rained __. Therefore,__ we stayed home.

3. We stayed home ___because of___ the bad weather.

4. The hurricane was moving directly toward a small coastal town _____ all residents were advised to move inland until it passed.

5. The residents moved inland _____ the hurricane.

6. _____ the hurricane was moving directly toward the town all residents were advised to move inland.

7. Piranhas, which are found in the Amazon River, are ferocious and bloodthirsty fish. When they attack in great numbers, they can devour an entire cow in several minutes _____ their extremely sharp teeth.

PART II. Complete the sentence with *due to, since,* or *consequently*. Add any necessary punctuation and capitalization.

8. _____ his poor eyesight John has to sit in the front row in class.

9. _____ John has poor eyesight he has to sit in the front row.

10. John has poor eyesight _____ he has to sit in the front row.

11. Sarah is afraid of heights _____ she will not walk across a bridge.

12. Sarah will not walk across a bridge _____ her fear of heights.

13. Mark is overweight _____ his doctor has advised him to exercise regularly.

14. _____ a diamond is extremely hard it can be used to cut glass.

◇ **PRACTICE 4. Periods and commas. (Charts 16-3 and 19-3)**

Directions: Punctuate the sentences properly, using periods and commas. Capitalize as appropriate.

1. Edward missed the final exam. Therefore, he failed the course.*

2. Edward failed the course because he missed the final exam. *(no change)*

3. Edward missed the final exam. He simply forgot to go to it.**

_____

*The use of a semicolon is also possible:
  Edward missed the final exam; therefore, he failed the course.
**The use of a semicolon is also possible:
  Edward missed the final exam; he simply forgot to go to it.

4. Because we forgot to make a reservation we couldn't get a table at our favorite restaurant last night.

5. The waitress kept dropping trays full of dishes therefore she was fired.

6. The waiter kept forgetting customers' orders so he was fired.

7. Ron is an unpleasant dinner companion because of his uncouth table manners.

8. The needle has been around since prehistoric times the button was invented about 2000 years ago the zipper wasn't invented until 1890.

9. It is possible for wildlife observers to identify individual zebras because the patterns of stripes on each zebra are unique no two zebras are alike.

10. When students are learning to type, they often practice the sentence "The quick brown fox jumps over the lazy dog" because it contains all the letters of the alphabet.

◇ **PRACTICE 5. Such . . . that and so . . . that.** (Chart 19-4)
Directions: Add *such* or *so* to the following sentences.

1. It was ___such___ a hot day that we canceled our tennis game.

2. The test was ___so___ easy that everyone got a high score.

3. The movie was _____ bad that we left early.

4. It was _____ a bad movie that we left early.

5. Professor James is _____ a stern taskmaster that lazy students won't take his class.

6. The restaurant patron at the table near us was _____ belligerent that we all felt embarrassed, especially when he swept everything off the table and demanded his money back.

7. The intricate metal lacework on the Eiffel Tower in Paris was _____ complicated that the structure took more than two and a half years to complete.

8. Charles and his brother are _____ hard-working carpenters that I'm sure they'll make a success of their new business.

9. The children had _____ much fun at the carnival that they begged to go again.

10. I feel like I have _____ little energy that I wonder if I'm getting sick.

◇ **PRACTICE 6. Such . . . that and so . . . that.** (Chart 19-4)
Directions: Combine the sentences by using *so . . . that* or *such . . . that*.

1. We took a walk. It was a nice day.
   → *It was such a nice day that we took a walk.*

2. The weather was hot. You could fry an egg on the sidewalk.

3. I couldn't understand her. She talked too fast.

4. It was an expensive car. We couldn't afford to buy it.

5. I don't feel like going to class. We're having beautiful weather.

6. Grandpa held me tightly when he hugged me. I couldn't breathe for a moment.

7. There were few people at the meeting. It was canceled.

8. The classroom has comfortable chairs. The students find it easy to fall asleep.

9. Ted couldn't get to sleep last night. He was worried about the exam.

10. Jerry got angry. He put his fist through the wall.

11. I have many problems. I can use all the help you can give me.

12. The tornado struck with great force. It lifted automobiles off the ground.

13. I can't figure out what this sentence says. His handwriting is illegible.

14. David has too many girlfriends. He can't remember all of their names.

15. Too many people came to the meeting. There were not enough seats for everyone.

◇ **PRACTICE 7. So that. (Chart 19-5)**
Directions: Combine the ideas using *so that*.

1. Rachel wanted to watch the news. She turned on the TV.
   → *Rachel turned on the TV so that she could watch the news.*

2. Alex wrote down the time and date of his appointment. He didn't want to forget to go.
   → *Alex wrote down the time and date of his appointment so that he wouldn't forget to go.*

3. Nancy is carrying extra courses every semester. She wants to graduate early.

4. Jason wants to travel in Europe. He's tired of work and school and is planning to take a semester off.

5. Suzanne didn't want to disturb her roommate. She lowered the volume on the TV set.

6. Whenever we are planning a vacation, we call a travel agent. We are able to get expert advice on our itinerary.

7. It's a good idea for you to learn how to type. You'll be able to type your own papers when you go to the university.

8. Lynn wanted to make sure that she didn't forget to take her book back to the library. She tied a string around her finger.

9. Ed took some change from his pocket. He wanted to buy a newspaper.

10. I wanted to listen to the news while I was making dinner. I turned on the TV.

11. I unplugged the phone. I didn't want to be interrupted while I was working.

12. Yesterday Linda was driving on the highway when her car started making strange noises. After she pulled over to the side of the road, she raised the hood of her car in order to make sure that other drivers knew that she had car trouble.

◇ **PRACTICE 8. Cause and effect. (Charts 16-3, 17-2, and 19-1 → 19-5)**
   Directions: Choose the correct completion.

   Example: ___B___ I was tired, I went to bed.
      A. Because of   B. Since   C. For   D. Due to

   1. The workers have gone on strike. _____, all production has ceased.
      A. Because   B. So that   C. Now that   D. Therefore

   2. A small fish needs camouflage to hide itself _____ its enemies cannot find it.
      A. so that   B. because   C. therefore   D. due to

   3. Our apartment building has had two robberies in the last month, _____ I'm going to put
      an extra lock on the door and install a telephone in my bedroom.
      A. now that   B. so that   C. so   D. since

   4. The Chippewas are Native North Americans. Their language is one of the most complex in
      the world, _____ it contains more than 6,000 verb forms.
      A. consequently   B. so   C. so that   D. for

   5. _____ the bad grease stain on the carpet, we had to rearrange the furniture before the
      company arrived.
      A. Because   B. Now that   C. For   D. Because of

   6. The price of airline tickets has gone down recently. _____ the tickets cost less, more
      people are flying than before.
      A. Consequently   B. Because of   C. Because   D. For

   7. Let's ask our teacher how to solve this problem _____ we can't agree on the answer.
      A. since   B. because of   C. consequently   D. so

   8. The fire raged out of control. It got _____ bad that more firefighters had to be called in.
      A. such   B. therefore   C. so   D. so that

   9. Dolphins are sometimes caught and killed in commercial fishing nets _____ they often
      swim in schools with other fish, such as tuna.
      A. due to   B. because   C. so   D. therefore

   10. We can finally afford to trade in the old car for a new one _____ I've gotten the raise I've
      been waiting for.
      A. so that   B. consequently   C. now that   D. so

   11. Two of the factories in our small town have closed. _____, unemployment is high.
      A. Consequently   B. Because   C. So that   D. For

   12. _____ I had nothing for lunch but an apple, I ate dinner early.
      A. For   B. Since   C. Due to   D. Therefore

   13. I needed to finish the marathon race _____ I could prove that I had the strength and
      stamina to do it. I didn't care whether I won or not.
      A. because of   B. so that   C. for   D. therefore

14. The Eskimo* way of life changed dramatically during the 1800s _____ the introduction of firearms and the influx of large numbers of European whalers and fur traders.

    A. because   B. for   C. due to   D. so

15. During extremely hot weather, elephants require both mud and water to keep their skin cool _____ they have no sweat glands.

    A. and   B. because of   C. so   D. due to the fact that

◇ PRACTICE 9. Showing contrast: punctuation. (Chart 19-6)
Directions: Add commas, periods, and capital letters as necessary. Do not add or omit any words. Do not change the order of the words.

1. Annie told the truth, but no one believed her.

2. Annie told the truth. **H**however, no one believed her.**

3. Even though Annie told the truth no one believed her.

4. No one believed Annie even though she told the truth.

5. Annie told the truth yet no one believed her.

6. Annie told the truth nevertheless no one believed her.

7. In spite of the fact that Annie told the truth no one believed her.

8. No one believed Annie despite the fact that she told the truth.

9. Even though all of my family friends have advised me not to travel abroad during this time of political turmoil I'm leaving next week to begin a trip around the world.

10. Some people think great strides have been made in cleaning up the environment in much of the world however others think the situation is much worse than it was twenty years ago.

◇ PRACTICE 10. *Despite/in spite of* vs. *even though/although.* (Chart 19-6)
Directions: Choose the correct completions.

1. a. *Even though, Despite* her doctor warned her, Carol has continued to smoke nearly three packs of cigarettes a day.

   b. *Even though, Despite* her doctor's warnings, Carol has continued to smoke nearly three packs of cigarettes a day.

   c. *Even though, Despite* the warnings her doctor gave her, Carol continues to smoke.

   d. *Even though, Despite* the fact that her doctor warned her of dangers to her health, Carol continues to smoke.

   e. *Even though, Despite* she has been warned about the dangers of smoking by her doctor, Carol continues to smoke.

_____

*Eskimos are people who live in the Arctic regions of northern Alaska, northern Canada, and Greenland.
**Also possible: *Annie told the truth; however, no one believed her.*

2. a. *Although, In spite of* an approaching storm, the two climbers continued their trek up the mountain.

   b. *Although, In spite of* a storm was approaching, the two climbers continued their trek.

   c. *Although, In spite of* there was an approaching storm, the two climbers continued up the mountain.

   d. *Although, In spite of* the storm that was approaching the mountain area, the two climbers continued their trek.

   e. *Although, In spite of* the fact that a storm was approaching the mountain area, the two climbers continued their trek.

3. a. *Although, Despite* his many hours of practice, George failed his driving test for the third time.

   b. *Although, Despite* he had practiced for many hours, George failed his driving test for the third time.

   c. *Although, Despite* practicing for many hours, George failed his driving test again.

   d. *Although, Despite* his mother and father spent hours with him in the car trying to teach him how to drive, George failed his driving test repeatedly.

   e. *Although, Despite* his mother and father's efforts to teach him how to drive, George failed his driving test.

4. a. *Even though, In spite of* repeated crop failures due to drought, the villagers are refusing to leave their traditional homeland for resettlement in other areas.

   b. *Even though, In spite of* their crops have failed repeatedly due to drought, the villagers are refusing to leave their traditional homeland for resettlement in other areas.

c. The villagers refuse to leave *even though, in spite of* the drought.

d. The villagers refuse to leave *even though, in spite of* the drought seriously threatens their food supply.

e. The villagers refuse to leave *even though, in spite of* the threat to their food supply because of the continued drought.

f. The villagers refuse to leave *even though, in spite of* the threat to their food supply is serious because of the continued drought.

g. The villagers refuse to leave *even though, in spite of* their food supply is threatened.

h. The villagers refuse to leave *even though, in spite of* their threatened food supply.

◇ **PRACTICE 11. Using *in spite of/despite* and *even though/though/although*. (Chart 19-6)**
   Directions: Choose the phrase from the list that best completes each sentence. Use each completion only once.

> A. *its many benefits*
> ✔B. *its inherent dangers*
> C. *it has been shown to be safe*
> D. *it has been shown to cause birth defects and sometimes death*
> E. *his fear of heights*
> F. *he is afraid of heights*
> G. *he is normally quite shy and sometimes inarticulate*
> H. *an inability to communicate well in any language besides English*
> I. *having excellent skills in the job category they were trying to fill*
> J. *he had the necessary qualifications*

1. In spite of ___B___, nuclear energy is a clean and potentially inexhaustible source of energy.

2. In spite of _____, Carl enjoyed his helicopter trip over the Grand Canyon in Arizona.

3. Because of his age, John was not hired even though _____.

4. Although _____, Mark rode an elevator to the top of the World Trade Center in New York for the magnificent view.

5. Although _____, many people avoid using a microwave oven for fear of its rays.

6. Jack usually has little trouble making new friends in another country despite _____.

7. In spite of _____, the use of chemotherapy to treat cancer has many severe side effects.

8. Though _____, Bob managed to give an excellent presentation at the board meeting.

9. Jerry continued to be denied a promotion despite _____.

10. DDT is still used in many countries as a primary insecticide even though _____.

◇ **PRACTICE 12. Direct contrast. (Chart 19-7)**
Directions: Connect the given ideas, using the words in parentheses. Add commas, periods, semicolons, and capital letters as necessary.

1. *(while)* red is bright and lively gray is a dull color
   → *Red is bright and lively, while gray is a dull color.* OR
   → *While red is bright and lively, gray is a dull color.*

2. *(on the other hand)* Jane is insecure and unsure of herself her sister is full of self-confidence

3. *(while)* a rock is heavy a feather is light

4. *(whereas)* some children are unruly others are quiet and obedient

5. *(on the other hand)* language and literature classes are easy and enjoyable for Alex math and science courses are difficult for him

6. *(however)* strikes can bring improvements in wages and working conditions strikes can also cause loss of jobs and bankruptcy

◇ **PRACTICE 13. Cause and effect; showing contrast. (Charts 16-3, 17-2, and 19-1 → 19-7)**
Directions: Show the relationship between the ideas by adding any of the following expressions, as appropriate. There may be more than one possible completion.

because	*because of*	*while/whereas*	*on the other hand*
since	*due to*	*nevertheless*	*in spite of*
now that	*even though*	*however*	*despite*
therefore	*although*		

1. It was still hot in the room __even though/although__ I had turned on the air conditioner.

2. Several people in the crowd became ill and fainted __due to/because of__ the extreme heat.

3. The gardener trimmed the branches on the cherry tree _____ I asked him not to.

4. The meat of the puffer fish can cause paralysis or even death if it is improperly prepared. _____, it remains a delicacy in Japan for brave diners.

5. _____ everyone disagreed with him, Brian went ahead with his original plan for the company.

6. The first mention of the game of chess appears in an Indian text written almost 1500 years ago. _____ its ancient beginnings, it remains one of the most widely played games in the world today.

7. Alice heard a siren and saw the flashing lights of a police car in her rear-view mirror. _____, she quickly pulled over to the side of the road and stopped.

8. Most adults carry around certain attitudes and prejudices about the world around them. Most children, _____, enter new situations without such preconceived notions.

9. They often have to close all of the ski areas in the mountains _____ severe weather conditions and avalanche danger.

10. _____ paper was first developed by the ancient Chinese, its English name comes from the word *papyrus*, the name of an Egyptian water plant.

11. The supervisor must know what everyone in the department is doing _____ all responsibility for error will fall on her shoulders.

12. _____ aspirin is relatively safe for most adults, it should be administered very carefully to children, if at all. It can be dangerous to children's health.

13. The peanut is used today to make everything from cosmetics to explosives _____ the pioneering scientific work of George Washington Carver in the 1910s and 1920s.

14. In ancient China, yellow was considered to be an imperial color. _____, only the emperor was allowed to wear it. No one else could have yellow clothing of any kind.

15. _____ the abacus had been in use in Asia since ancient times, many in the Western world credited 19-year-old Blaise Pascal, a Frenchman, with inventing the first calculating machine in 1642.

16. _____ she thought she heard the telephone ringing, Marge turned the TV down—only to discover it had been a telephone on the show she was watching.

◇ **PRACTICE 14. Using *otherwise*. (Chart 19-8)**
Directions: Make two sentences. Show the relationship between them by using *otherwise*. In the first sentence, use a modal auxiliary or phrasal modal. *should, had better, have to, must*, etc.

1. If you don't eat less and get more exercise, you won't lose weight.
   → *You should (had better/have to/must) eat less and get more exercise. Otherwise, you won't lose weight.*

2. The children can watch TV tonight only if they finish all of their chores.
   → *The children have to (had better/should/must) finish all of their chores. Otherwise, they cannot watch TV tonight.*

3. Unless you speak up now, the boss will go ahead without knowing that you don't agree.

4. If you don't stop at the store on your way home from work, we won't have anything to eat for dinner tonight.

5. Unless you think it through very carefully, you won't come up with the right answer.

6. If we don't catch any fish this morning, we're going to have beans for dinner again.

7. It's going to be very difficult to finish on time if you don't get someone to help you.

8. Maria is probably going to lose her job unless she finds a way to convince the boss that the error was unavoidable.

◇ **PRACTICE 15. Expressing conditions. (Charts 17-6 → 17-9 and 19-8)**
   Directions: Complete the sentences with any appropriate form of the verb **pass**.

   1. Keith will graduate if he ___*passes*___ all of his courses.

   2. Sam won't graduate if he ___*doesn't pass*___ all of his courses.

   3. Ed won't graduate unless he _____ all of his courses.

   4. Sue will graduate only if she _____ all of her courses.

   5. Jessica will graduate even if she _____ all of her courses.

   6. Alex won't graduate even if he _____ all of his courses.

   7. Jennifer will graduate unless she _____ all of her courses.

   8. Amy won't graduate in the event that she _____ all of her courses.

   9. Jerry _____ all of his courses. Otherwise, he won't graduate.

   10. Carolyn _____ all of her courses, or else she won't graduate.

Directions: Choose the best completion.

1. I have to eat breakfast in the morning. _____, I get grouchy and hungry before my lunch break.
   A. Consequently   B. And   C. Otherwise   D. However

2. My mouth is burning! This is _____ spicy food that I don't think I can finish it.
   A. such   B. so   C. very   D. too

3. I couldn't use the pay phone, _____ I didn't have any coins with me.
   A. yet   B. despite   C. for   D. even though

4. Bats are fascinating _____ have many interesting and amazing qualities.
   A. animals. Therefore, they   C. animals. They
   B. animals, they   D. animals. Because they

5. I need to find an apartment before I can move. _____ I can find one in the next week or so, I will move to Chicago the first of next month.
   A. If   B. Even if   C. Whether   D. Only if

6. Sam and I would love to meet you at a restaurant tonight, but we can do that _____ we can find a babysitter.
   A. if   B. unless   C. only if   D. even if

7. _____ want to take a train trip across western Canada, but my traveling companion wants to fly to Mexico City for our vacation.
   A. Although I   B. Even if I   C. I   D. Despite I

8. Timmy doesn't do well in school _____ his inability to concentrate on any one thing for longer than a minute or two.
   A. as   B. because of   C. because   D. therefore

9. Tony spent _____ money buying movie tickets that he didn't have enough left to buy a soft drink or candy bar.
   A. such   B. a lot of   C. too much   D. so much

10. You should learn how to change a tire on your car _____ you can handle an emergency situation if necessary.
    A. so that   B. if   C. for that   D. therefore

11. Cars have become much more complicated. _____, mechanics need more training than in the past.
    A. Because   B. Therefore   C. So that   D. For

12. Not wanting to be late my first day of class, _____ to school after I missed my bus.
    A. so I ran   B. because I ran   C. I ran   D. therefore, I ran

13. It was raining _____ I couldn't go outside.
    A. because   B. so hard that   C. so that   D. too hard that

14. The Northern Hemisphere has mostly westerly winds _____ the rotation of the earth toward the east.
    A. due to   B. because   C. therefore   D. so

15. Emily is motivated to study _____ she knows that a good education can improve her life.
    A. therefore   B. because of   C. because   D. so

16. Sonia broke her leg in two places. _____, she had to wear a cast and use crutches for three months.
    A. Nevertheless   B. Consequently   C. For that   D. Because

17. Carol showed up for the meeting _____ I asked her not to be there.
    A. even though   B. despite   C. because of   D. because

18. Peter works hard at everything he does. His brother, _____, seldom puts out much effort.
    A. on the other hand   C. even though
    B. otherwise   D. consequently

19. The road will remain safe _____ the flood washes out the bridge.
    A. as long as   B. unless   C. if   D. since

20. _____ I can't make the presentation myself, I've asked my assistant to be prepared to do it for me.
    A. For   C. Only if
    B. In the event that   D. On the other hand

21. I have to go to the meeting _____ I want to or not.
    A. because   B. whether   C. even though   D. only if

22. I asked Angela to run the office while I'm gone _____ I know I can depend on her.
    A. unless   B. since   C. Although   D. so that

23. I think I did okay in my speech last night _____ I'd had almost no sleep for 24 hours.
    A. in spite of   B. unless   C. so that   D. despite the fact that

24. I talked to Anna throughout the evening, _____ nothing I said changed her opinion.
    A. yet   B. and   C. otherwise   D. so that

25. After getting home from elementary school, _____.
    A. our house buzzes with the children's many activities
    B. the dog greets the children at the front door with wagging tail
    C. the children have an hour to play before they begin their homework
    D. the school bus drops the children at the corner near their house

◇ **PRACTICE 17. TEST B: Connecting ideas. (Chapters 16 → 19)**
Directions: Choose the best completion.

1. _____ the extremely bad weather in the mountains, my friends decided not to cancel their trip across the mountain pass.
   A. Because of   B. In spite of   C. Even if   D. Even though

2. Even though a duck lives on water, it stays dry _____ the oil on its feathers, which prevents water from reaching its skin.
   A. because of   B. since   C. because   D. for

3. Alex cannot express himself clearly and correctly in writing. He will never advance in his job _____ he improves his language skills.
   A. otherwise   B. if   C. only if   D. unless

4. _____ there was no electricity, I was able to read because I had a candle.
   A. Unless   B. Even though   C. Even   D. Only if

5. A fire must have a readily available supply of oxygen. _____, it will stop burning.
   A. Consequently   B. Therefore   C. Otherwise   D. However

6. I studied Spanish for four years in high school. _____, I had trouble talking with people when I was traveling in Spain.
   A. Therefore   C. Otherwise
   B. On the other hand   D. Nonetheless

7. I'm sorry you've decided not to go with us on the river trip, but _____ you change your mind, there will still be enough room on the boat for you.
   A. even   C. in the event that
   B. nevertheless   D. although

8. I like to keep the windows open at night no matter how cold it gets. My wife, _____, prefers a warm bedroom with all windows tightly shut.
   A. nevertheless   C. on the other hand
   B. consequently   D. whereas

9. You must lend me the money for the trip. _____, I won't be able to go.
   A. Consequently   B. Nevertheless   C. Otherwise   D. Although

10. I don't understand why, but my neighbor Mr. Morrow doesn't seem to like me. He never smiles at me or speaks to me _____ the many efforts I have made to be friendly and neighborly.
    A. because of   B. in spite of   C. for   D. so

11. _____ the salary meets my expectations, I will accept the job offer.
    A. Due to   B. Even if   C. If   D. Unless

12. Camels have either one hump or two humps. The Arabian camel has one hump. The Bactrian camel, _____, has two humps.
    A. nevertheless   B. however   C. therefore   D. otherwise

13. Ms. Moore, the school counselor, has had years of experience dealing with student problems. _____, she is sometimes confronted by a problem that she cannot handle by herself.

    A. Therefore   B. Nevertheless   C. Otherwise   D. On the other hand

14. Right now all the seats on that flight are taken, sir. _____ there is a cancelation, I will call you.

    A. In the event that   C. Unless

    B. Nevertheless   D. Even if

15. A newborn baby can neither walk nor crawl. A newborn antelope, _____, can run within minutes of birth.

    A. however   B. neverthcless   C. otherwise   D. even though

16. Jason has become _____ famous that he now ignores his old friends. He shouldn't do that.

    A. such   B. so   C. so much   D. too

17. Joan worked in a vineyard last summer _____ money for school expenses.

    A. because to earn   C. for she earned

    B. so she earns   D. so that she could earn

18. Watching the children fly their kites in the park, _____.

    A. suddenly a gust of wind blew my hat off my head

    B. one of the kites got stuck in a tree

    C. I thought of the times long ago when I did the same thing

    D. it looked like a lot of fun

19. I guess I'm a soft touch. I just lent Jan some money for lunch _____ she never paid me back my last loan.

    A. even though   B. unless   C. or else   D. only if

20. Hundreds of species of Hawaiian flowers have become extinct or rare _____ extensive land development and the grazing of wild goats.

    A. now that   B. due to   C. because   D. for

21. It looks like they're going to succeed _____ their present difficulties.

    A. despite   B. because of   C. even though   D. yet

22. The professor told me that I was doing well, _____ my final grade was awful.

    A. so   B. therefore   C. in spite of   D. yet

23. _____ Beth has a new car, she no longer takes the commuter train to work. She drives to work every day.

    A. Now that   B. While   C. Although   D. In case

24. Our village had _____ money available for education that the schools had to close.

    A. so little   B. such little   C. so much   D. such much

25. I hadn't understood his _____ asked him to repeat what he'd said.

    A. directions. I   C. directions, I

    B. directions because I   D. directions. However, I

CHAPTER 20
Conditional Sentences and Wishes

◇ **PRACTICE 1. Conditional sentences: present/future. (Charts 20-1 → 20-3)**
Directions: Complete the sentences with the correct form of the verbs in parentheses. Some of the sentences are contrary to fact, and some are not.

1. I am not an astronaut. If I *(be)* ___were___ were an astronaut, I *(take)* ___would take___ my camera with me on the rocket ship next month.

2. That sounds like a good job offer. I *(accept)* _____ it if I *(be)* _____ you.

3. Don't throw aerosol cans into a fire. An aerosol can *(explode)* _____ if you *(throw)* _____ it into a fire.

4. It is expensive to call across the ocean. However, if transoceanic telephone calls *(be)* _____ cheap, I *(call)* _____ my family every day and *(talk)* _____ for hours.

5. The teacher was absent today, so class was canceled. If she *(be)* _____ absent again tomorrow, class *(cancel)* _____ tomorrow, too.

6. Sea water is salty. If the oceans *(consist)* _____ of fresh water, there *(be)* _____ plenty of water to irrigate all of the deserts in the world to provide an abundant food supply for the entire population of the earth.

◇ **PRACTICE 2. Conditional sentences: past time. (Chart 20-4)**
Directions: Complete the sentences with the words in parentheses. All of the sentences to complete are contrary to fact.

1. I'm sorry you had to take a cab to the airport. I didn't know you needed a ride. If you *(tell)* ___had told___ me, I *(give)* ___would have given___ you a ride gladly.

2. I got wet because I didn't take my umbrella. However, I *(get, not)* _____ _____ wet if I *(remember)* _____ to take my umbrella with me yesterday.

3. Many people were not satisfied with the leader after he took office. If they *(know)* _____ more about his planned economic program, they *(vote, not)* _____ for him.

4. You made a lot of unnecessary mistakes in your composition. You *(get)* _____ _____ a better grade if you *(use)* _____ either a dictionary or the spell checker on your computer to check your spelling.

5. A: Oh, no! I've lost it!

   B: Lost what?

   A: The address for my job interview this afternoon. I wrote it on a match book.

   B: A match book! If you *(write)* _____ the address in your appointment book where it belongs, you *(lose, not)* _____ it. When are you going to get organized?

6. A: Ann, *(you, take)* _____ that job if you *(know)* _____ _____ that you had to work nights?

   B: No way. I had no idea I'd have to work the late night hours they've had me working.

◇ **PRACTICE 3. Conditional sentences: present/future and past time. (Charts 20-1 → 20-4)**
Directions: Complete the sentences with the words in parentheses.

1. If I *(have)* _____ wings, I *(have to, not)* _____ take an airplane to fly home.

2. *(people, be)* _____ able to fly if they *(have)* _____ feathers instead of hair?

3. This box has got to be in Chicago tomorrow. I'm going to send it by express mail. I'm sure if I *(send)* _____ it today by overnight express, it *(arrive)* _____ _____ in time.

4. I didn't know the Newtons were going to bring two other people to dinner last night. If anyone else *(bring)* _____ an extra guest, we *(have, not)* _____ _____ enough seats at the table.

5. A: I don't understand anything in this class. It's boring. And I'm getting a failing grade.

   B: If I *(feel)* _____ the way you do about it, I *(drop)* _____ _____ the class as soon as possible.

6. I've never understood why people build houses on flood plains. If we *(have)* _____ heavy rains in the spring, the river through my hometown *(rise, always)* _____ _____ above its banks and *(flood)* _____ the low-lying areas of the town. Some houses have been flooded a half-dozen times in the last 20 years.

7. A: I'm exhausted, and we're no closer to a solution to this problem after nine hours of work.

   B: Why don't you go home and get some sleep, and I'll keep working. If I *(discover)*
   _____ a solution before morning, I *(call)* _____
   you immediately. I promise.

8. A: I can't believe that you haven't finished that report. What will I use in the committee
   meeting at noon today?

   B: I'm really sorry. If I *(know)* _____ you needed it today, I *(stay)*
   _____ up all night last night and *(finish)*
   _____ it.

◇ **PRACTICE 4. Conditional sentences. (Charts 20-1 → 20-4)**
Directions: Using the given information, create conditional sentences. Use *if*.

1. I was sick yesterday, so I didn't go to class.
   → *If I hadn't been sick yesterday, I would have gone to class.*

2. Because Alan never eats breakfast, he always overeats at lunch.
   → *If Alan ate breakfast, he wouldn't overeat at lunch.*

3. Kostas was late to his own wedding because his watch was slow.

4. I don't ride the bus to work every morning because it's always so crowded.

5. Sara didn't know that highway 57 was closed, so she didn't take an alternative route.

6. Camille couldn't finish unloading the truck because no one was there to help her.

◇ **PRACTICE 5. Using progressive forms and "mixed time" in conditional sentences.
(Charts 20-5 and 20-6)**
Directions: Using the given information, complete the conditional sentences.

1. *It is raining, so we won't finish the game.*
   → If it ___ *weren't raining* ___, we ___ *would finish* ___ the game.

2. *I didn't eat lunch, and now I'm hungry.*
   → If I ___ *had eaten* ___ lunch, I ___ *wouldn't be* ___ hungry now.

3. *Bob left his wallet at home this morning, and now he doesn't have any money for lunch.*
   → If Bob _____ his wallet at home this morning, he _____
   _____ some money for lunch now.

4. *Carol didn't answer the phone because she was studying.*
   → Carol _____ the phone if she _____.

5. *The sun was shining, so we went to the beach yesterday.*
   → If the sun _____, we _____ to the
   beach yesterday.

6. *Every muscle in my body aches today because I played basketball for three hours last night.*

   → Every muscle in my body _____ today if I _____

   _____ basketball for three hours last night.

7. *Barry stops to shake everyone's hand because he's running for political office.*

   → Barry _____ to shake everyone's hand if he _____

   _____ for political office.

8. *We didn't eat all of the turkey at dinner last night, so we have to have turkey again tonight.*

   → If we _____ all of the turkey at dinner last night, we

   _____ turkey again tonight.

9. *The music was playing loudly at the restaurant, so I didn't hear everything Mr. Lee said during
   dinner.*

   → If the music _____ so loudly, I _____

   everything Mr. Lee said during dinner.

10. *The library is closing now, so Abdul will have to leave before finishing his research.*

    → If the library _____ now, Abdul _____

    _____ before finishing his research.

◇ **PRACTICE 6. Using progressive forms and "mixed time" in conditional sentences.
   (Charts 20-5 and 20-6)**

Directions: Using the given information, make conditional sentences. Use *if*.

1. The wind is blowing hard, so I won't take the boat out for a ride.
   → *If the wind weren't blowing hard, I would take the boat out for a ride.*

2. I feel better now because you talked to me about my problems last night.

   → *I wouldn't feel better now if you hadn't talked to me about my problems last night.*

3. Ann carried heavy furniture when she helped her friend move. Her back hurts now.

4. Paulo is working on two jobs right now, so he doesn't have time to help you with your
   remodeling.

5. I wasn't working at the restaurant last night. I didn't wait on your table.

6. Because Diane asked questions every time she didn't understand a problem, she has a good
   understanding of geometry now.

7. A fallen tree was blocking the road, so we didn't arrive on time.

8. Rita is exhausted today because she didn't get any sleep last night.

9. Olga and Ivan weren't paying attention, so they didn't see the sign marking their exit from
   the highway.

10. The doctor doesn't really care about his patients. He didn't explain the medical procedure
    to me before surgery.

◇ **PRACTICE 7. Omitting *if*. (Chart 20-7)**
  Directions: Make sentences with the same meaning by omitting *if*.

  1. *If you should need my help, please call.*

     → _____Should you need_____ my help, please call.

  2. *If I were you, I wouldn't go there.*

     → _____ you, I wouldn't go there.

  3. *If I had been offered a job at the law office, I would have gladly accepted.*

     → _____ a job at the law office, I would have gladly accepted.

  4. *If anyone should call, would you please take a message?*

     → _____ , would you please take a message?

  5. *If I were your doctor, I'd insist that you stop smoking.*

     → _____ your doctor, I'd insist you stop smoking.

  6. *They wouldn't have visited her house if they had known about her illness.*

     → They wouldn't have visited her house _____ about her illness.

  7. *I would start giving my sister driving lessons if she were just a little older.*

     → I would start giving my sister driving lessons _____ just a little
        older.

  8. *If I had not opened the door when I did, I wouldn't have seen you walk by.*

     → _____ the door when I did, I wouldn't have seen you walk by.

◇ **PRACTICE 8. Omitting *if*. (Chart 20-7)**
  Directions: Make sentences with the same meaning by omitting *if*.

  1. If I were your age, I'd do things differently.
     → *Were I your age, I'd do things differently.*

  2. If Bob should show up while I'm away, please give him my message.

  3. If my uncle had stood up to sing, I'd have been embarrassed.

  4. If she were ever in trouble, I'd do anything I could to help her.

  5. If the manager should question these figures, have her talk to the bookkeeper.

  6. I wouldn't have known about your new job if I hadn't talked to your mother.

◇ **PRACTICE 9. Implied conditions. (Chart 20-8)**
  Directions: Notice the conditional verbs in the sentences. Then, using the given information,
  complete the implied *if*-clauses.

  1. *Sara's dad **would have picked** her up, but I forgot to tell him that she needed a ride.*

     → Sara's dad would have picked her up if _____I hadn't forgotten to tell him that_____
        _____she needed a ride._____

2. *I couldn't have made it* without your help.

   → I couldn't have made it if _____

3. *I opened the door slowly. Otherwise, I could have hit* someone.

   → If _____, I could have hit someone.

4. *Doug would have gone* with me, but he couldn't get time off from work.

   → Doug would have gone with me if _____

5. *Carol:* Why didn't Oscar tell his boss about the problem?

   Alice: He **would have gotten** into a lot of trouble.

   → Oscar would have gotten into a lot of trouble if _____

   _____

◇ **PRACTICE 10. Review: conditional sentences. (Charts 20-1 → 20-8)**
   Directions: Choose the correct completion.

   1. If I could speak Spanish, I _____ next year studying in Mexico.
      A. will spend   C. had spent
      B. would have spent   D. would spend

   2. It would have been a much more serious accident _____ fast at the time.
      A. was she driving   C. she had driven
      B. had she been driving   D. if she drove

   3. "Can I borrow your car for this evening?"
      "Sure, but Nora's using it right now. If she _____ it back in time, you're welcome to borrow it."
      A. brought   B. would bring   C. will bring   D. brings

   4. I didn't get home until well after midnight last night. Otherwise, I _____ your call.
      A. returned   B. had returned   C. would return   D. would have returned

   5. If energy _____ inexpensive and unlimited, many things in the world would be different.
      A. is   B. will be   C. were   D. would be

   6. We _____ the game if we'd had a few more minutes.
      A. could have won   C. had won
      B. won   D. will win

   7. I _____ William with me if I had known you and he didn't get along with each other.
      A. hadn't brought   C. wouldn't have brought
      B. didn't bring   D. won't bring

   8. The lecturer last night didn't know what he was talking about, but if Dr. Mason _____,
      I would have listened carefully.
      A. lectured   C. was lecturing
      B. had been lecturing   D. would lecture

   9. If you _____ to my advice in the first place, you wouldn't be in this mess right now.
      A. listen   B. will listen   C. had listened   D. listened

10. _____ interested in that subject, I would try to learn more about it.
   A. If I am   B. Should I   C. I was   D. Were I

11. If I _____ the same problems you had as a child, I might not have succeeded in life as well as you have.
   A. have   B. would have   C. had had   D. should have

12. I _____ you sooner had someone told me you were in the hospital.
   A. would have visited   C. had visited
   B. visited   D. visit

13. _____ more help, I could call my neighbor.
   A. Needed   B. Should I need   C. I have needed   D. I should need

14. _____ then what I know today, I would have saved myself a lot of time and trouble over the years.
   A. If I know   B. If I would know   C. Did I know   D. Had I known

15. Do you think there would be less conflict in the world if all people _____ the same language?
   A. speak   B. will speak   C. spoke   D. had spoken

16. If you can give me one good reason for your acting like this, _____ this incident again.
   A. I don't mention   C. I never mention
   B. I will never mention   D. will I never mention

17. I didn't know you were asleep. Otherwise, I _____ so much noise when I came in.
   A. didn't make   C. won't make
   B. wouldn't have made   D. don't make

18. Unless you _____ all of my questions, I can't do anything to help you.
   A. answered   B. answer   C. would answer   D. are answering

19. Had you told me that this was going to happen, I _____ it.
   A. would never have believed   C. hadn't believed
   B. don't believe   D. can't believe

20. If Jake _____ to go on the trip, would you have gone?
   A. doesn't agree   B. didn't agree   C. hadn't agreed   D. wouldn't agree

◇ **PRACTICE 11. Review: conditional sentences. (Charts 20-1 → 20-8)**
Directions: Complete the sentences with the words in parentheses.

1. I'm broke, but I *(have)* _____ plenty of money now if I

   (spend, not) _____ so much yesterday.

2. That child had a narrow escape. She *(hit)* _____ by a car if her

   mother *(pull, not)* _____ her out of the street.

3. A: Why were you late for the meeting?

   B: Well, I *(be)* _____ there on time, but I had a flat tire on the way.

4. A: Did you know that Bob got 100% on the test?

   B: Really? That surprises me. If I didn't know better, I *(think)* _____

      he cheated.

5. A: How did you do on the test?

   B: Not so well. I *(do)* _____ much better, but I misread the

      directions for the last section.

6. A: Do you really mean it?

   B: Of course! I *(say, not)* _____ it unless I *(mean)*

      _____ it.

7. A: When did Mark graduate?

   B: He didn't.

   A: Oh?

   B: He had to quit school because of some trouble at home. Otherwise, he *(graduate)*

      _____ last June.

8. A: I hear Dorothy had an accident. Was it serious?

   B: No. Luckily, she wasn't driving fast at the time of the accident. If she *(drive)* _____

      _____ fast, I'm sure it *(be)* _____

      a more serious accident.

9. Tom's hobby is collecting stamps from all over the world. If he *(travel)* _____

    _____ to a new country, he *(spend, always)* _____

    _____ time looking for new stamps. That's how he has acquired such a large

collection of valuable stamps.

◇ **PRACTICE 12.** *As if/as though.* **(Chart 20-9)**

   Directions: Using the information in parentheses, complete the sentences.

1. Tim acts as if he __were__ the boss. *(Truth: Tim isn't the boss.)*

2. This hole in my shirt looks as if it ___had been made___ by a bullet. *(Truth: The hole*

   wasn't made by a bullet.)

3. Barbara looked at me as though she _____ never _____ me before.

   (Truth: She has met me many times before.)

4. They treat their dog as if it _____ a child. *(Truth: The dog isn't a child.)*

5. She went right on talking as though she _____ a word I'd said.

   (Truth: She heard everything I said.)

6. You look so depressed. You look as if you _____ a friend in the world.

   (Truth: You have many friends.)

7. He looked right through me as if I _____. *(Truth: I exist.)*

8. Craig bumped the other car and then continued as though nothing _____.
   (Truth: Something happened.)

9. A: Have Joe and Diane ever met?

   B: I don't think so. Why?

   A: He came in and started talking to her as if they _____ old friends.
   (Truth: They aren't old friends.)

10. I can hear his voice so clearly that it's as if he _____ here in this room.
    (Truth: He isn't here in this room; he's next door.)

11. It was so quiet that it seemed as if the earth _____. *(Truth: The earth
    didn't stop.)*

12. I turned, and there she was. It was as though she _____ out of nowhere.
    (Truth: She didn't appear out of nowhere.)

◇ **PRACTICE 13. Using *wish*. (Charts 20-10 and 20-11)**
   Directions: Using the information in parentheses, complete the sentences.

   1. *(The sun isn't shining.)* I wish the sun _____ were shining _____ right now.

   2. *(I wanted you to go.)* I wish you _____ had gone _____ with us to the concert last night.

   3. *(Spiro didn't drive.)* I wish Spiro _____ to work. I'd ask him for a ride
      home.

   4. *(I can't swim.)* I wish I _____ so I would feel safe in a boat.

   5. *(I want you to stop fighting.)* I wish you _____ fighting and try to work
      things out.

   6. *(I wanted to win.)* I wish we _____ the game last night.

   7. *(Bill didn't get the promotion.)* I wish Bill _____ the promotion. He feels
      bad.

   8. *(I quit my job.)* I wish I _____ my job until I'd found another one.

   9. *(It isn't winter.)* I wish it _____ winter so that I could go skiing.

   10. *(I want Al to sing.)* I wish Al _____ a couple of songs. He has a good voice.

   11. *(Natasha can't bring her children.)* I wish Natasha _____ her children
       with her tomorrow. They would be good company for mine.

   12. *(No one offered to help.)* I wish someone _____ to help us find our way
       when we got lost in the middle of the city.

◇ **PRACTICE 14. Using *wish*. (Charts 20-10 and 20-11)**
Directions: Complete the sentences with the words in parentheses.

1. Pedro's in trouble with the teacher. Now he wishes he *(miss, not)* ___hadn't missed___
    class three times this week.

2. A: It's raining. I wish it *(stop)* _would stop_.
    B: Me too. I wish the sun *(shine)* _were shining_ so that we could go swimming.

3. Heinrich doesn't like his job as a house painter. He wishes he *(go)* _____ to
    art school when he was younger. He wishes he *(can paint)* _____
    canvasses instead of houses for a living.

4. I wish I *(move, not)* _____ to this town. I can't seem to make any
    friends, and everything is so congested. I wish I *(take)* _____ the job I
    was offered in the small town near here.

5. I know I should quit smoking. I wish you *(stop)* _____ nagging me
    about it.

6. A: Did you get your car back from the garage?
    B: Yes, and it still isn't fixed. I wish I *(pay, not)* _____ them in full
       when I picked up the car. I should have waited to be sure that everything was all right.

7. A: I wish you *(hurry)* _____! We're going to be late.
    B: I wish you *(relax)* _____. We've got plenty of time.

8. I wish my husband *(invite, not)* _____ the neighbors over for dinner
    when he talked to them this afternoon. I don't feel like cooking a big dinner.

9. A: How do you like the new president of our association?
    B: Not much. I wish she *(elect, not)* _____. I never should
       have voted for her.
    A: Oh, really? Then you probably wish I *(vote, not)* _____ for her. If
       you recall, she won by only one vote. You and I could have changed the outcome of the
       election if we'd known then what we know now.

10. A: I wish we *(buy)* _____ everything we wanted all the time.
    B: In that case, you probably wish money *(grow)* _____ on trees. We'd plant
       some in the back yard, and just go out and pick a little from the branches every morning.

11. A: My thirteen-year-old daughter wishes she *(be, not)* _____ so tall and that her
       hair *(be)* _____ black and straight.
    B: Really? My daughter wishes she *(be)* _____ taller and that her hair *(be)* _____
       blond and curly.

12. A: I wish most world leaders *(meet)* _____ in the near future and reach

    some agreement on environmental issues. I'm worried the earth is running out of time.

   B: I wish I *(disagree)* _____ with you and *(prove)* _____

    _____ your fears groundless, but I'm afraid you might be right.

13. A: I can't go to the game with you this afternoon.

   B: Really? That's too bad. But I wish you *(tell)* _____ me sooner so

    that I could have found someone else to go with.

14. A: How long have you been sick?

   B: For over a week.

   A: I wish you *(go)* _____ to see a doctor today. You should find out

    what's wrong with you.

   B: Maybe I'll go tomorrow.

◇ **PRACTICE 15. Conditionals. (Charts 20-1 → 20-11)**   *have + 3V*

Directions: Complete the sentences with the words in parentheses.

TOM: What's wrong, Bob? You look awful! You look as if you *(1. run)* _*have been run*_

    over by a truck!

BOB: Well, you *(2. look)* _____ this bad today, too, if you *(3. have)*

    _____ a day like mine yesterday. My car slid into a tree because the

    roads were icy.

TOM: Oh? I was driving on the icy roads yesterday, and I didn't slide into a tree. What happened?

BOB: Well, I suppose if I *(4. drive, not)* _____ so fast, I *(5. slide, not)*

    _____ into the tree.

TOM: Icy roads and speed don't mix. If drivers *(6. step)* _____ on the gas on

    ice, they're likely to spin their car in a circle.

BOB: I know! And not only is my car a mess now, but I didn't have my driver's license with me,

    so now I'll have to pay an extra fine when I go to court next month.

TOM: Why were you driving without your license?

BOB: Well, I lost my wallet a few days ago. It slipped out of my pocket while I was riding the bus

    to work.

TOM: What a tale of woe! If you *(7. take not)* _____ that bus, you *(8. lose, not)*

    _____ your wallet. If you *(9. lose, not)* _____

    your wallet, you *(10. have)* _____ your driver's license with you when you hit a tree. If you *(11. have)* _____ your license with you, you

(12. have to pay, not) _____ a big fine when you go to court

next week. And of course, if you *(13. drive, not)* _____ too

fast, you *(14. run into, not)* _____ a tree, and you *(15. be, not)*

_____ in this mess now. If I *(16. be)* _____ you, I

(17. take) _____ it easy for a while and just *(18. stay)* _____

home where you're safe and sound.

BOB: Enough about me! How about you?

TOM: Well, things are really looking up for me. I'm planning to take off for Florida as soon as I
finish my finals. I'm sick of all this cold, rainy weather we've been having. I *(19. stay)*
_____ here for vacation if the weather *(20. be, not)* _____
so bad. But I need some sun!

BOB: I wish I *(21. go)* _____ with you. How are you planning on getting
there?

TOM: If I have enough money, I *(22. fly)* _____. Otherwise, I *(23. take)*
_____ the bus. I wish I *(24. drive)* _____ my own
car there because it *(25. be)* _____ nice to have it to drive around in
once I get there, but it's such a long trip. I've been looking for a friend to go with me and
share the driving.

BOB: Hey, I have a super idea! Why don't I go with you? I can share the driving. I'm a great
driver!

TOM: Didn't you just get through telling me that you'd wrapped your car around a tree?

Directions: Choose the correct answer.

Example: If I ___C___ you, I would get some rest before the game tomorrow.
    A. am   B. could be   C. were   D. had been

1. When I stopped talking, Sam finished my sentence for me as though he _____ my mind.
    A. would read   B. had read   C. reads   D. can read

2. If you _____, I would have brought my friends over to your house this evening to watch TV, but I didn't want to bother you.
    A. had studied   C. hadn't been studying
    B. studied   D. didn't study

3. I wish I _____ you some money for your rent, but I'm broke myself.
    A. can lend   B. would lend   C. could lend   D. will lend

4. If someone _____ into the store, smile and say, "May I help you?"
    A. comes   B. came   C. would come   D. could come

5. "Are we lost?"
   "I think so. I wish we _____ a map with us today."
    A. were bringing   B. brought   C. had brought   D. would bring

6. "Here's my phone number."
   "Thanks. I'll give you a call if I _____ some help tomorrow."
    A. will need   B. need   C. would need   D. needed

7. If I weren't working for an accounting firm, I _____ in a bank.
    A. work   B. will work   C. have worked   D. would be working

8. Ed invested a lot of money with a dishonest advisor, and lost nearly all of it. Now he is having serious financial problems. He _____ in this position if he'd listened to some of his friends.
    A. will be   B. wouldn't be   C. will be   D. hadn't been

9. The world _____ a better place if we had known a hundred years ago what we know today about the earth's environment.
    A. will be   B. was   C. should be   D. might be

10. The medicine made me feel dizzy. I felt as though the room _____ around and around.
    A. were spinning   C. spins
    B. will spin   D. would be spinning

11. "I'm really sorry about what happened during the meeting. I felt I had no choice."
   "It's okay. I'm sure you wouldn't have done it if you _____."
    A. should have   B. had to   C. hadn't had to   D. have to

12. _____ you, I'd think twice about that decision. It could be a bad move.
    A. If I had been   B. Were I   C. Should I be   D. If I am

13. "Was Pam seriously injured in the automobile accident?"
   "She broke her arm. It _____ much worse if she hadn't been wearing her seat belt."
    A. will be   B. would have been   C. was   D. were

14. If my candidate had won the election, I _____ happy now.
    A. am   B. would be   C. was   D. can be

15. I wish Janet _____ to the meeting this afternoon.
    A. came   B. will come   C. can come   D. could come

16. I _____ you to the woman I was speaking with, but I couldn't think of her name.
    A. will introduce   C. would have introduced
    B. would introduce   D. couldn't have introduced

17. "What _____ today if you hadn't come here this weekend?"
    "I guess I'd be putting in extra hours at my office."
    A. are you doing   C. will you be doing
    B. can you do   D. would you be doing

18. Page 12 of the manual that came with the appliance says, "_____ any problem with the
    merchandise, contact your local dealer."
    A. Do you have   C. Had you
    B. Should you have   D. You have

19. Marge walked away from the discussion. Otherwise, she _____ something she would
    regret later.
    A. will say   B. said   C. might say   D. might have said

20. I would never have encouraged you to go into this field _____ it would be so stressful for you.
    I'm sorry it's been so difficult for you.
    A. had I known   C. should I know
    B. and I have known   D. but I knew

Directions: Choose the correct answer.

Example: If I ___C___ you, I would get some rest before the game tomorrow.
   A. am   B. could be   C. were   D. had been

1. Please keep your voice down in this section of the library. If you _____ to talk loudly, I will have to ask you to leave.
   A. continued   B. could continue   C. will continue   D. continue

2. Gloria never seems to get tired. I sure wish I _____ her energy.
   A. would have   B. have   C. have had   D. had

3. "Why didn't Bill get the promotion he was expecting?"
   "He may not be qualified. If he were, he _____ that promotion last year."
   A. would have been given   C. would be given
   B. was given   D. had been given

4. If I could find Rob's phone number, I _____ him about the change in plans. Maybe somebody else will call him.
   A. called   B. had called   C. could call   D. will call

5. "How do you like your new apartment?"
   "The apartment itself is great, but I wish I _____ used to the constant noise from the street below."
   A. got   B. could get   C. had gotten   D. am

6. I was very engrossed in that presentation on Australia. The videotapes were so realistic that it was as though we _____ there, driving through the outback.
   A. were   B. have been   C. are   D. will be

7. If I _____ following that other car too closely, I would have been able to stop in time instead of running into it.
   A. wasn't   B. would have been   C. was   D. hadn't been

8. "Why aren't you going mountain climbing with the rest of us next weekend?"
   "To be honest with you, I'm lazy. If I weren't, I _____ with you."
   A. would have gone   C. go
   B. would go   D. will go

9. "Will you see Tom at lunch today? I'd like you to give him a message for me."
   "I'm not going to lunch, but if I _____ him later, I'll give him your message."
   A. should see   B. will see   C. would see   D. could see

10. I'm really sleepy today. I wish I _____ Bob to the airport late last night.
    A. didn't have to take   C. hadn't had to take
    B. weren't taking   D. didn't take

11. Hurry! We've got to leave the house immediately. Otherwise, _____ the opening ceremony.
    A. we'd miss   C. we miss
    B. we'd have missed   D. we're going to miss

12. "Why didn't you tell me you were having so many problems?"
"I _____ you, but I figured you had enough to worry about without my problems, so I said nothing."

    A. would tell   B. would have told   C. would be telling   D. had told

13. A nation's balance of trade is considered unfavorable if it _____ more money on imports than it gains from exports.

    A. will spend   B. would spend   C. can spend   D. spends

14. Many people who live near nuclear plants are concerned. _____ go wrong, the impact on the surrounding area could be disastrous.

    A. Something would   C. Should something
    B. Something will   D. Does something

15. Had I known the carpenter was going to take three days to show up, I _____ the materials and done the work myself. It would be finished by now.

    A. will get   C. might get
    B. would have gotten   D. will have gotten

16. I wish you _____ making that noise. It's bothering me.

    A. would stop   C. stop
    B. are going to stop   D. can stop

17. A huge tree crashed through the bedroom roof and broke my bed and most of the other furniture. _____ in the room, I would have been killed.

    A. Should I be   C. Would I have been
    B. Had I been   D. Would I be

18. If everyone _____, how would we control air traffic? Surely, we'd all be crashing into each other.

    A. can fly   B. will fly   C. flies   D. could fly

19. If the world's tropical forests continue to disappear at their present rate, many animal species _____ extinct.

    A. became   C. will become
    B. would have become   D. would become

20. When my lost briefcase was returned with my year-long research results intact, I felt tremendously relieved. It was as if a huge, heavy weight _____ from my shoulders.

    A. had been lifted   C. would be lifted
    B. is being lifted   D. is lifting

APPENDIX
Supplementary Grammar Units

◇ **PRACTICE 1. Subjects, verbs, and objects. (Chart A-1)**
    Directions: <u>Underline</u> and identify the subject (S), verb (V), and object of the verb (O) in each sentence.

        S   V   O
    1. <u>Airplanes</u> <u>have</u> <u>wings</u>.

    2. The teacher explained the problem.

    3. Children enjoy games.

    4. Jack wore a blue suit.

    5. Some animals eat plants. Some animals eat other animals.

    6. According to an experienced waitress, you can carry full cups of coffee without spilling them just by never looking at them.

◇ **PRACTICE 2. Transitive vs. intransitive verbs. (Chart A-1)**
    Directions: <u>Underline</u> and identify the verb in each sentence. Write **VT** if it is transitive. Write **VI** if it is intransitive.

          VI
    1. Alice <u>arrived</u> at six o'clock.

         VT
    2. We <u>drank</u> some tea.

    3. I agree with you.

    4. I waited for Sam at the airport for two hours.

    5. They're staying at a resort hotel in San Antonio, Texas.

    6. Chanchai is studying English.

    7. The wind is blowing hard today.

    8. I walked to the theater, but Janice rode her bicycle.

    9. Amphibians hatch from eggs.

    10. Rivers flow toward the sea.

◇ **PRACTICE 3. Identifying prepositions. (Chart A-2)**
Directions: <u>Underline</u> the prepositions.

1. Jim came to class <u>without</u> his books.

2. We stayed at home during the storm.

3. Sonya walked across the bridge over the Cedar River.

4. When Alex walked through the door, his little sister ran toward him and put her arms around his neck.

5. The two of us need to talk to Tom, too.

6. Animals live in all parts of the world. Animals walk or crawl on land, fly in the air, and swim in the water.

7. Scientists divide living things into two main groups: the animal kingdom and the plant kingdom.

8. Asia extends from the Pacific Ocean in the east to Africa and Europe in the west.

◇ **PRACTICE 4. Sentence elements. (Charts A-1 and A-2)**
Directions: <u>Underline</u> and identify the subject (**S**), verb (**V**) object (**O**), and prepositional phrases (**PP**) in the following sentences.

```
        S     V      O       PP
```
1. <u>Jack</u> <u>put</u> the <u>letter</u> <u>in the mailbox</u>.

2. The children walked to school.

3. Mary did her homework at the library.

4. Chinese printers created the first paper money in the world.

5. Dark clouds appeared on the horizon.

6. Mary filled the shelves of the cabinet with boxes of old books.

◇ **PRACTICE 5. Adjectives and adverbs. (Charts A-3 and A-4)**
Directions: <u>Underline</u> and identify the adjectives (**ADJ**) and adverbs (**ADV**) in these sentences.

```
             ADJ       ADV
```
1. Jack opened the <u>heavy</u> door <u>slowly</u>.

2. Chinese jewelers carved beautiful ornaments from jade.

3. The old man carves wooden figures skillfully.

4. A busy executive usually has short conversations on the telephone.

5. The young woman had a very good time at the picnic yesterday.

◇ **PRACTICE 6. Adjectives and adverbs. (Charts A-3 and A-4)**
  Directions: Complete each sentence with the correct adjective or adverb.

  1. *quick, quickly*   We ate ___quickly___ and ran to the theater.

  2. *quick, quickly*   We had a ___quick___ dinner and ran to the theater.

  3. *polite, politely*   I've always found Fred to be a _____ person.

  4. *polite, politely*   He responded to my question _____ .

  5. *regular, regularly* Mr. Thomas comes to the store _____ for cheese and
                           bread.

  6. *regular, regularly* He is a _____ customer.

  7. *usual, usually*   The teacher arrived at the _____ time.

  8. *usual, usually*   She _____ comes to class five minutes before it begins.

  9. *good, well*   Jennifer Cooper paints _____ .

  10. *good, well*   She is a _____ artist.

  11. *gentle, gently*   A _____ breeze touched my face.

  12. *gentle, gently*   A breeze _____ touched my face.

  13. *annual, annually*   Many birds migrate _____ to a warm climate for the
                           winter.

  14. *annual, annually*   Many birds fly long distances in their _____ migration to
                           a warm climate for the winter.

  15. *bad, badly*   The audience booed the actors' _____ performance.

  16. *bad, badly*   The audience booed and whistled because the actors performed
                           _____ throughout the show.

◇ **PRACTICE 7. Midsentence adverbs. (Chart A-4)**
  Directions: Put the adverb in parentheses in its usual midsentence position.

                        always
  1. *(always)*   Sue ∧ takes a walk in the morning.

  2. *(always)*   Tim is a hard worker.

  3. *(always)*   Beth has worked hard.

  4. *(always)*   Jack works hard.

  5. *(always)*   Do you work hard?

  6. *(usually)*   Taxis are available at the airport.

7. *(rarely)* Youssef takes a taxi to his office.

8. *(often)* I have thought about quitting my job and sailing to Alaska.

9. *(probably)* Yuko needs some help.

10. *(ever)* Have you attended the show at the planetarium?

11. *(seldom)* Al goes out to eat at a restaurant.

12. *(hardly ever)* The students are late.

13. *(usually)* Do you finish your homework before dinner?

14. *(generally)* In India, the monsoon season begins in April.

15. *(usually)* During the monsoon season, Mr. Singh's hometown receives around

610 centimeters (240 inches) of rain, which is an unusually large amount.

◇ **PRACTICE 8. Linking verbs. (Charts A-1 → A-6)**
Directions: Some of the *italicized* words in the following are used as linking verbs. Identify which ones are linking verbs by underlining them. Also underline the adjective that follows the linking verb.

1. Olga *looked* at the fruit. *(no underline)*

2. It *looked* fresh.

3. Dan *noticed* a scratch on the door of his car.

4. Morris *tasted* the candy.

5. It *tasted* good.

6. The crowd *grew* quiet as the official began her speech.

7. Felix *grows* tomatoes in his garden.

8. Sally *grew* up in Florida.

9. I can *smell* the chicken in the oven.

10. It *smells* delicious.

11. Barbara *got* a package in the mail.

12. Al *got* sleepy after dinner.

13. During the storm, the sea *became* rough.

14. Nicole *became* a doctor after many years of study.

15. Diana *sounded* her horn to warn the driver of the other car.

16. Helen *sounded* happy when I talked to her.

17. The weather *turns* hot in July.

18. When Bob entered the room, I *turned* around to look at him.

19. I *turned* a page in the book.

20. It *appears* certain that Mary Hanson will win the election.

21. Dick's story *seems* strange. Do you believe it?

◇ **PRACTICE 9. Linking verbs; adjectives and adverbs. (Charts A-3 → A-6)**
   Directions: Complete each sentence with the correct adjective or adverb.

1. *clean, cleanly*   The floor looks ___clean___ .

2. *slow, slowly*   The bear climbed ___slowly___ up the tree.

3. *safe, safely*   The plane landed _____ on the runway.

4. *anxious, anxiously*   When the wind started to blow, I grew _____ .

5. *complete, completely*   This list of names appears _____ . No more names
                             need to be added.

6. *wild, wildly*   The crowd yelled _____ when we scored a goal.

7. *honest, honestly*   The merchant looked _____ , but she wasn't. I
                             discovered when I got home that she had cheated me.

8. *thoughtful, thoughtfully* Jane looked at her book _____ before she
                             answered the teacher's question.

9. *good, well*   Most of the students did _____ on their tests.

10. *fair, fairly*   The contract offer sounded _____ to me, so I accepted
                             the job.

11. *terrible, terribly*   Jim felt _____ about forgetting his son's birthday.

12. *good, well*   A rose smells _____ .

13. *light, lightly*   As dawn approached, the sky became _____ .

14. *confident, confidently* Beth spoke _____ when she delivered her speech.

15. *famous, famously*   The actor became _____ throughout much of the
                             world.

16. *fine, finely*   I don't think this milk is spoiled. It tastes _____ to me.

◇ **PRACTICE 10. Review: basic question forms. (Chart B-1)**
   Directions: From the <u>underlined</u> sentences, make questions for the given answers. Fill in the blank spaces with the appropriate words. If no word is needed, write Ø.

1. <u>*Bob can live there*</u>.

	Question word	Auxiliary verb	Subject	Main verb	Rest of question	→	Answer
1a.	Ø	Can	Bob	live	there ?	→	Yes.
1b.	Where	can	Bob	live	Ø ?	→	There.
1c.	Who	can	Ø	live	there ?	→	Bob.

2. <u>*Don is living there*</u>.

	Question word	Auxiliary verb	Subject	Main verb	Rest of question	→	Answer
2a.	Ø				there ?	→	Yes.
2b.	Where				Ø ?	→	There.
2c.	Who				there ?	→	Don.

3. <u>*Sue lives there*</u>.

	Question word	Auxiliary verb	Subject	Main verb	Rest of question	→	Answer
3a.	Ø				there ?	→	Yes.
3b.	Where				Ø ?	→	There.
3c.	Who				there ?	→	Sue.

4. <u>*Ann will live there*</u>.

	Question word	Auxiliary verb	Subject	Main verb	Rest of question	→	Answer
4a.	Ø				there ?	→	Yes.
4b.	Where				Ø ?	→	There.
4c.	Who				there ?	→	Ann.

5. <u>*Jack lived there*</u>.

	Question word	Auxiliary verb	Subject	Main verb	Rest of question	→	Answer
5a.					there ?	→	Yes.
5b.					Ø ?	→	There.
5c.					there ?	→	Jack.

6. <u>*Mary has lived there*</u>.

	Question word	Auxiliary verb	Subject	Main verb	Rest of question	→	Answer
6a.					?	→	Yes.
6b.					?	→	There.
6c.					?	→	Mary.

◇ **PRACTICE 11. Yes/no and information questions. (Charts B-1 and B-2)**

Directions: Create questions to fit the dialogues. There are two speakers in each dialogue: A and B. Notice in the examples that in each dialogue there is a short answer and then in parentheses a long answer. Your questions should produce those answers.

1. A: _____ When are you going to the zoo? _____
   B: Tomorrow. *(I'm going to the zoo tomorrow.)*

2. A: _____ Are you going downtown later today? _____
   B: Yes. *(I'm going downtown later today.)*

3. A: _____
   B: Yes. *(I live in an apartment.)*

4. A: _____
   B: In a condominium. *(Sue lives in a condominium.)*

5. A: _____
   B: Jack. *(Jack lives in that house.)*

6. A: _____
   B: Yes. *(I can speak French.)*

7. A: _____
   B: Don. *(Don can speak Arabic.)*

8. A: _____
   B: Two weeks ago. *(Olga arrived two weeks ago.)*

9. A: _____
   B: Ali. *(Ali arrived late.)*

10. A: _____
    B: The window. *(Ann is opening the window.)*

11. A: _____
    B: Opening the window. *(Ann is opening the window.)*

12. A: _____
    B: Her book. *(Mary opened her book.)*

13. A: _____
    B: Tom. *(Tom opened the door.)*

14. A: _____
    B: Yes. *(The mail has arrived.)*

15. A: _____
    B: Yes. *(I have a bicycle.)*

16. A: _____
    B: A pen. *(Alex has a pen in his hand.)*

17. A: _____

    B: Yes. *(I like ice cream.)*

18. A: _____

    B: Yes. *(I would like an ice cream cone.)*

19. A: _____

    B: A candy bar. *(Joe would like a candy bar.)*

20. A: _____

    B: Ann. *(Ann would like a soft drink.)*

◇ **PRACTICE 12. Yes/no and information questions. (Charts B-1 and B-2)**

Directions: Create questions to fit the dialogues. There are two speakers in each dialogue: A and B. Notice in the examples that in each dialogue there is a short answer and then in parentheses a long answer. Your questions should produce those answers.

1. A: _____How long has Pierre been living here?_____

    B: Since last September. *(Pierre has been living here since last September.)*

2. A: I need some information. Maybe you can help me. ___Which (city) is farther north, London or Paris?___

    B: London. *(London is farther north than Paris.)*

3. A: Is that your umbrella?

    B: No.

    A: _____

    B: Jane's. *(It's Jane's.)*

4. A: I haven't seen you for weeks. How are you? _____

    B: Going to school and studying hard. *(I've been going to school and studying hard.)*

5. A: Did you call Sally?

    B: Yes, but she wasn't in.

    A: _____

    B: Her roommate. *(Her roommate answered the phone.)*

6. A: Do the villagers have tractors in the rural areas?

    B: No. They don't have any modern farm machinery.

    A: _____

    B: With oxen or water buffaloes. *(They plow their fields with oxen or water buffaloes.)*

7. A: I really like having my own computer.

    B: _____

    A: Since last December. *(I've had it since last December.)*

8. A: _____ I've never seen one quite like it.

   B: A myna. It's common in warm climates. *(That kind of bird is a myna.)*

9. A: _____

   B: I missed my bus. *(I was late for work this morning because I missed my bus.)*

10. A: Last summer we painted the outside of our house.

    B: That must have been a big job. _____

    A: About four days. *(It took about four days.)*

11. A: Jack was late last night, wasn't he? _____

    B: At 11:30. *(He finally got home at 11:30.)*

12. A: Would you like a cup of coffee?

    B: Thanks. That sounds good.

    A: _____

    B: With cream and sugar. *(I take it with cream and sugar.)*

13. A: _____

    B: Around 250 million. *(The population of the United States is around 250 million.)*

14. A: _____

    B: The red one. *(Of those two coats, I like the red one better than the black one.)*

15. A: We spent a relaxing weekend in a small village in the mountains.

    B: _____

    A: By bus. *(We got there by bus.)*

16. A: I'm sending a letter to the consulate about the problems I'm having with my visa.

    _____

    B: Mr. Ho. *(You should address it to Mr. Ho.)*

17. A: _____

    B: Over 800 miles. *(It's over 800 miles from here to Los Angeles.)*

18. A: _____

    B: Ann, Susan, and Alice. *(Ann, Susan, and Alice are going to be at the meeting tonight.)*

19. A: In my country, we eat rice every day. _____

    B: About once a week. *(People in my country have rice about once a week.)*

20. A: _____

    B: Silly looking hat?! I think it's a great hat! I got it at the shopping mall. *(I got that silly looking hat at the shopping mall.)*

21. A: _____

    B: To say you're sorry. *(Apologize means "to say you're sorry.")*

22. A: _____

   B: Twelve. *(There are twelve edges on a cube.)*

   A: _____

   B: Eight. *(There are eight edges on a pyramid.)*

23. A: I've never met Bob. _____

   B: *He has dark hair, a mustache, wears glasses, and is about average height.*

24. A: You know Ann Green, don't you? _____

   B: *She's energetic, bright, very friendly. A really nice person.*

◇ **PRACTICE 13. Information questions. (Charts B-1 and B-2)**
   Directions: Create questions from these sentences. The *italicized* words in parentheses should be the answers to your questions.

   1. I take my coffee *(black)*. → *How do you take your coffee?*

   2. I have *(an English-Spanish)* dictionary.

   3. He *(runs a grocery store)* for a living.

   4. Margaret was talking to *(her uncle)*.

   5. *(Only ten)* people showed up for the meeting.

   6. *(Due to heavy fog)*, none of the planes could take off.

   7. She was thinking about *(her experiences as a rural doctor)*.

   8. I was driving *(sixty-five miles per hour)* when the policeman stopped me.

   9. I like *(hot and spicy Mexican)* food best.

   10. *(The)* apartment *(at the end of the hall on the second floor)* is mine.

   11. Oscar is *(friendly, generous, and kindhearted)*.

   12. Oscar is *(tall and thin and has short black hair)*.

   13. *(Ann's)* dictionary fell to the floor.

   14. Abby isn't here *(because she has a doctor's appointment)*.

   15. All of the students in the class will be informed of their final grades *(on Friday)*.

   16. I feel *(awful)*.

   17. Of those three books, I preferred *(the one by Tolstoy)*.

   18. I like *(rock)* music.

   19. The plane is expected to be *(an hour)* late.

   20. The driver of the stalled car lit a flare *(in order to warn oncoming cars)*.

   21. I want *(the felt-tip)* pen, *(not the ballpoint)*.

   22. The weather is *(hot and humid)* in July.

23. I like my steak *(medium rare)*.

24. I did *(very well)* on the test.

25. There are *(31,536,000)* seconds in a year.

◇ **PRACTICE 14. Information questions. (Charts B-1 and B-2)**
Directions: Create questions from the following sentences. The words in parentheses should be the answers to your questions.

1. I need *(five dollars)*. → *How much money do you need?*

2. Roberto was born *(in Panama)*.

3. I go out to eat *(at least once a week)*.

4. I'm waiting for *(Maria)*.

5. *(My sister)* answered the phone.

6. I called *(Benjamin)*.

7. *(Benjamin)* called.

8. She bought *(twelve gallons of)* gas.

9. "Deceitful" means *("dishonest")*.

10. An abyss is *(a bottomless hole)*.

11. He went *(this)* way, *(not that way)*.

12. These are *(Jim's)* books and papers.

13. They have *(four)* children.

14. He has been here *(for two hours)*.

15. It is *(two hundred miles)* to New Orleans.

16. The doctor can see you *(at three on Friday)*.

17. Her roommate is *(Jane Peters)*.

18. Her roommates are *(Jane Peters and Sue Lee)*.

19. My parents have been living there *(for three years)*.

20. This is *(Alice's)* book.

21. *(Fred and Jack)* are coming over for dinner.

22. Ann's dress is *(blue)*.

23. Anne's eyes are *(brown)*.

24. *(Bob)* can't go on the picnic.

25. Bob can't go *(because he is sick)*.

26. I didn't answer the phone *(because I didn't hear it ring)*.

27. I like *(classical)* music.

28. I don't understand *(the chart on page 50)*.

29. Janet is *(studying)* right now.

30. You spell "sitting" *(with two "t's" S-I-T-T-I-N-G)*.

31. Tom *(is about medium height and has red hair and freckles)*.

32. Tom is *(very serious and hardworking)*.

33. Ron *(works as a civil engineer for the railroad company)*.

34. Mexico is *(eight hundred miles)* from here.

35. I take my coffee *(black with sugar)*.

36. Of Stockholm and Moscow, *(Stockholm)* is farther north.

37. *(Fine.)* I'm getting along *(just fine)*.

◇ **PRACTICE 15. Negative questions. (Chart B-4)**
  Directions: In these dialogues, make negative questions from the words in parentheses, and determine the expected response.

  1. A: Your infected finger looks terrible. *(you, see, not)* __Haven't you seen__ a doctor yet?

     B: __No__. But I'm going to. I don't want the infection to get any worse.

  2. A: You look pale. What's the matter? *(you, feel)* _____ well?

     B: _____ . I think I might be coming down with something.

  3. A: Did you see Mark at the meeting?

     B: No, I didn't.

     A: Really? *(he, be, not)* _____ there?

     B: _____ .

     A: That's funny. I've never known him to miss a meeting before.

  4. A: Why didn't you come to the meeting yesterday afternoon?

     B: What meeting? I didn't know there was a meeting.

     A: *(Mary, tell, not)* _____ you about it?

     B: _____ . No one said a word to me about it.

  5. A: I have a package for Janet. *(Janet and you, work, not)* _____

     _____ in the same building?

     B: _____ . I'd be happy to take the package to her tomorrow when I go to work.

  6. A: Frank didn't report all of his income on his tax forms.

     B: *(that, be, not)* _____ against the law?

     A: _____ . And that's why he's in a lot of legal trouble. He might even go to jail.

  7. A: Did you give Linda my message when you went to class this morning?

     B: No. I didn't see her.

     A: Oh? *(she, be)* _____ in class?

     B: _____ . She didn't come today.

8. A: Do you see that woman over there, the one in the blue dress? *(she, be)* _____

   Mrs. Robbins?

   B: _____ .

   A: I thought so. I wonder what she is doing here.

◇ **PRACTICE 16. Tag questions. (Chart B-5)**
   Directions: Add tag questions to the following.

   1. You live in an apartment, _don't you_ ?

   2. You've never been in Italy, _have you_ ?

   3. Sally turned in her report, _____ ?

   4. There are more countries north of the equator than south of it, _____ ?

   5. You've never met Jack Freeman, _____ ?

   6. You have a ticket to the game, _____ ?

   7. You'll be there, _____ ?

   8. Tom knows Alice Reed, _____ ?

   9. We should call Rita, _____ ?

   10. Ostriches can't swim, _____ ?

   11. These books aren't yours, _____ ?

   12. That's Bob's, _____ ?

   13. No one died in the accident, _____ ?

   14. I'm right, _____ ?

   15. This grammar is easy, _____ ?

◇ **PRACTICE 17. Contractions. (Chart C)**
   Directions: Write the contraction of the pronoun and verb if appropriate. Write Ø if the pronoun and verb cannot be contracted.

   1. He is (_He's_) in my class.

   2. He was (_Ø_) in my class.

   3. He has (_He's_) been here since July.

   4. He has (_Ø_) a Volvo.★

   _____

   ★NOTE: **has, have** and **had** are NOT contracted when they are used as main verbs. They are contracted only
   when they are used as helping verbs.

5. She had (_____) been there for a long time before we arrived.

6. She had (_____) a bad cold.

7. She would (_____) like to go to the zoo.

8. I did (_____) well on the test.

9. We will (_____) be there early.

10. They are (_____) in their seats over there.*

11. It is (_____) going to be hot tomorrow.

12. It has (_____) been a long time since I've seen him.

13. A bear is a large animal. It has (_____) four legs and brown hair.

14. We were (_____) on time.

15. We are (_____) always on time.

16. She has (_____) a good job.

17. She has (_____) been working there for a long time.

18. She had (_____) opened the window before class began.

19. She would (_____) have helped us if we had (_____) asked her.

20. He could (_____) have helped us if he had (_____) been there.

◇ **PRACTICE 18. Using *not* and *no*. (Chart D-1)**
Directions: Change each sentence into the negative in two ways: use ***not . . . any*** in one sentence and ***no*** in the other.

1. I have some problems. → *I don't have any problems. I have no problems.*

2. There was some food on the shelf.

3. I received some letters from home.

4. I need some help.

5. We have some time to waste.

6. You should have given the beggar some money.

7. I trust someone. → *I don't trust anyone. I trust no one.***

8. I saw someone.

9. There was someone in his room.

10. She can find somebody who knows about it.

*****They're, their,*** and ***there*** all have the same pronunciation.

**Also spelled with a hyphen in British English: *no-one*

◇ **PRACTICE 19. Avoiding double negatives. (Chart D-2)**
    Directions: Correct the errors in these sentences, all of which contain double negatives.

    1. We don't have no time to waste.

      → *We have no time to waste.* OR: *We don't have any time to waste.*

    2. I didn't have no problems.

    3. I can't do nothing about it.

    4. You can't hardly ever understand her when she speaks.

    5. I don't know neither Ann nor her husband.

    6. Don't never drink water from that river without boiling it first.

    7. Because I had to sit in the back row of the auditorium, I couldn't barely hear the speaker.

◇ **PRACTICE 20. Beginning a sentence with a negative word. (Chart D-3)**
    Directions: Change each sentence so that it begins with a negative word.

    1. I had hardly stepped out of bed when the phone rang.

      → *Hardly had I stepped out of bed when the phone rang.*

    2. I will never say that again.

    3. I have scarcely ever enjoyed myself more than I did yesterday.

    4. She rarely makes a mistake.

    5. I will never trust him again because he lied to me.

    6. It is hardly ever possible to get an appointment to see him.

    7. I seldom skip breakfast.

    8. I have never known a more generous person than Samantha.

◇ **PRACTICE 21. Preposition combinations. (Chart E)**
    Directions: Complete the sentences with prepositions.

    1. There is no excuse ___for___ lying to your friends.

    2. The children are excited _____ their upcoming trip to the zoo.

    3. I wasn't aware _____ any problems with the new design.

    4. Are you satisfied _____ your accommodations?

    5. Cubs are protected _____ danger by the mother bear.

    6. Registration for the conference is limited _____ 300 participants.

    7. I'm very fond _____ my nieces and nephews.

    8. Do you regularly contribute _____ worthwhile causes?

    9. We thanked the contributors _____ their donations.

10. The famous actor gladly answers questions that are relevant _____ her work.

11. She does not respond _____ questions about her personal life.

12. I am envious _____ no one.

13. Did Sara apologize _____ being late?

14. Lemonade is composed _____ lemon juice, water, and sugar.

15. Our apartment is furnished _____ kitchen appliances, but not a washer and dryer.

◇ **PRACTICE 22. Preposition combinations. (Chart E)**
  Directions: Complete the sentences with prepositions.

1. It's important to believe _____ yourself.

2. Would you be willing to fight _____ your ideals?

3. The spy was involved _____ a dangerous conspiracy.

4. For many people it's difficult to distinguish a dolphin _____ a porpoise.

5. Gandhi was committed _____ nonviolence.

6. He will be remembered throughout the ages _____ his commitment to nonviolence.

7. If you're done _____ your dictionary, could I borrow it for a minute?

8. Usually people will be polite _____ you if you are polite _____ them.

9. Oliver is grateful _____ his parents _____ giving him the opportunity for a good education.

10. Many people are very concerned _____ global warming.

11. It took Natasha almost a year to recover _____ her automobile accident.

12. The driver of the other car was accused _____ reckless driving.

13. I do not agree _____ your political views.

14. I refuse to argue _____ you _____ politics ever again.

15. My mother introduced me _____ classical music when I was quite young.

◇ **PRACTICE 23. Preposition combinations. (Chart E)**
  Directions: Complete the sentences with prepositions.

1. Susan took advantage _____ having a roommate from Chile by practicing speaking Spanish with her as often as she could.

2. The president is innocent _____ the charges leveled against him by his political opponents.

3. Under what circumstances, if any, would you be capable _____ killing another human being?

4. There is no substitute _____ good home cooking.

5. Showing that he was faithful _____ his campaign promises, the governor approved the building of ten new schools.

6. After studying the evidence, I am convinced _____ his innocence.

7. So you subscribe _____ the theory that the universe began as a Big Bang?

8. I'd like to get a high-paying job, but I'm not qualified _____ much of anything. Maybe I'd better go back to school.

9. If you need me, I'll be there. You can count _____ me.

10. The brave firefighter rescued two small children _____ a burning building.

11. A locked gate prevented us _____ entering the park.

12. The bride wore white, and the bridesmaids were dressed _____ yellow silk.

13. Ms. Fields' office is cluttered _____ stacks and stacks of papers.

14. New computers are equipped _____ all sorts of things I don't understand and never use.

15. Professor Armsley was invited to participate _____ a panel discussion on the role of business in protecting the environment.

◇ **PRACTICE 24. Preposition combinations. (Chart E)**
   Directions: Complete the sentences with prepositions.

   1. Would you approve _____ a law allowing 13-year-olds to drive?

   2. I myself would be opposed _____ such a law.

   3. Olga's heart was filled _____ happiness on her wedding day.

   4. Please don't be upset _____ me. I didn't mean to hurt your feelings.

   5. Would you be interested _____ joining a hiking club?

   6. I know little about the ancient Greek philosophers. I'm not acquainted _____ the works of Plato.

   7. Anna, who works twelve-hour days, is dedicated _____ her research into possible cures for cancer.

   8. While we're all hoping _____ better weather, we don't expect it.

   9. The nightly news on TV exposes watchers _____ acts of violence that leave them fearful and horrified.

10. Sam can't keep any secrets _____ his wife. Sometimes he even feels that she knows what he's thinking.

11. My uncle stopped my cousin _____ marrying the man she loves.

12. Larry started with one small store and now has twenty stores. He has succeeded _____ business.

13. Are you complaining _____ the neighbors' children again? Maybe we should move to another apartment.

14. Are you related _____ anyone famous?

15. Mr. Adams tried to hide his gambling losses _____ his wife, but she found out.

◇ **PRACTICE 25. Preposition combinations. (Chart E)**
Directions: Complete the sentences with prepositions.

1. Would you vote _____ a woman to lead your country?

2. Stop staring _____ me! What are you doing? Is something wrong?

3. Mrs. Jefferson is known _____ her sharp intellect.

4. I look forward _____ meeting your parents.

5. The city of Kigali is located _____ Ruwanda.

6. This sentence consists _____ six words.

7. We are blessed _____ three healthy, happy, rambunctious children.

8. If you can't depend _____ your family to help you in times of trouble, who can you rely _____?

9. Don't blame other people _____ your own failures in life.

10. We have a date for tomorrow evening. You haven't forgotten _____ it, have you?

11. I think it's important to become familiar _____ cultures and customs different from our own.

12. We barely escaped _____ the war-torn country with our lives.

13. Do you believe that children should never be allowed to argue _____ adults _____ anything?

14. Your doctor can provide you _____ information about any health concerns you might have. Be sure to ask questions.

15. Some countries try to prohibit their citizens _____ traveling abroad.

◇ **PRACTICE 26. Preposition combinations. (Chart E)**

Directions: Complete the sentences with prepositions.

1. My boss demanded to know why I was absent _____ work last Friday.

2. My neighbor takes care _____ my two children while I'm at work.

3. At first it was hard to leave my children with a babysitter, but now I'm used _____ it.

4. As a last resort, I covered my face _____ a scarf to keep the flies away.

5. I applied _____ several companies _____ positions in their accounting department.

6. As soon as I was finished _____ my dessert, we paid the bill and left the restaurant.

7. Please forgive me _____ not getting back to you sooner.

8. Who is responsible _____ ordering supplies in the mail room?

9. We arrived _____ Paris around noon, but we didn't arrive _____ our friends' apartment until well after three.

10. I'm not accustomed _____ drinking coffee. I'm a tea drinker.

11. Siblings are often jealous _____ each other, but these jealousies usually decrease as the children mature.

12. I'm exhausted _____ all the hard work of the past week.

13. Would you object _____ watching a different station for the news tonight?

14. Please be patient _____ me. I'm trying very hard to understand what you're saying, but your meaning isn't clear to me yet.

15. It is good to be pleased _____ ourselves and proud _____ ourselves when we have done a good job.

SPECIAL WORKBOOK SECTION
Phrasal Verbs

PHRASAL VERBS (TWO-WORD AND THREE-WORD VERBS)

The term *phrasal verb* refers to a verb and particle which together have a special meaning. For example, ***put + off*** means "postpone." Sometimes a phrasal verb consists of three parts. For example, ***put + up + with*** means "tolerate." Phrasal verbs are also called *two-word verbs* or *three-word verbs*.

SEPARABLE PHRASAL VERBS (a) ***I handed*** my paper ***in*** yesterday. (b) ***I handed in*** my paper yesterday. (c) ***I handed*** it ***in*** yesterday. (INCORRECT: I *handed in* it yesterday.)	A phrasal verb may be either *separable* or *nonseparable*. With a separable phrasal verb, a noun may come either between the verb and the preposition or after the preposition, as in (a) and (b). A pronoun comes between the verb and the preposition if the phrasal verb is separable, as in (c).
NONSEPARABLE PHRASAL VERBS (d) ***I ran into*** an old friend yesterday. (e) ***I ran into*** her yesterday. (INCORRECT: I *ran* an old friend *into*.) (INCORRECT: I *ran* her *into* yesterday.)	With a nonseparable phrasal verb, a noun or pronoun must follow the preposition, as in (d) and (e).

Phrasal verbs are especially common in informal English. Following is a list of common phrasal verbs and their usual meanings. This list contains only those phrasal verbs used in the exercises in the text. The phrasal verbs marked with an asterisk (★) are nonseparable.

A   ask out . . . . *ask someone to go on a date*

B   bring about, bring on . . . . *cause*
       bring up . . . . *(1) rear children; (2) mention or introduce a topic*

C   call back . . . . *return a telephone call*
       call in . . . . *ask to come to an official place for a specific purpose*
       call off . . . . *cancel*
       ★call on . . . . *(1) ask to speak in class; (2) visit*
       call up . . . . *call on the telephone*
       ★catch up (with) . . . . *reach the same position or level*
       ★check in, check into . . . . *register at a hotel*
       ★check into . . . . *investigate*
       ★check out . . . . *(1) take a book from the library; (2) investigate*
       ★check out (of) . . . . *leave a hotel*
       cheer up . . . . *make (someone) feel happier*
       clean up . . . . *make clean and orderly*
       ★come across . . . . *meet/find by chance*
       cross out . . . . *draw a line through*
       cut out . . . . *stop an annoying activity*

D	do over	*do again*
	*drop by, drop in (on)	*visit informally*
	drop off	*leave something/someone at a place*
	*drop out (of)	*stop going to school, to a class, to a club, etc.*
F	figure out	*find the answer by reasoning*
	fill out	*write the answers to a questionnaire or complete an official form*
	find out	*discover information*
G	*get along (with)	*exist satisfactorily*
	get back (from)	*(1) return from a place; (2) receive again*
	*get in, get into	*(1) enter a car; (2) arrive*
	*get off	*leave an airplane, a bus, a train, a subway, a bicycle*
	*get on	*enter an airplane, a bus, a train, a subway, a bicycle*
	*get out of	*(1) leave a car; (2) avoid work or an unpleasant activity*
	*get over	*recover from an illness*
	*get through (with)	*finish*
	*get up (from)	*arise from a bed, a chair*
	give back	*return an item to someone*
	give up	*stop trying*
	*go over	*review or check carefully*
	*grow up	*become an adult*
H	hand in	*submit an assignment*
	hang up	*(1) conclude a telephone conversation; (2) put clothes on a hanger or a hook*
	have on	*wear*
K	keep out (of)	*not enter*
	*keep up (with)	*stay at the same position or level*
	kick out (of)	*force (someone) to leave*
L	*look after	*take care of*
	*look into	*investigate*
	*look out (for)	*be careful*
	look over	*review or check carefully*
	look up	*look for information in a reference book*
M	make up	*(1) invent; (2) do past due work*
N	name after, name for	*give a baby the name of someone else*
P	*pass away, *pass on	*die*
	pass out	*distribute*
	*pass out	*lose consciousness*
	pick out	*select*
	pick up	*(1) go to get someone (e.g., in a car); (2) take in one's hand*
	point out	*call attention to*
	put away	*remove to a proper place*
	put back	*return to original place*
	put off	*postpone*
	put on	*put clothes on one's body*
	put out	*extinguish a cigarette, cigar, or fire*
	*put up with	*tolerate*
R	*run into, *run across	*meet by chance*
	*run out (of)	*finish a supply of something*
S	*show up	*appear, come*
	shut off	*stop a machine, light, faucet*

T *take after . . . . *resemble*
　　take off . . . . *(1) remove clothing; (2) leave on a trip*
　　take out . . . . *(1) take someone on a date; (2) remove*
　　take over . . . . *take control*
　　take up . . . . *begin a new activity or topic*
　　tear down . . . . *demolish, reduce to nothing*
　　tear up . . . . *tear into many little pieces*
　　think over . . . . *consider carefully*
　　throw away, throw out . . . . *discard, get rid of*
　　throw up . . . . *vomit, regurgitate food*
　　try on . . . . *put on clothing to see if it fits*
　　turn down . . . . *decrease volume or intensity*
　　turn in . . . . *(1) submit an assignment; (2) go to bed*
　　turn off . . . . *stop a machine, light, faucet*
　　turn on . . . . *start a machine, light, faucet*
　　turn out . . . . *extinguish a light*
　　turn up . . . . *increase volume or intensity*

◇ **PRACTICE 1. Phrasal verbs.**

　　Directions: Supply appropriate prepositions for these two-word and three-word verbs.

　　1. A: Where did you grow ___up___ ?

　　　 B: In Seattle, Washington.

　　2. A: I'm trying to find yesterday's newspaper. Have you seen it?

　　　 B: I'm afraid I threw it _____ . I thought you had finished reading it.

　　3. A: Don't forget to turn the lights _____ before you go to bed.

　　　 B: I won't.

　　4. A: I have a car, so I can drive us to the festival.

　　　 B: Good.

　　　 A: What time should I pick you _____ ?

　　　 B: Any time after five would be fine.

　　5. A: We couldn't see the show at the outdoor theater last night.

　　　 B: Why not?

　　　 A: It was called _____ on account of rain.

　　　 B: Did you get a raincheck?

　　6. A: Thomas looks sad.

　　　 B: I think he misses his girlfriend. Let's try to cheer him _____ .

　　7. A: I would like to check this book _____ . What should I do?

　　　 B: Take the book to the circulation desk and give the librarian your student I.D.

　　8. A: What brought _____ your decision to quit your present job?

　　　 B: I was offered a better job.

　　9. A: How many people showed _____ for the meeting yesterday?

　　　 B: About twenty.

10. A: How was your vacation?

B: I had a great time.

A: When did you get _____ home?

B: A couple of days ago. I had planned to stay a little longer, but I ran _____ _____ money.

◇ **PRACTICE 2. Phrasal verbs.**

Directions: Supply appropriate prepositions for these two-word and three-word verbs.

1. A: When do we have to turn _____ our assignments?

B: They're due next Tuesday.

2. A: How does this tape recorder work?

B: Push this button to turn it _____ , and push that button to shut it _____ .

3. A: May I borrow your dictionary?

B: Sure. But please be sure to put it _____ on the shelf when you're finished.

4. A: I'm going to be in your neighborhood tomorrow.

B: Oh? If you have time, why don't you drop _____ to see us?

5. A: Look _____ ! A car is coming!

6. A: I got very irritated at one of my dinner guests last night.

B: Why?

A: There was an ashtray on the table, but she put her cigarette _____ on one of my good plates!

7. A: I need to talk to Karen.

B: Why don't you call her _____ ? She's probably at home now.

8. A: Oh-oh. I made a mistake on the check I just wrote.

B: Don't try to correct the mistake. Just tear _____ the check and throw it _____ .

9. A: Are you here to apply for a job?

B: Yes.

A: Here is an application form. Fill it _____ and then give it _____ to me when you are finished.

10. A: Look. There's Mike.

B: Where?

A: At the other end of the block, walking toward the administration building. If we run, we can catch _____ with him.

11. A: Is your roommate here?

   B: Yes. She decided to come to the party after all. Have you ever met her?

   A: No, but I'd like to.

   B: She's the one standing over there by the far window. She has a blue dress _____. Come on. I'll introduce you.

12. A: Do you have a date for Saturday night?

   B: Yes. Jim Brock asked me _____. We're going bowling.

◇ **PRACTICE 3. Phrasal verbs.**

Directions: Supply appropriate prepositions for these two-word and three-word verbs.

1. A: I think we should increase the membership dues from one dollar to two.

   B: That might solve some of our financial problems. Why don't you bring that _____ at the next meeting?

2. A: Did you hand _____ your composition?

   B: No. I didn't like it, so I decided to do it _____ .

3. A: What time did you get _____ this morning?

   B: I slept late. I didn't drag myself out of bed until after nine.

4. A: What's the baby's name?

   B: Helen. She was named _____ her paternal grandmother.

5. A: I need to get more exercise.

   B: Why don't you take _____ tennis?

6. A: You can't go in there.

   B: Why not?

   A: Look at that sign. It says, "Keep _____. No trespassing."

7. A: I can't reach Fred. There's a busy signal.

   B: Then hang _____ and try again later.

8. A: The radio is too loud. Would you mind if I turned it _____ a little?

   B: No.

9. A: I can't hear the radio. Could you turn it _____ a little?

   B: Sure.

10. A: What are you doing Saturday night, Bob?

   B: I'm taking Virginia _____ for dinner and a show.

◇ **PRACTICE 4. Phrasal verbs.**

Directions: Supply appropriate prepositions for these two-word and three-word verbs.

1. A: Omar, would you please pass these papers _____ to the rest of the class?

   B: I'd be happy to.

2. A: When are we expected to be at the hotel?

   B: According to our reservation, we are supposed to check _____ the hotel before 6 P.M. Monday and check _____ before noon Tuesday.

3. A: How do you get _____ with your roommate?

   B: Fine. He's a nice guy.

4. A: Thanks for the ride. I appreciate it.

   B: Where should I drop you _____?

   A: The next corner would be fine.

5. A: I'm going to be out of town for a couple of days. Would you mind looking _____ my cat?

   B: Not at all. I'd be happy to. Just tell me what I'm supposed to do.

6. A: I think I'm going to turn _____ now. Good night.

   B: 'Night. See you in the morning. Sleep well.

7. A: Don't you think it's hot in here?

   B: Not especially. If you're hot, why don't you take your sweater _____?

8: A: How do you spell "occasionally"?

   B: I'm not sure. You'd better look it _____ in your dictionary.

9. A: How much lettuce should we get?

   B: I think we could use two heads. Pick _____ two that feel fresh and firm.

10. A: Why are you sniffling?

    B: I had a cold last week, and I can't seem to get _____ it.

◇ **PRACTICE 5. Phrasal verbs.**

Directions: Supply appropriate prepositions for these two-word and three-word verbs.

1. A: Are you ready to leave?

   B: Almost. I'll be ready to go just as soon as I get _____ putting the clean dishes away.

2. A: I'm going crazy! I've been trying to solve this math problem for the last hour, and I still can't get it.

   B: Why don't you give _____ for a while? Take a break and then go back to it.

3. A: I hear you had a frightening experience yesterday. What happened?

   B: Ed suddenly got dizzy and then passed _____ . I tried to revive him, but he was out cold. Luckily there was a doctor in the building.

4. A: What happened when the pilot of the plane passed out during the flight?

   B: The co-pilot took _____ .

5. A: Cindy is only three. She likes to play with the older kids, but when they're running and playing, she can't keep _____ with them.

   B: Does she mind?

   A: She doesn't seem to.

6. A: I made a mistake in my composition. What should I do?

   B: Since it's an in-class composition, just cross it _____ .

7. A: I need my dictionary, but I lent it to Jose.

   B: Why don't you get it _____ from him?

8. A: I wish the teacher wouldn't call _____ me in class.

   B: Why not?

   A: I get nervous.

   B: Why?

   A: I don't know.

9. I took a plane from Atlanta to Miami. I got _____ the plane in Atlanta. I got _____ the plane in Miami.

10. It was a snowy winter day, but I still had to drive to work. First I got _____ the car to start the engine. Then I got _____ of the car to scrape the snow and ice from the windows.

11. Last year I took a train trip. I got _____ the train in Chicago. I got _____ the train in Des Moines.

12. Phyllis takes the bus to work. She gets _____ the bus at Lindbergh Boulevard and gets _____ the bus about two blocks from her office on Tower Street.

◇ **PRACTICE 6. Phrasal verbs.**
   Directions: Supply appropriate prepositions for these two-word and three-word verbs.

   1. A: Why don't we try to call _____ the O'Briens sometime this weekend? We haven't seen them for a long time.

      B: Good idea. I'd like to see them again.

2. A: Did you go _____ your paper carefully before you handed it _____?

   B: Yes. I looked it _____ carefully.

3. A: Do you believe his story about being late because he had a flat tire?

   B: No. I think he made it _____.

4. A: Could you pick _____ a newspaper on your way home from work tonight?

   B: Sure.

5. A: Did you hear the bad news?

   B: About what?

   A: Gary's grandmother passed _____. Gary went home to be with his family and attend the funeral.

6. A: I like your new shoes.

   B: Thanks. I had to try _____ almost a dozen pairs before I decided to get these.

7. A: Have you decided to accept that new job?

   B: Not yet. I'm still thinking it _____.

8. A: I'm tired. I wish I could get _____ of going to the meeting tonight.

   B: Do you have to go?

9. A: Why hasn't Mary been in class for the last two weeks?

   B: She dropped _____ _____ school.

10. A: What time does your plane take _____?

    B: 10:40.

    A: How long does the flight take?

    B: I think we get _____ around 12:30.

11. A: Do you like living in the dorm?

    B: It's okay. I've learned to put _____ with all the noise.

12. A: What brought _____ your decision to quit your job?

    B: I couldn't get _____ _____ my boss.

◇ **PRACTICE 7. Phrasal verbs.**

Directions: Supply appropriate prepositions for each of these two-word verbs.

1. A: Guess who I ran _____ today as I was walking across campus.

   B: Who?

   A: Ann Keefe.

   B: You're kidding!

2. A: There will be a test on Chapters Eight and Nine next Friday.

   B: *(Groan.)* Couldn't you put it _____ until Monday?

3. A: You'd better put _____ your coat before you leave. It's chilly out.

   B: What's the temperature?

4. A: I smell something burning in the kitchen. Can I call you _____ in a minute?

   B: Sure. I hope your dinner hasn't burned.

   A: So do I! Bye.

   B: Good-bye.

5. A: I think that if I learn enough vocabulary I won't have any trouble using English.

   B: That's not necessarily so. I'd like to point _____ that language consists of much more than just vocabulary.

6. A: One billion seconds ago, World War II was being fought. One billion minutes ago, Jesus Christ was living. One billion hours ago, the human race had not yet discovered agriculture.

   B: How did you figure that _____?

   A: I didn't. I came _____ that information while I was reading the newspaper.

7. A: Your children certainly love the outdoors.

   B: Yes, they do. We brought them _____ to appreciate nature.

8. A: What forms do I have to fill out to change my tourist visa to a student visa?

   B: I don't know, but I'll look _____ it first thing tomorrow and try to find _____.
   I'll let you know.

9. A: How long were you in the hospital?

   B: About a week. But I've missed almost two weeks of classes.

   A: It's going to be hard for you to make _____ all the work you've missed, isn't it?

   B: Very.

10. A: Would you mind turning _____ the light?

    B: Not at all.

◇ **PRACTICE 8. Phrasal verbs.**

Directions: Supply appropriate prepositions for these two-word verbs.

1. A: Who do you take _____ the most, your father or your mother?

   B: My mother, I think. I can see many similarities between the two of us.

2. A: Hey, cut it _____, you guys! I'm trying to sleep.

   B: What's the matter? Are we making too much noise?

3. A: Could I help you clean _____?

   B: Sure. Would you mind taking _____ the garbage?

4. A: Miss Ward, what seems to be the problem?

   B: Well, Doctor, for the last two days I haven't been able to keep any food down. Every time I try to eat something, I throw _____ soon afterward.

5. A: Where's my jacket?

   B: I hung it _____ the closet.

6. A: Why are you going to see Professor Kelly?

   B: He called me _____ to talk about my research project.

7. A: Is that man's story true?

   B: Yes. A newspaper reporter checked _____ his story and found that it was true.

8. A: The city government is planning to redevelop a large section of the inner city.

   B: What's going to happen to the buildings that are there now?

   A: They are going to be torn _____ .

9. A: Some people tried to crash our party last night.

   B: What did you do?

   A: We kicked them _____ .

10. The test is about to begin. Please put _____ all of your books and notebooks.

Index

Answer Key

To the student: To make it easy to correct your own answers, remove this answer key along the perforations and make a separate answer key booklet for yourself.

Chapter 1: OVERVIEW OF VERB TENSES

◇ PRACTICE 1, p. 1.
1. do you do . . . eat
2. did you do . . . ate . . . visited . . . wrote
3. are you doing . . . am talking . . . am answering
4. was looking
5. have I asked . . . have asked
6. have you been doing . . . have been talking
7. will you be (OR: are you going to be) . . . will be (OR: am going to be)
8. will you be doing   will he sitting
9. had you done . . . had eaten
10. will you have done . . . will have eaten

◇ PRACTICE 2, p. 2.
1. eats
2. ate
3. will eat (OR: is going to eat)
4. am eating
5. was eating
6. will be eating
7. have already eaten
8. had already eaten
9. will have already eaten (OR: will already have eaten)
10. has been eating
11. had been eating
12. will have been eating

◇ PRACTICE 3, p. 4.
PART A.
1. shouting, shouted
2. sloping, sloped
3. stopping, stopped
4. stooping, stooped
5. answering, answered
6. referring, referred
7. returning, returned
8. enjoying, enjoyed
9. copying, copied
10. dying, died

PART B.
11. pointing
12. beating
13. betting
14. exciting
15. exiting
16. regretting
17. attempting
18. shouting
19. flitting
20. interesting

PART C.
21. bothered
22. blurred
23. scared
24. scarred
25. feared
26. starred
27. stared
28. ordered
29. suffered
30. occurred

PART D.
31. dreaming
32. filing
33. filling
34. failing
35. annoying
36. denying
37. scrubbing
38. draining
39. fanning
40. interrupting

PART E.
41. combed
42. wrapped
43. groaned
44. occupied
45. sprayed
46. wiped
47. whipped
48. accepted
49. permitted
50. merited
51. whispered
52. inferred

1

Chapter 2: PRESENT AND PAST, SIMPLE AND PROGRESSIVE

◇ PRACTICE 1, p. 5.

1. isn't shining
2. own
3. am trying
4. belongs
5. is sleeping
6. is bleeding
7. am failing
8. shrinks
9. is biting
10. isn't blowing
11. are always fighting
12. is he screaming
13. means
14. are you whispering
15. is taping

◇ PRACTICE 2, p. 6.

1. has
2. is having
3. weighs
4. is weighing . . . needs
5. am doing . . . consists
6. am thinking . . . think
7. is looking . . . look
8. is currently appearing
9. appears
10. are seeing
11. doesn't see
12. am imagining
13. imagine
14. Aren't you forgetting
15. forget
16. is costing/costs
17. costs
18. am smelling . . . smells
19. Are you being
20. is
21. am being . . . am not

◇ PRACTICE 3, p. 7.

1. usually drinks . . . is drinking
2. takes . . . usually waits
3. is raining . . . is standing . . . is holding . . . is waiting
4. is taking . . . studies . . . has . . . is also taking . . . likes . . . has
5. are you doing . . . am tasting . . . tastes
6. are you writing . . . am making . . . Do you always prepare . . . always try
7. are the children being . . . are cleaning . . . (are) picking
8. am preparing . . . don't need

◇ PRACTICE 4, p. 8.

1. /əd/	7. /əd/	13. /t/
2. /t/	8. /t/	14. /d/
3. /d/	9. /d/	15. /t/
4. /t/	10. /əd/	16. /d/
5. /əd/	11. /əd/	
6. /d/	12. /t/	

◇ PRACTICE 5, p. 9.

GROUP 1A:

begin	began	begun
drink	drank	drunk
ring	rang	rung
shrink	shrank	shrunk
sing	sang	sung
sink	sank	sunk
spring	sprang	sprung
stink	stank	stunk
swim	swam	swum

GROUP 1B:

blow	blew	blown
draw	drew	drawn
grow	grew	grown
know	knew	known
throw	threw	thrown
fly	flew	flown
break	broke	broken
choose	chose	chosen
drive	drove	driven
freeze	froze	frozen
ride	rode	ridden
rise	rose	risen
speak	spoke	spoken
steal	stole	stolen
swear	swore	sworn
tear	tore	torn
wear	wore	worn
weave	wove	woven
write	wrote	written
get	got	got/gotten
forget	forgot	forgot/forgotten
mistake	mistook	mistaken
shake	shook	shaken
take	took	taken
bite	bit	bitten
hide	hid	hidden
be	was, were	been
eat	ate	eaten
fall	fell	fallen
forgive	forgave	forgiven
give	gave	given
lie	lay	lain
see	saw	seen
do	did	done
go	went	gone

GROUP 2A:

sell	sold	sold
tell	told	told
flee	fled	fled
bleed	bled	bled
breed	bred	bred
feed	fed	fed
lead	led	led
read	read	read
speed	sped	sped
lay	laid	laid
pay	paid	paid
say	said	said
find	found	found
grind	ground	ground
wind	wound	wound

have	had	had
hear	heard	heard

GROUP 2B:

creep	crept	crept
deal	dealt	dealt
feel	felt	felt
keep	kept	kept
kneel	knelt	knelt
leave	left	left
mean	meant	meant
meet	met	met
sleep	slept	slept
sweep	swept	swept
weep	wept	wept
lose	lost	lost
bring	brought	brought
buy	bought	bought
catch	caught	caught
fight	fought	fought
seek	sought	sought
teach	taught	taught
think	thought	thought
bend	bent	bent
build	built	built
lend	lent	lent
send	sent	sent
spend	spent	spent

GROUP 2C:

cling	clung	clung
dig	dug	dug
hang	hung	hung
spin	spun	spun
stick	stuck	stuck
sting	stung	stung
strike	struck	struck/stricken
swing	swung	swung
hold	held	held
shoot	shot	shot
sit	sat	sat
stand	stood	stood
understand	understood	understood
win	won	won

GROUP 2D:

become	became	become
come	came	come
run	ran	run

GROUP 3:

bet	bet	bet
bid	bid	bid
broadcast	broadcast	broadcast
burst	burst	burst
cost	cost	cost
cut	cut	cut
hit	hit	hit
hurt	hurt	hurt
let	let	let
put	put	put
quit	quit	quit
shed	shed	shed
shut	shut	shut
slit	slit	slit

split	split	split
spread	spread	spread
upset	upset	upset

◇ **PRACTICE 6, p. 11.**

1. swore
2. shook
3. drew
4. burst
5. hid
6. stuck
7. slit
8. slid
9. spread
10. won
11. dug
12. bought

◇ **PRACTICE 7, p. 12.**

1. bit
2. clung
3. meant
4. blew
5. quit
6. felt
7. stung
8. swam
9. paid
10. caught
11. shed
12. wove

◇ **PRACTICE 8, p. 13.**

1. spent
2. led
3. bet
4. wept
5. upset
6. split
7. sank
8. flew
9. spun
10. rang
11. chose
12. froze

◇ **PRACTICE 9, p. 14.**

1. fell
2. struck
3. broadcast
4. sought
5. lost
6. dealt
7. held
8. shot
9. cost
10. swept
11. stole
12. fled

◇ **PRACTICE 10, p. 14.**

1. raises
2. rose
3. set
4. sat
5. lays
6. lying
7. lay
8. laid
9. hung
10. lies

◇ **PRACTICE 11, p. 15.**

1. had
2. were at home having
3. was in his garage working . . . exploded . . . caused . . . lit/lighted
4. didn't see . . . was thinking . . . were you thinking
5. didn't want . . . was waiting
6. didn't hear . . . was in her room listening
7. stopped . . . fell . . . spilled
8. came . . . didn't hear . . . was in her room drying
9. served . . . went
10. looked . . . was sleeping . . . was dreaming . . . was smiling

◇ **PRACTICE 12, p. 16.**

1. was crossing . . . turned . . . hit
2. was . . . was humming
3. were in our living room watching . . . went . . . went . . . got . . . turned . . . listened . . . was
4. outwitted [= outsmarted, were more clever] . . . surrounded . . . was still inside stuffing
5. rang . . . came . . . were still playing . . . was pulling . . . ran . . . told
6. was looking . . . Did you find . . . took
7. is always interrupting . . . is always asking
8. was trying . . . interrupted . . . asked . . . refused

PRACTICE 13, p. 17.

Possible answers:

1. was cleaning . . . found/came upon/discovered
2. took/withdrew . . . bought/purchased . . . was driving . . . collided with/hit . . . demolished/destroyed/ wrecked
3. woke/got . . . heard . . . was walking/running/ crawling
4. visited/called on . . . were doing/were washing . . . came/knocked/arrived . . . finished . . . sat . . . talked/chatted/ reminisced
5. got to/arrived at . . . was waiting/was watching . . . saw . . . waved/raised . . . said/shouted . . . were making
6. was . . . watering/sprinkling/tending . . . began/ started . . . shut/turned

Chapter 3: PERFECT AND PERFECT PROGRESSIVE TENSES

PRACTICE 1, p. 18.

1. have already eaten
2. have won
3. haven't written
4. has improved
5. hasn't started
6. have already swept
7. have you known
8. have made
9. have never ridden
10. Have you ever swum
11. has grown
12. have driven
13. has forgotten
14. has cost . . . have saved

PRACTICE 2, p. 19.

1. for . . . since
2. since
3. for
4. for . . . since
5. for
6. since
7. for
8. since
9. for . . . for
10. since
11. since . . . since
12. since

PRACTICE 3, p. 20.

1. knew . . . have known
2. agreed . . . have agreed
3. took . . . has taken
4. has played . . . played
5. wrote . . . has written
6. sent . . . have sent
7. has flown . . . flew
8. overslept . . . has overslept

PRACTICE 4, p. 20.

1. have been playing
2. has played
3. has been sleeping
4. has slept
5. haven't flown
6. have been flying
7. have been searching
8. has raised
9. has been lecturing
10. has never missed
11. have finally made . . . have chosen

PRACTICE 5, p. 21.

1. have never understood
2. have met
3. has been standing
4. have always wanted
5. has been painting
6. have been travel(l)ing
7. has grown
8. have already spent
9. has been cooking
10. have never heard
11. have been waiting
12. has been digging

PRACTICE 6, p. 22.

1. had already finished
2. turned on
3. had already invented
4. had burned
5. had never spent
6. stung
7. had never designed
8. helped
9. had never been
10. had flown
11. had never taught
12. had already left

PRACTICE 7, p. 23.

1. went . . . had never been . . . didn't take . . . was
2. ate . . . had never eaten
3. saw . . . did . . . Had you ever acted . . . started
4. went . . . moved . . . took . . . had arrived . . . laughed . . . invited . . . was
5. was . . . studied . . . had never had . . . spoke . . . enjoyed
6. traveled . . . had never lived . . . had . . . became . . . had never lived

PRACTICE 8, p. 25.

1. had been listening to . . . have been dancing . . . singing
2. have been waiting
3. had been waiting
4. has been training
5. had been running
6. had been trying . . . has been teaching
7. has been performing
8. have been working . . . had been building

Chapter 4: FUTURE TIME

PRACTICE 1, p. 26.

1. will
2. are going to
3. will
4. Are you going to . . . are going to
5. am going to

6. will
7. will/am going to
8. am going to
9. will
10. am going to
11. is going to . . . is he going to/will he
12. will
13. am going to . . . will
14. am going to

◇ **PRACTICE 2, p. 27.**
1. will not/are not going to return . . . get
2. hear . . . will let
3. will lend . . . finish
4. gets . . . will be/is going to be
5. isn't going to be/won't be . . . learns . . . comes . . . asks
6. returns . . . will start/is going to start
7. is going to build/will build . . . will be/is going to be . . . complete
8. will be/is going to be . . . is

◇ **PRACTICE 3, p. 29.**
1. I'm sending
2. *(no change)*
3. I'm having
4. are you doing . . . am studying
5. *(no change)* [*I'm getting it* would have a present, not future, meaning.]
6. are . . . getting
7. *(no change)*
8. are moving
9. Is . . . teaching
10. am not sending . . . are coming

◇ **PRACTICE 4, p. 29.**
1. heals . . . will be playing
2. clear . . . will be standing
3. start . . . will be attending
4. have . . . will be shopping
5. will be attending . . . return

◇ **PRACTICE 5, p. 30.**
1. will already have risen (OR: will have already risen)
2. will have been riding
3. will already have arrived (OR: will have already arrived)
4. will have been listening
5. will have smoked
6. will have been flying
7. will have saved
8. will have taught

Chapter 5: ADVERB CLAUSES OF TIME AND SUMMARY OF VERB TENSES

◇ **PRACTICE 1, p. 31.**
1. When I reached my 21st birthday, I didn't feel any older.
2. I had a cup of tea before I left for work.
Before I left for work, I had a cup of tea.

3. After I get home from work, I like to read the evening newspaper.
I like to read the evening newspaper after I get home from work.
4. Since my watch broke, I have been late to work three times.
I have been late to work three times since my watch broke.
5. My cat hides under the house whenever it rains.
Whenever it rains, my cat hides under the house.
6. I'm going to get a job once I finish school.
Once I finish school, I'm going to get a job.
7. While I was waiting for my bus, I heard a gunshot.
I heard a gunshot while I was waiting for my bus.
8. The village will have no electric power until a new generator is installed.
Until a new generator is installed, the village will have no electric power.
9. The last time I was in Taipei, I saw Mr. Wu.
I saw Mr. Wu the last time I was in Taipei.
10. As soon as we saw the tornado heading toward our town, we ran to the basement of the town hall.
We ran to the basement of the town hall as soon as we saw the tornado heading toward our town.

◇ **PRACTICE 2, p. 32.**
1. As soon as our taxi **gets** here, we can leave.
2. I turned off the TV before I left the room.
3. The first time I parachuted from a plane, I was both terrified and exhilarated.
4. My boss stormed into my office while I was talking on the phone to an important client.
5. After Ceylon had been independent for 24 years, its name was changed to Sri Lanka.
6. Since Jack fell off his bicycle, he's had to use crutches to walk.
7. Ms. Johnson will return your call as soon as she **has** some free time.
8. Once John **learns** how to use a computer, he'll be able to work more efficiently.
9. I won't return this book to the library until I finish my research project.
10. Sue dropped a carton of eggs as she was leaving the store.
11. The next time Anna **goes** to class, she'll remember to take her grammar book.
12. When the flooding river raced down the valley, it destroyed everything in its path.
13. Just as soon as the rice **is** done, we can eat.
14. When I go to bed at night, I like to read until I get sleepy.

◇ **PRACTICE 3, p. 32.**

1. C	6. D	11. A
2. C	7. B	12. A
3. D	8. B	13. A
4. C	9. C	14. C
5. C	10. A	15. B

◇ PRACTICE 4, p. 33.

1. has never flown
2. have been waiting . . . hasn't arrived
3. are . . . reach
4. will have already left (OR: will already have left) . . . get
5. are having . . . has been
6. went . . . got . . . were dancing . . . were talking . . . was standing . . . had never met . . . introduced
7. was lying . . . heard . . . got . . . looked . . . had just backed
8. am planning . . . am going/am going to go/will go . . . leave . . . am going/am going to go/will go . . . is studying . . . has been living/has lived . . . knows . . . promised/has promised . . . have never been . . . am looking
9. was sitting . . . got . . . was sitting . . . tried . . . was lecturing . . . had been hiccupping *(also possible: had hiccupped)* . . . raised . . . excused
10. has been raining . . . has dropped . . . is . . . was shining . . . was . . . changes . . . wake . . . will be snowing

◇ PRACTICE 5, p. 34.

1. had been
2. met
3. had missed
4. was
5. got
6. took
7. was
8. had grown
9. was
10. was wearing
11. had changed
12. was still
13. asked
14. had gained
15. had turned
16. looked
17. were

◇ PRACTICE 6, p. 35.

1. will have been
2. will meet
3. will have missed
4. will be
5. get
6. will take
7. will no longer be
8. will have grown
9. will be
10. will probably be wearing
11. will have changed
12. will still be
13. will ask
14. will probably have gained
15. will have turned
16. will look
17. will be

◇ PRACTICE 7, p. 35.

PART I.
1. seems
2. sent
3. haven't received
4. is not functioning
5. are working
6. will start

PART II.
1. haven't seen
2. is at home recuperating/is recuperating at home
3. is she recuperating
4. hurt
5. was playing
6. did she hurt
7. was trying
8. collided
9. fell
10. landed
11. twisted
12. has been wearing
13. hasn't been
14. will not/won't be
15. Will her doctor allow/Is her doctor going to allow
16. will have had

PART III.
1. Did you enjoy
2. I've never gone
3. had never gone
4. didn't know
5. were still trying
6. appeared
7. started
8. was singing
9. was

PART IV.
1. grew up
2. greatly admired/had greatly admired
3. had become
4. became
5. contained
6. died
7. had been working
8. never finished
9. has become

◇ PRACTICE 8. Test A, p. 38.

1. C	11. D
2. C	12. A
3. A	13. D
4. A	14. A
5. B	15. B
6. C	16. B
7. C	17 D
8. C	18. B
9. B	19. D
10. C	20. C

◇ PRACTICE 9. Test B, p. 40.

1. A	11. D
2. A	12. A
3. B	13. A
4. C	14. A
5. C	15. D
6. A	16. D
7. B	17. C
8. B	18. B
9. C	19. A
10. B	20. D

Chapter 6: SUBJECT-VERB AGREEMENT

◇ PRACTICE 1, p. 42.

1. My mother <u>wears</u> glasses.
2. <u>Elephants</u> <u>are</u> large animals. OR: <u>An</u> elephant is <u>a</u> large <u>animal</u>.
3. Your heart <u>beats</u> faster when you exercise.
4. Healthy hearts <u>need</u> regular exercise.
5. Every child in the class <u>knows</u> the alphabet.
6. Some of the <u>magazines</u> at the dentist's office are two <u>years</u> old.
7. A number of the <u>students</u> in my class <u>are</u> from Mexico.
8. One of my favorite <u>subjects</u> in school is algebra.
9. There <u>are</u> many different <u>kinds</u> of insects in the world.
10. Writing compositions <u>is</u> difficult for me.
11. The United <u>States</u> <u>has</u> a population of more than 250 <u>million</u>.
12. Most of the people in my factory division <u>like</u> and <u>get</u> along with one another, but a few of the <u>workers</u> <u>don't</u> fit in with the rest of us very well.

◇ PRACTICE 2, p. 42.

1. s	/z/	9. s	/s/
2. es	/əz/	10. es	/əz/
3. s	/s/	11. s	/z/
4. s	/z/	12. ies	/z/
5. s	/s/	13. s	/z/
6. es	/əz/	14. s	/s/
7. s	/s/	15. s	/s/
8. s	/z/	16. s	/z/

◇ PRACTICE 3, p. 43.

1. is	6. are	11. is
2. are	7. is	12. is
3. barks	8. are	13. are
4. bark	9. is	14. is
5. is	10. are	15. is

◇ PRACTICE 4, p. 43.

1. is	10. is
2. are	11. is
3. is	12. has
4. are	13. has
5. has	14. has/have
6. have	15. is
7. were	16. is/are
8. was	17. is
9. was	18. are

◇ PRACTICE 5, p. 44.

1. is	9. is . . . is . . . is
2. are	10. isn't
3. aren't	11. isn't
4. isn't	12. is
5. are	13. are
6. is	14. is
7. is	15. are
8. is	16. are

◇ PRACTICE 6, p. 44.

1. vote
2. have
3. was
4. knows
5. Isn't
6. speak and understand
7. are
8. do
9. are
10. have
11. has . . . have
12. confirms
13. is . . . is
14. are
15. is
16. Aren't
17. Is
18. begin *[Answer: 4 (Alabama, Alaska, Arizona, Arkansas)]*
19. consists
20. have
21. is
22. Was

Chapter 7: NOUNS

◇ PRACTICE 1, p. 46.

1. cares . . . feathers
2. occupations . . . Doctors . . . Pilots . . . airplanes . . . Farmers . . . crops . . . Shepherds
3. designs . . . buildings . . . digs . . . objects
4. computers . . . Computers
5. factories . . . employs
6. Kangaroos . . . animals . . . continents . . . zoos
7. Mosquitos/Mosquitoes
8. tomatoes
9. Birds . . . insects . . . mammals . . . forms . . . characteristics
10. creatures . . . five senses . . . these senses . . . Birds . . . Animals . . . dogs . . . human beings

◇ PRACTICE 2, p. 47.

1. feet
2. heroes
3. knives
4. qualities
5. doorways
6. gentlemen
7. wolves
8. quizzes
9. customs
10. videos
11. potatoes
12. deer
13. oxen
14. donkeys
15. mysteries
16. chiefs
17. thieves
18. flashes
19. memos
20. memoranda
21. crises
22. mouths

PRACTICE 3, p. 47.

1. theses
2. phenomena
3. hypotheses
4. crises
5. memoranda
6. media
7. criteria
8. curricula
9. stimuli
10. bacteria
11. oases
12. data

PRACTICE 4, p. 48.

1. secretary's
2. secretaryies'
3. cats'
4. cat's
5. child's
6. children's
7. supervisors'
8. supervisor's
9. people's
10. month's
11. actors'
12. actor's

PRACTICE 5, p. 49.

1. Mary's father . . . He's a dentist.
2. Jack's parents live . . . His parents' home . . . .
3. Our teacher's last name . . . She's one of the best teachers . . . .
4. Our teachers' last names . . . They're all good teachers.
5. Ms Wells' (OR: Wells's) husband . . . Ms. Hunt's husband . . . .
6. It's well known that a bear likes . . . .
7. Ann's telephone number . . . . [Note: No apostrophes are used with possessive pronouns, e.g., *hers, ours*). See Chart 8-1.]
8. Although it's found . . . our children's and grandchildren's lives . . . .

PRACTICE 6, p. 49.

PART I.

1. toys . . . toy
2. tomato . . . tomatoes
3. vegetable . . . vegetables
4. drugs . . . drug
5. two lanes . . . two-lane
6. five-minute . . . five minutes
7. sixty-year-old . . . sixty years old

PART II.

8. student handbook.
9. ten-month-old baby.
10. three-day trip.
11. child psychologist.
12. fifty-dollar check.
13. three-credit course.
14. nine-room house.
15. dog food.
16. guest room.
17. five-page paper.
18. ten-year-old sister and a twelve-year-old brother.

PRACTICE 7, p. 50.

1. a bank robber
2. a bullfighter
3. a stamp collector
4. an animal trainer
5. a storyteller
6. a tax collector
7. a can opener
8. a windshield wiper
9. a wage earner
10. an office manager
11. a computer programmer
12. a bookkeeper
13. a spot remover
14. a pot holder
15. a troublemaker
16. a mind reader
17. a hair dryer (OR: hair drier)
18. a potato peeler
19. a tennis player
20. a firefighter
21. a mail carrier

PRACTICE 8, p. 51.

1. *(no change)* . . . eyes
2. *(no change)*
3. *(no change)*
4. sandwiches
5. *(no change)*
6. *(no change)*
7. photographs
8. *(no change)*
9. ideas
10. *(no change)*
11. *(no change)*
12. *(no change)*
13. words
14. *(no change)*
15. *(no change)*
16. gloves
17. cars . . . minutes . . . *(no change)*
18. *(no change)* . . . rings . . . bracelets . . . *(no change)*
19. *(no change)* . . . *(no change)* . . . vegetables . . . *(no change)*
20. Butterflies . . . caterpillars . . . insects . . . wings
21. *(no change)* . . . *(no change)* . . . *(no change)* . . . *(no change)* . . . *(no change)* . . . *(no change)* . . . *(no change)* . . . *(no change)* . . . customs
22. *(no change)* . . . *(no change)*
23. *(no change)* . . . products . . . vegetables . . . *(no change)* . . . sardines . . . vitamins . . . *(no change)* . . . pills
24. *(no change)* . . . *(no change)* . . . *(no change)* . . . facts . . . *(no change)*
25. *(no change)* . . . *(no change)* . . . *(no change)*

PRACTICE 9, p. 53.

1. Ø . . . a . . . Ø
2. a . . . the
3. Ø . . . Ø
4. A . . . a . . . the . . . the
5. The . . . the
6. Ø . . . Ø . . . Ø
7. Ø . . . Ø . . . Ø
8. the
9. The . . . the . . . the
10. an

11. a . . . a . . . an . . . an . . . a
12. the . . . a . . . the . . . an/a . . . The . . . Ø
13. a . . . The . . . the . . . a . . . a . . . the . . . the . . . a
14. the . . . a . . . a
15. Ø . . . a . . . an
16. Ø . . . a . . . a
17. Ø . . . a . . . a . . . a . . . the
18. the . . . A . . . Ø
19. a . . . the . . . the . . . the . . . the . . . the . . . a . . . the
20. a . . . the . . . the
21. a . . . Ø . . . Ø . . . The . . . The
22. a . . . a . . . Ø . . . Ø . . . Ø . . . an . . . a . . . the . . . a
    . . . a . . . Ø . . . Ø . . . Ø . . . a
23. a . . . a . . . The . . . a . . . the . . . The . . . the . . .
    The . . . the . . . Ø
24. the . . . the

◇ **PRACTICE 10, p. 55.**
1. many watch**es**
2. much . . . Ø
3. many **teeth**
4. much . . . Ø is
5. much . . . Ø
6. much . . . Ø
7. many videos
8. is much . . . Ø
9. many witness**es**
10. much . . . Ø
11. many villages
12. much . . . Ø
13. much . . . Ø
14. many **mice**
15. isn't much . . . Ø
16. many adventures
17. was , . . much . . . Ø
18. much . . . Ø . . . many . . . textbook**s**
19. are . . . many . . . thie**ves**, muggers . . . pickpockets
20. isn't much . . . Ø . . . much
21. many . . . volcano**es** are
22. many speech**es**

◇ **PRACTICE 11, p. 56.**
1. a little
2. (very) few
3. a little
4. a few
5. (Very) Few
6. (very) few
7. a few
8. (very) little
9. a few
10. a little
11. A few
12. a little . . . a little
13. (very) little
14. (very) few

◇ **PRACTICE 12, p. 56.**
1. Ø
2. of
3. Ø
4. of
5. Ø
6. of
7. of
8. Ø

9. Ø
10. of
11. Ø
12. Ø
13. of
14. Ø
15. of
16. Ø
17. Ø
18. Ø   OR: of
19. Ø   OR: of
20. Ø
21. of
22. Ø
23. Ø . . . Ø
24. of
25. Ø
26. Ø
27. of
28. Ø
29. Ø
30. of

◇ **PRACTICE 13, p. 58.**
1. student
2. students
3. rooms
4. room
5. window
6. windows
7. item
8. items
9. countries
10. country
11. person
12. question
13. children . . . child
14. problems
15. applicants

Chapter 8: PRONOUNS

◇ **PRACTICE 1, p. 59.**
1. them
2. me
3. I
4. me . . . his
5. his . . . her
6. its . . . them
7. They . . . it
8. your . . . them
9. I . . . him . . . me
10. My . . . I . . . She . . . her . . . mine
11. its
12. it . . . it
13. them
14. me . . . them . . . us . . . our
15. she . . . me . . . us . . . his

◇ **PRACTICE 2, p. 60.**
1. his/her; his or her; his; her
2. their
3. their
4. his/her; his or her; his; her
5. his/her; his or her; his; her

6. their
7. them; him or her; him; her
8. their; his/her; his or her; his; her
9. Their
10. They have . . . they
11. They
12. It was

◇ **PRACTICE 3, p. 60.**
1. himself
2. myself
3. himself
4. yourself
5. yourselves
6. themselves
7. myself
8. themselves
9. myself
10. herself
11. himself
12. yourself
13. ourselves
14. myself
15. himself
16. yourself
17. herself
18. myself
19. ourselves
20. themselves
21. yourself
22. yourselves
23. himself . . . himself

◇ **PRACTICE 4, p. 62.**
1. ourselves . . . we are . . . our
2. yourself . . . you are . . . your
3. yourselves . . . you are . . . your
4. themselves . . . they are . . . their
5. and 6. INFORMAL: themselves . . . they are . . . their
FORMAL: himself . . . he is . . . his OR: herself . . . she is
. . . her *(also possible:* him/herself . . . s/he is . . . his/her)

◇ **PRACTICE 5, p. 62.**
1. another
2. Others
3. The other
4. another
5. the others
6. the other *(Answer: The other states are Oregon,
   California, Hawaii, and Alaska.)*
7. other
8. others . . . others . . . Other
9. another
10. another
11. the others
12. other
13. The others
14. the other
15. The others . . . another
16. Others . . . other . . . others
17. other . . . the other
18. Another . . . Others
19. The others

20. other
21. other
22. another
23. another
24. others

◇ **PRACTICE 6, p. 64.**

Potatoes are grown in most **countries**. They are one of the most widely grown **vegetables** in the world. They are very versatile; they can be prepared in many different **ways**. French **fries** are popular almost everywhere. Besides frying **them**, **potatoes** can be baked or boiled. **Another** way people use potatoes is to make potato flour for making bread and **other** kinds of dishes. **It's** also possible to make alcoholic beverages from **potatoes**. There are still **other** ways potatoes are used by commercial food **processers** to make **products** such as potato **chips** and freeze-dried **potatoes**.

Potatoes originated in South America, where **they** were cultivated by the Incas as early as 5000 **years** ago. It is believed that potatoes were the **world's** first freeze-dried food. Over 4000 years ago the Incas carried **their** harvested **potatoes** up into the mountains and spread them on the ground to freeze overnight. After the sun came up and heated the potatoes the next day, the Incas squeezed the water out of the potatoes by stepping on **them**. This process **was** repeated for four or five **days** until almost all the moisture was gone from the potatoes. The Incas then dried the potatoes and stored **them** in **pots**. Some Indians of South America still **do** this today.

◇ **PRACTICE 7. Test A, p. 65.**
1. C	11. A
2. D	12. A
3. A	13. D
4. C	14. A
5. C	15. A
6. B	16. B
7. B	17. C
8. C	18. D
9. A	19. D
10. C	20. B

◇ **PRACTICE 8. Test B, p. 67.**
1. C	11. C
2. B	12. D
3. A	13. B
4. C	14. B
5. B	15. C
6. C	16. D
7. D	17. A
8. A	18. C
9. D	19. B
10. B	20. B

Chapter 9: MODALS, PART 1

◇ PRACTICE 1, p. 69.

1. C	7. C
2. C	8. C
3. C	9. C
4. B	10. C
5. C	11. C
6. C	12. C

◇ PRACTICE 2, p. 70.

1. Would you (please) hand me that book?
2. Could you (please) give me some advice about buying a computer?
3. Could I (please) borrow your wheelbarrow?
4. May I (please) have a cup of coffee?
5. Can I (please) use your bicycle tomorrow?
6. Would you (please) read over my composition for spelling errors?
7. Would you mind opening the door for me?
8. Would you mind if I left early?

◇ PRACTICE 3, p. 70.

1. closing
2. if I closed
3. taking
4. if I showed
5. drying
6. finishing
7. if I used
8. waiting
9. if I borrowed
10. if I gave

◇ PRACTICE 4, p. 71.

1. B	6. C
2. A	7. B
3. A	8. C
4. B	9. A
5. A	10. B

◇ PRACTICE 5, p. 72.

1. Do you have to . . . have to
2. had to . . . Did you have to
3. doesn't have to
4. don't have to / won't have to
5. have had to
6. did Tom have to
7. don't have to / won't have to
8. Did John have to
9. has had to
10. will have had to
11. Don't you have to
12. will have to / is going to have to . . . Does she have to / Will she have to
13. didn't have to
14. haven't had to

◇ PRACTICE 6, p. 73.

Expected completions:

1. I think she should/ought to join some clubs to meet people with similar interests.
2. She'd better find a chemistry major to tutor her.
3. You should have stopped for gas.
4. They'd better clean it up right away.
5. I should have taken it back sooner.
6. He'd better change clothes before he goes.
7. She should/ought to make her own decision about her career and go to architecture school.
8. Richard should/ought to get his roommate a pair of earphones.
9. He should/ought to call home and talk to his family.
10. I shouldn't have eaten so much.
11. He should have listened to Tom before he fired him.
12. He shouldn't have left the room. He should have apologized immediately and signaled to a waiter for help.

◇ PRACTICE 7, p. 74.

1. The students are supposed to write a composition.
2. The are supposed to write it about a person they admire.
3. They're supposed to write it in ink.
4. They aren't supposed to write it in pencil.
5. When are they supposed to hand it in?

◇ PRACTICE 8, p. 74.

1. You are not supposed to smoke.
2. You are supposed to keep off the grass.
3. You are not supposed to eat or drink in this room.
4. You are supposed to move to the rear of the bus.
5. You are not supposed to joke with airport personnel while your hand luggage is being inspected.
6. You are supposed to use the stairs in case of fire. You are not supposed to use the elevator.
7. You are not supposed to litter.
8. Slower traffic is supposed to keep right.

◇ PRACTICE 9, p. 75.

1. A: we
    B: Ø
    A: we
    B: I
	3. A: you
	    B: Ø
	    A: we/you
	    B: I

2. B: Ø
    A: I/you/we
    B: you
	4. B: we
	    A: we
	    A: I/we
	    A: I/we
	    A: you

◇ PRACTICE 10, p. 76.

Possible completions:

1. He could hide under his bed.
   He could pick up his baseball bat and go looking for the intruder.
   He should leave the house and go to his neighbor's to call the police.

2. He could jump from the moving train.
   He could stay on the train, but hide from the conductor.
   He should buy a ticket from the conductor to the next stop, get off, then take the next train back home.

3. She could take a warm bath to relax her before she
   goes to bed.
   She could take sleeping pills.
   She should see a doctor and find out if there is a
   physical reason for her insomnia.

4. I could have called the police and asked for help in
   getting gas.
   I could have continued driving to see if I could
   make it to the next town without running out of
   gas.
   I should have found a place to stay overnight and
   waited until the gas station opened in the morning.

Chapter 10: MODALS, PART 2

◇ **PRACTICE 1, p. 78.**

1. A	5. B	9. C
2. B	6. A	10. A
3. B	7. B	11. B
4. A	8. B	12. C

◇ **PRACTICE 2, p. 79.**

1. could be visiting
2. should watch
3. must have thrown
4. should be working . . . shouldn't be wasting
5. must be playing
6. might be taking
7. should have bought . . . shouldn't have waited
8. must have been driving
9. must not have planned
10. may have borrowed . . . couldn't have borrowed
11. could not have been listening
12. couldn't have told
13. must not have . . . must have been sleeping
14. must be making

◇ **PRACTICE 3, p. 80.**

Possible logical conclusions:
1. They must not be at home.
2. He must have studied for the test.
3. He must have seen the movie before.
4. She must be asleep.
5. She must not have heard them.
6. He must like to listen to classical music when he's
   in the car.
7. She must not like classical music.
8. She must not have paid her phone bill.
9. The mushrooms must have been poisonous.
10. The cat must have knocked it over.

◇ **PRACTICE 4, p. 81.**

1. can't
2. could
3. can't
4. could . . . can't
5. couldn't
6. can
7. couldn't
8. couldn't

◇ **PRACTICE 5, p. 82.**

1. would always yell . . . would come
2. would fall . . . would throw
3. would never call . . . wouldn't even knock
4. would always bring
5. would take
6. would always wipe
7. would tell . . . would listen
8. would drive

◇ **PRACTICE 6, p. 83.**

1. have gone to an opera
2. have studied Chinese
3. be an environmental lawyer
4. not tell you
5. go out with their friends . . . stay home with their
   parents
6. not have gone out . . . have stayed home

◇ **PRACTICE 7. Test A, p. 84.**

1. B	11. D
2. D	12. C
3. D	13. C
4. A	14. D
5. B	15. C
6. C	16. A
7. D	17. D
8. C	18. C
9. D	19. D
10. A	20. A

◇ **PRACTICE 8. Test B, p. 86.**

1. A	11. D
2. B	12. C
3. A	13. A
4. C	14. B
5. D	15. C
6. C	16. A
7. D	17. B
8. B	18. D
9. C	19. C
10. C	20. A

Chapter 11: THE PASSIVE

◇ **PRACTICE 1, p. 88.**

1. are
2. is being
3. has been
4. was
5. was being
6. had been
7. will be
8. is going to be
9. will have been
10. has been
11. was
12. are being
13. will be
14. had been
15. will have been
16. are
17. is going to be
18. were being

◇ **PRACTICE 2, p. 89.**

1. a. Was that report written by Tom?
   b. No, it wasn't written by him.
   c. It was written by Alice.
2. a. Is your house being painted by Mr. Brown?
   b. No, it isn't being painted by him.
   c. It's being painted by my uncle.
3. a. Will the dishes be washed by Steve?
   b. No, they won't be washed by him.
   c. They'll be washed by the children.
4. a. Has the meeting been planned by Sue?
   b. No, it hasn't been planned by her.
   c. It has been planned by the committee.
5. a. Is that violin played by Mr. Parr?
   b. No, it isn't played by him.
   c. It is played by his son.
6. a. Are the books going to be returned to the library by Jack?
   b. No, they aren't going to be returned by him.
   c. They're going to be returned by his sister.
7. a. Was the ancient skeleton discovered by the archeologists?
   b. No, it wasn't discovered by them.
   c. It was discovered by a farmer.

8. a. Was the food being prepared by Sally?
   b. No, it wasn't being prepared by her.
   c. It was being prepared by her mother.
9. a. Will the letters have been typed by Ms. Anderson?
   b. No, they won't have been typed by her.
   c. They will have been typed by the secretary.

◇ **PRACTICE 3, p. 89.**

1. was . . . discovered
2. was written
3. won't be paid
4. was refilled
5. Was . . . knocked
6. wasn't broken
7. am not impressed
8. is being taped
9. Is . . . being flown
10. will be won
11. won't be influenced
12. is going to be decided
13. has been discovered
14. hasn't been taught
15. Had . . . been delivered
16. was being affected

◇ **PRACTICE 4, p. 91.**

	Verb	Object of Verb	Passive Sentence
1.	will pay	the bill	The bill will be paid by Al.
2.	will come	Ø	Ø
3.	supplies	towels	Towels are supplied by the hotel.
4.	happen	Ø	Ø
5.	noticed	my mistake	My mistake was noticed by everyone.
6.	arrived	Ø	Ø
7.	didn't	me	I wasn't surprised by the news.
8.	Did . . . surprise	you	Were you surprised by the news?
9.	wasn't shining	Ø	Ø
10.	interrupted	my story	My story was interrupted by Ann.
11.	Do . . . exist	Ø	Ø
12.	fly	Ø	Ø
13.	Will . . . come	Ø	Ø
14.	died	Ø	Ø
15.	Did . . . throw	the ball	Was the ball thrown by Bob?
16.	laughed	Ø	Ø
17.	told	the story	The story was told by an old man.
18.	rained	Ø	Ø

◇ **PRACTICE 5, p. 91.**

1. You will be met at the airport by my uncle.
2. (no change)
3. (no change)
4. (no change)
5. The food will be prepared by the chef.
6. (no change)
7. (no change)
8. The subway is ridden by thousands of people every day.
9. (no change)
10. (no change)
11. (no change)
12. The phone was answered by the office manager.

◇ **PRACTICE 6, p. 92.**

1. will be notified
2. didn't remember
3. is being restored
4. was built
5. was ruled . . . walked . . . stood
6. is visited
7. do not use
8. do not agree
9. will be invaded / are going to be invaded
10. live . . . lives
11. Had you already been accepted
12. was being followed . . . felt
13. was felt
14. died
15. is influenced
16. was stolen . . . was caught

PRACTICE 7, p. 93.

1. Rice is grown in India.
2. This rug was made by my aunt.
3. My car is being fixed today.
4. French is spoken in Quebec.
5. That bridge was designed by Mr. Eads in the 1870s.
6. The wheel was invented thousands of years ago.
7. Was the telephone invented by Thomas Edison?
8. A new hospital is going to be built just outside of town.
9. How are candles made?
10. That TV show is watched by very few people.
11. Look! The seals are being fed.
12. That pie was made by Sally.
13. Jack is being considered for that job.
14. The Mediterranean Sea is surrounded by three continents.
15. I got upset when I was interrupted in the middle of my story.
16. Rome wasn't built in a day.
17. Are those tractors made in this country, or are they imported?
18. While I was walking down the street, I was approached by a nice young man in a military uniform.

PRACTICE 8, p. 94.

1. (I.O. = Jack) Jack is going to be served breakfast in bed on his birthday.
2. (I.O. = Mike) Mike had been offered the opportunity to study abroad.
3. (I.O. = babysitters) Babysitters aren't paid a lot of money.
4. (I.O. = me) When I was living in Kuwait, I was taught Arabic by my neighbor.
5. (I.O. = Jason) Jason was awarded a medal for distinguished service in the military.
6. (I.O. = you) You will be sent a copy of the sales contract by the real estate office.
7. (I.O. = me) I was handed a telegram when I answered the door.
8. (I.O. = the schoolchildren) The schoolchildren are going to be given a special tour of the modern art exhibit by the director of the museum, Ms. Cynthia Hall.
9. (I.O. = Mr. French) Mr. French was given a gold watch upon his retirement from the company.

PRACTICE 9, p. 94.

1. will be told
2. completed
3. was assisted
4. applied . . . was hired
5. lie . . . are fed
6. will probably be eroded OR: is probably going to be eroded
7. were introduced . . . were eaten . . . are exported . . . are enjoyed
8. is going to be interviewed (OR: will be interviewed) . . . has collected
9. have complained . . . has been done [to date = until now]
10. went . . . had piled . . . had been shoved
11. are intimidated . . . buy

12. put . . . sold . . . was bought . . . was/had been looking . . . had already been sold
13. was invented . . . has assisted
14. occurred . . . were crossing . . . were swept . . . left . . . were found . . . were/had been seriously injured . . . took

PRACTICE 10, p. 96.

1. redecorated
2. threading
3. smuggled
4. dragged
5. exposed
6. scrubbing
7. wound
8. broadcast
9. shoved
10. financed
11. leaning
12. mined
13. stretched
14. bred

PRACTICE 11, p. 97.

1. memorized
2. photographing
3. equipped
4. destroyed
5. rubbing
6. whispering
7. erased
8. performed
9. predicting
10. vaccinated
11. rehearsing
12. billed [= The dentist will send him a bill.]

PRACTICE 12, p. 97.

1. Pandas should be saved from extinction.
2. All traffic laws must be obeyed.
3. This broken window ought to be repaired.
4. The hotel guests should have been supplied with clean towels.
5. This garbage had better be taken to the dump soon.
6. Tomatoes can be picked before they are completely ripe.
7. The profits are supposed to be divided among the shareholders.
8. Bob's feelings must have been hurt.
9. This work has to be finished today.
10. The accident ought to have been reported to the police.
11. Fresh bananas shouldn't be put in the freezer.

PRACTICE 13, p. 98.

1. be told
2. repeated
3. be wrapped
4. forgotten
5. been discovered
6. sew
7. been replaced
8. cost
9. whisper
10. be polluted
11. be considered
12. be worn
13. be signed
14. read

◇ PRACTICE 14, p. 99.

1. be obtained
2. been won
3. scrub
4. be taught
5. been vaccinated
6. replied
7. been stopped
8. be revised
9. trade
10. participate
11. be established
12. eat
13. be distinguished
14. be killed

◇ PRACTICE 15, p. 101.

1. are excited
2. are covered
3. is cracked
4. are exhausted
5. Are . . . finished
6. was insured
7. is polluted
8. is closed
9. is stuck
10. is dressed
11. am . . . confused
12. are buried

◇ PRACTICE 16, p. 102.

1. is located
2. are summarized
3. isn't listed
4. is forbidden
5. am . . . acquainted
6. is scheduled
7. is overdrawn
8. is cancel(l)ed [*canceled;* = American; *cancelled* = British]
9. is wrinkled [*iron* = press]
10. are equipped [*automobile* = American; *motor car* = British]
11. is made
12. is clogged

◇ PRACTICE 17, p. 103.

1. with
2. for
3. in
4. with
5. to
6. with
7. against
8. of
9. with
10. in/with . . . with
11. for
12. to
13. at/with
14. with
15. of
16. to
17. with . . . about
18. to
19. from
20. of

◇ PRACTICE 18, p. 104.

1. concerned about
2. explaining
3. known for
4. provided with
5. laughing
6. satisfied with
7. connected to
8. crossing
9. involved in
10. composed of
11. accompanying
12. blessed with
13. limited to
14. annoyed at/with
15. blowing

◇ PRACTICE 19, p. 105.

1. got torn
2. get broken
3. got lost
4. get hired
5. get hurt
6. was getting worried
7. got . . . soaked
8. get started
9. got buried
10. got stuck

◇ PRACTICE 20, p. 106.

1. got hit
2. get accepted
3. got cheated
4. got fired
5. got mugged [*to mug* = to rob; *scruffy* = unkempt, dirty]
6. get invited
7. get dressed
8. got caught
9. got elected
10. get electrocuted
11. got ruined
12. got embarrassed

◇ PRACTICE 21, p. 107.

1. (a) interesting (b) interested
2. (a) irritating (b) irritated
3. (a) tired (b) tiring
4. (a) boiling (b) boiled
5. (a) upset (b) upsetting
6. (a) confusing (b) confused
7. (a) disappointing (b) disappointed
8. (a) reassuring (b) reassured
9. (a) frustrating (b) frustrated
10. (a) disturbing (b) disturbed
11. (a) convincing (b) convinced
12. (a) moving (b) moved
13. (a) shocking (b) shocked
14. (a) depressed (b) depressing
15. (a) humiliated (b) humiliating
16. (a) intriguing (b) intrigued

◇ PRACTICE 22, p. 108.

1. running
2. invited
3. suggested
4. written
5. exhausting
6. stimulating
7. spoken

8. falling
9. Frozen
10. invading
11. thrilling
12. intended
13. amusing
14. manufactured
15. relaxing
16. expected
17. approaching
18. inquiring
19. visiting . . . winning . . . disappointed
20. encouraging
21. invigorating
22. contaminated

◇ PRACTICE 23, p. 109.

1. were served
2. has been training
3. are lost
4. received
5. are given
6. are discriminated . . . have been enacted
7. had been offered
8. finish [time clause]
9. are returned [time clause] . . . will be given
10. were allowed
11. was not fooled
12. established . . . be followed
13. irritating . . . will be replaced
14. vending . . . kicked . . . fell . . . was seriously injured
   . . . ended . . . is still wearing/still wears . . . vending
   [In fact, in the decade of the 1980s, eight people in
   the United States were reported to have died from a
   vending machine falling on them.]
15. proposed . . . is not being offered (*also possible:* is
   not / will not be / is not going to be offered)
16. jogged/has been jogging . . . plans/is planning
17. is conducted . . . are sent . . . are asked . . . is
   collected . . . is published . . . use

◇ PRACTICE 24. Test A, p. 112.

1. A	11. A
2. C	12. C
3. A	13. B
4. C	14. D
5. D	15. B
6. D	16. C
7. C	17. A
8. D	18. B
9. C	19. D
10. B	20. A

◇ PRACTICE 25. Test B, p. 114.

1. C	11. D
2. B	12. A
3. A	13. C
4. B	14. A
5. B	15. C
6. A	16. A
7. B	17. C
8. A	18. C
9. C	19. A
10. C	20. D

Chapter 12: NOUN CLAUSES

◇ PRACTICE 1, p. 116.

1. Q (?)
2. N.Cl. (.)
3. Q (?)
4. N.Cl. (.)
5. Q (?)
6. N.Cl. (.)
7. N.Cl. (.)
8. Q (?)
9. Q (?)
10. N.Cl. (?) [Note: *who she is* is a noun clause; the
   whole sentence is a question.]
11. Q (?)
12. N.Cl. (.)

◇ PRACTICE 2, p. 116.

1. Where (?)
2. I don't know (.)
3. I don't know (.)
4. What (?)
5. How (?)
6. I don't know (.)
7. Where (?)
8. I don't know (.)
9. I don't know (.)
10. Why (?)
11. I don't know (.)
12. Who (?)
13. When (?)
14. I don't know (.)
15. Who (?)
16. I don't know (.)

◇ PRACTICE 3, p. 117.

1. Who is that man? . . . who that man is.
2. Where does George live? . . . where George lives.
3. What did Ann buy? . . . what Ann bought.
4. How far is it to Denver from here? . . . how far it is
   to Denver from here.
5. Why was Jack late to class? . . . why Jack was late to
   class.
6. Whose pen is that? . . . whose pen that is.
7. Who(m) did Alex see at the meeting? . . . who(m)
   Alex saw at the meeting.
8. Who saw Ms. Frost at the meeting? . . . who saw
   Ms. Frost at the meeting.
9. Which book does Alice like best? . . . which book
   Alice likes best.
10. When/What time is the plane supposed to land? . . .
   when/what time the plane is supposed to land.

◇ PRACTICE 4, p. 118.

1. A: *Where* does Fred live?
   B: (. . .) wants to know where Fred lives.
2. A: *What* time is it?
   B: (. . .) wants to know what time it is.
3. A: *What* does Tom want for his birthday?
   B: (. . .) wants to know what Tom wants for his
   birthday.
   C. He wants a watch.
4. A: *How* does Jane get to school?
   B: (. . .) wants to know how Jane gets to school.
   C: By bus.

5. A: *When* does vacation start?
   B: . . . wants to know when vacation starts.
   C: On June 3rd [= third].
6. A: *Why* did Sue leave class early?
   B: . . . wants to know why Sue left class early.
   C: Because she didn't feel well.
7. A: *How* long is the movie going to last?
   B: . . . wants to know how long the movie is going to last.
   C: Two hours and ten minutes
8. A: *Who(m)* did Mary call?
   B: . . . wants to know who(m) Mary called.
   C: Jim
9. A: *Who* called Jim?
   B: . . . wants to know who called Jim.
   C: Mary.
10. A: *What* did Alice talk to the teacher about?
    B: . . . wants to know what Alice talked to the teacher about.
    C: The test.
11. A: *Who(m)* did Alice talk to about the test?
    (Formal: To whom did Alice talk about the test?*)*
    B: (. . .) wants to know who(m) Alice talked to about the test. *(Formal:* (. . .) wants to know to whom Alice talked about the test.*)*
    C: The teacher.
12. A: *Who* talked to the teacher about the test?
    B: (. . .) wants to know who talked to the teacher about the test.
    C: Alice.
13. A: *When/At what time* will Sue's plane arrive?
    B: (. . .) wants to know when/at what time Sue's plane will arrive.
    C: At 8:05.
14. A: *How many* students will be absent from class tomorrow?
    B: (. . .) wants to know how many students will be absent from class tomorrow.
    C: Two.
15. A: *How many* lakes are there in Minnesota?
    B: (. . .) wants to know how many lakes there are in Minnesota.
    C: 10,000.
16. A: *How far/How many miles* is it to Springfield from here?
    B: (. . .) wants to know how far/how many miles it is to Springfield from here.
    C: 25.
17. A: *What* did Jane do last night?
    B: (. . .) wants to know what Jane did last night.
    C: Studied.
18. A: *Which* book are we supposed to buy?
    B: (. . .) wants to know which book we're supposed to buy.
    C: This book.
19. A: *What kind of* ice cream does Ann like the best?
    B: (. . .) wants to know what kind of ice cream Ann likes the best.
    C: Chocolate.
20. A: *What* color is a robin's egg?
    B: (. . .) wants to know what color a robin's egg is.
    C: Turquoise blue. [TURQUOISE is pronounced /ˈtɜrkwɔɪz/]
21. A: *Who* is that woman?
    B: (. . .) wants to know who that woman is.
    C: Mrs. Anderson.

22. A: *Who* is talking on the telephone?
    B: (. . .) wants to know who is talking on the telephone.
    C: Mr. Anderson.
23. A: *Whose* notebook is that?
    B: (. . .) wants to know whose notebook that is.
    C: Sam's.
24. A: *Whose* car was stolen?
    B: (. . .) wants to know whose car was stolen.
    C: Jessica's.

◇ **PRACTICE 5, p. 119.**
1. A: he's looking for
   B: are you looking for
2. A: did he decide
   B: he decided
3. A: is this
   B: it is
4. A: did he buy
   B: he bought
5. A: John's tutor is
   B: is John's tutor
6. A: didn't you study
   B: I didn't study

◇ **PRACTICE 6, p. 120.**
1. if/whether it will rain
2. when it will rain
3. if/whether Sam is
4. where Sam is
5. if/whether Jane called
6. what time she called
7. why the earth is called
8. how far it is
9. if/whether Susan has ever been
10. if/whether she speaks
11. who Ann played
12. who won
13. if/whether Ann won
14. if/whether all creatures, including fish and insects, feel
15. if/whether birds can communicate
16. how birds communicate
17. where the nearest post office is
18. if/whether there is a post office

◇ **PRACTICE 7, p. 122.**
1. where to buy
2. whether to stay . . . go
3. how to fix
4. whether (or not) to look
5. where to get
6. whether (or not) to go
7. what time to pick
8. who to talk
9. whether to take . . . to do
10. how to solve
11. where to tell
12. how long to cook
13. what to wear
14. how much coffee to make
15. which essay to use
16. whether to take . . . travel . . . (to) keep . . . save

◇ **PRACTICE 8, p. 123.**

1. It is surprising that no one stopped to help Sam when he had car trouble.
   That no one stopped to help Sam when he had car trouble is surprising.
2. It is unfortunate that people in modern cities are distrustful of each other.
   That people in modern cities are distrustful of each other is unfortunate.
3. It is still true that people in my village always help each other.
   That people in my village always help each other is still true.
4. It is undeniably true that people need each other and need to help each other.
   That people need each other and need to help each other is undeniably true.
5. It seems obvious to me that people have a moral duty to help others in need.
   That people have a moral duty to help others in need seems obvious to me.
6. It is a pity that people today are afraid to help strangers.
   That people today are afraid to help strangers is a pity.
7. It seems strange to me that people in cities live in densely populated areas but don't know their neighbors.
   That people in cities live in densely populated areas but don't know their neighbors seems strange to me.

◇ **PRACTICE 9, p. 123.**

1. *Regardless of **the fact that** I studied for three months for the examination,* I barely passed.
2. There's nothing we can do *about **the fact that** Jim lost our tickets to the concert.*
3. ***The fact that** we are going to miss one of the best concerts of the year because of Jim's carelessness* makes me a little angry.
4. *In view of **the fact that** we can't go to the concert,* let's plan to go to a movie.
5. *Except for **the fact that** I couldn't speak a word of Italian and understood very little,* I had a wonderful time visiting my Italian cousins in Rome.
6. When I first visited Florida, I was surprised *by **the fact that** many people living in Miami speak only Spanish.*
7. ***The fact that** Bobby broke my grandmother's antique flower vase* isn't important.
8. ***The fact that** he lied about it* is what bothers me.
9. At first, some of us objected *to **the fact that** Prof. Brown, who had almost no teaching experience, was hired to teach the advanced physics course,* but she has proven herself to be one of the best.
10. I am impressed *by **the fact that** that automobile has the best safety record of any car manufactured this year* and would definitely recommend that you buy that make.

◇ **PRACTICE 10, p. 124.**

1. The athlete said**, "W**here is my uniform?**"**
2. "I can't remember**,"** Margaret said**,** "where I put my purse.**"**
3. Sandy asked her sister**, "H**ow can I help you get through this difficulty?**"**

4. "I'll answers your question later**,"** he whispered. **"**I'm trying to hear what the speaker is saying.**"**
5. As the students entered the room, the teacher said**, "P**lease take your seats quickly.**"**
6. "Why did I ever take this job?**"** Barry wondered aloud.
7. After crashing into me and knocking all of my packages to the ground, the man stopped abruptly, turned to me, and said softly**, "E**xcuse me.**"**
8. "Do we want four more years of corruption and debt?**"** the candidate shouted into the microphone. **"**No!**"** the crowd screamed.
9. The woman behind the fast-food counter shouted**, "W**ho's next?**"**
   "I am**,"** three people replied at the same time.
   "Which one of you is really next?**"** she asked impatiently.
   "I was here first**,"** said a young woman elbowing her way up to the counter. **"**I want a hamburger.**"**
   "You were not!**"** hollered an older man standing next to her. **"**I was here before you were. **G**ive me a chicken sandwich and a cup of coffee.**"**
   "Wait a minute! I was in line first**,"** said a young man. **"G**ive me a cheeseburger and a chocolate shake.**"**
   The woman behind the restaurant counter spotted a little boy politely waiting his turn. **S**he turned to him and said**, "H**i, Sonny. **W**hat can I get for you?**"**

◇ **PRACTICE 11, p. 126.**

1. was
2. needed
3. was having
4. had finished
5. had finished
6. would arrive
7. was going to be/would be
8. could solve
9. might come
10. might come
11. had to leave
12. had to leave
13. should go
14. ought to go
15. to stay
16. not to move
17. was
18. had arrived

◇ **PRACTICE 12, p. 126.**

1. if/whether she was planning
2. what time the movie begins
3. if/whether we could still get
4. how he can help
5. if/whether he could help
6. when the final decision would be made
7. where she had been
8. what Kim's native language is
9. what the problem was
10. if/whether I was doing
11. when this terrible drought is going
12. what time he had
13. who(m) she should give the message to
14. (that) we would be leaving
15. why we hadn't called

◇ PRACTICE 13, p. 127.

1. knew . . . had known . . . wanted
2. still smoked . . . had tried . . . didn't seem
3. what the capital of Australia was/is . . . wasn't . . . thought it was
4. would be . . . would . . . left
5. was pouring . . . had better take . . . would stop . . . didn't need
6. was going . . . was . . . asked/invited . . . would like . . . had . . . had . . . was . . . could . . . were
7. The passenger sitting next to me on the plane *asked* me where I *was* from. I *told* her I *was* from Chicago. She *said* that she *was* from Mapleton, a small town in northern Michigan. She wondered if I *had heard* of it, and I told her that I *had*. [British: *had done*] I went on to say that I thought Michigan *was* a beautiful state and explained that I had *been* there on vacation many times. She *asked* me if I *had been* in Michigan on vacation this year. I replied that I *hadn't (been)* and *told* her that I *had gone* far away, to India. Then she asked me if it *was* a long drive . . . .

◇ PRACTICE 14, p. 129.

1. organize
2. be divided
3. call
4. be told
5. open
6. take
7. be
8. be mailed
9. obey
10. be given

◇ PRACTICE 15, p. 130.

1. whenever
2. wherever
3. whatever
4. whichever
5. whatever
6. who(m)ever
7. whichever
8. Whoever
9. whatever
10. wherever

◇ PRACTICE 16. Test A, p. 131.

1. B
2. C
3. B
4. D
5. A
6. A
7. D
8. D
9. A
10. B
11. B
12. A
13. D
14. D
15. D
16. B
17. C
18. C
19. A
20. B

◇ PRACTICE 17. Test B, p. 133.

1. A
2. C
3. D
4. D
5. C
6. B
7. B
8. C
9. C
10. A
11. D
12. D
13. B
14. D
15. A
16. D
17. B
18. C
19. A
20. C

Chapter 13: ADJECTIVE CLAUSES

◇ PRACTICE 1, p. 135.

1. a. that are marked with a small red dot
   b. which are marked with a small red dot
2. a. who sits at the first desk on the right
   b. that sits at the first desk on the right
3. a. that I bought
   b. which I bought
   c. I bought
4. a. that I met at the meeting
   b. who(m) I met at the meeting
   c. I met at the meeting
5. a. we listened to last night
   b. that we listened to last night
   c. which we listened to last night
   d. to which we listened last night
6. a. I told you about
   b. who(m) I told you about
   c. that I told you about
   d. about whom I told you
7. whose parents you just met
8. who played at the concert last night
9. a waiter has to serve
10. Bob recommended
11. whose book on time and space has been translated into dozens of languages
12. who lives next door to us

◇ PRACTICE 2, p. 136.

1. who(m)/that/Ø
2. who/that
3. which/that/Ø
4. which
5. who(m)/that/Ø
6. who/that
7. whose
8. whom
9. which/that

◇ PRACTICE 3, p. 137.

1. which/that
2. who/that
3. which/that
4. which/that
5. who/that
6. which/that/Ø
7. who(m)/that/Ø
8. which/that/Ø
9. which
10. which/that/Ø
11. whom
12. who(m)/that/Ø

◇ PRACTICE 4, p. 138.

1. Louis knows the woman *who/that is meeting us at the airport.*
2. The chair *which/that/Ø Sally inherited from her grandmother* is an antique.
3. The bench *which/that/Ø I sat on* was wet. OR: The bench *on which I sat* was wet.
4. The man *who(m)/that/Ø I hired to paint my house* finished the job in four days.

5. I miss seeing the old woman *who/that used to sell flowers on that street corner.*
6. The architect *who(m)/that/Ø Mario works with* is brilliant. OR: The architect *with whom Mario works* is brilliant.
7. Mary tutors students *who/that need extra help in geometry.*
8. I took a picture of the rainbow *which/that appeared in the sky after the shower.*

◇ **PRACTICE 5, p. 138.**
1. Do you know the man *whose car is parked over there?*
2. I know a woman *whose name is May Day.*
3. The people *whose home we visited* were very hospitable.
4. The school principal walked down the hallway to find the boy *whose parents had been injured in an automobile accident.*
5. Mrs. Lake is the teacher *whose class I enjoy the most.*
6. Any company *whose employees are in constant fear of losing their jobs* is stifling the creativity of its workforce.

◇ **PRACTICE 6, p. 139.**
1. That is the room where we have class.
2. That is the restaurant where we ate dinner.
3. That is the building where Anna works.
4. That is the year when I was born.
5. That is the cafeteria where you eat lunch.
6. That is the month when the monsoons arrive.
7. That is the street where Alex lives.
8. That is the island where you spent your vacation.
9. That is the lake where you went swimming.
10. That is the town where you grew up.
11. That is the day when the space flight to Mars is scheduled to leave.
12. That is the country where the earthquake occurred.
13. That is the room where the examination will be given.
14. That is the city where you lived until you were ten years old.
15. That is the time when you felt the happiest.

◇ **PRACTICE 7, p. 139.**
1. A, D
2. B, C, D
3. C, D
4. B
5. D
6. B, C
7. A
8. C, D
9. B, C, D
10. B
11. A
12. A

◇ **PRACTICE 8, p. 140.**
1. speak
2. speaks
3. are . . . don't
4. offers are
5. measures . . . walks
6. suffer
7. have
8. have
9. are
10. state . . . wish

◇ **PRACTICE 9, p. 140.**
1. NO
2. YES . . . I made an appointment with Dr. Raven, who is considered an expert on eye disorders.
3. NO

4. NO
5. YES . . . Bogota, which is the capital of Colombia, is a cosmopolitan city.
6. YES . . . They climbed Mount Rainier, which is in the state of Washington, twice last year.
7. YES . . . Emeralds, which are valuable gemstones, are mined in Colombia.
8. YES . . . The company offered the position to John, whose department performed best this year.
9. YES . . . On our trip to Africa we visited Nairobi, which is near several fascinating game reserves, and then traveled to Egypt to see the pyramids.
10. NO
11. NO
12. YES . . . Larry was very close to his only brother, who was a famous social historian.
13. NO
14. NO
15. YES . . . A typhoon, which is a violent tropical storm, can cause great destruction.
16. NO

◇ **PRACTICE 10, p. 141.**
1. A
2. A, D
3. C
4. A
5. A, B, D, E
6. B
7. A
8. C
9. A, D
10. A
11. A, D
12. A
13. C, D, E

◇ **PRACTICE 11, p. 142.**
1. a
2. b
3. a
4. b
5. b
6. a
7. b
8. a

◇ **PRACTICE 12, p. 143.**
1. YES . . . Thirty people, two of whom were members of the crew, were killed in the ferry accident.
2. NO
3. YES . . . Over 500 students took the entrance examination, the results of which will be posted in the administration building at the end of the month.
4. NO
5. NO
6. YES . . . The new supervisor was not happy with his work crew, none of whom seemed interested in doing quality work.
7. YES . . . My oldest brother, in whose house I lived for six months when I was ten, has been a father to me in many ways.
8. YES . . . Tom is always interrupting me, which makes me mad.
9. YES . . . To express the uselessness of worrying, Mark Twain once said, "I've had a lot of problems in my life, most of which never happened."

◇ **PRACTICE 13, p. 143.**
1. . . . offers, **neither of which** I accepted.
2. . . . three brothers, **two of whom** are professional athletes.
3. . . . business ventures, **only one of which** is profitable.

4. . . . fifty states, **the majority of which** are located . . . .
5. The two women, **both of whom** are changing careers, have already dissolved . . . .
6. . . . success, **much of which** has been due to hard work, but **some of which** has been due to good luck.

◇ **PRACTICE 14, p. 143.**

1. Only a few of the movies *shown at the Gray Theater* are suitable for children.
2. We visited Madrid, *the capital of Spain.*
3. The couple *living in the house next door* are both college professors.
4. Astronomy, *the study of planets and stars,* is one of the world's oldest sciences.
5. Only a small fraction of the eggs *laid by a fish* actually hatch and survive to adulthood.
6. Jasmine, *a viny plant with fragrant flowers,* grows only in warm places.
7. Arizona, *once thought to be a useless desert,* is today a rapidly growing industrial and agricultural state.
8. Simon Bolivar, *a great South American general,* led the fight for independence early in the 19th century.
9. In hot weather, many people enjoy lemonade, *a drink made from lemon juice, water, and sugar.*
10. I was awakened by the sound of laughter *coming from the room next to mine at the motel.*
11. Few tourists ever see a jaguar, *a spotted cat native to tropical America.*

◇ **PRACTICE 15, p. 144.**

1. A national holiday has been established in memory of Martin Luther King, Jr., the leader of the civil rights movement in the United States in the 1950s and 1960s.
2. Neil Armstrong, the first person to set foot on the moon, reported that the surface was fine and powdery.
3. Mark Twain is an author known far and wide as one of the greatest American humorists. *(no commas)*
4. Susan B. Anthony, one of the first leaders of the campaign for women's rights, worked tirelessly during her lifetime to gain the right to vote for women.

◇ **PRACTICE 16, p. 144.**

1. Louisville, the largest city in Kentucky, was founded in 1778.
2. John Quincy Adams, the sixth president of the United States, was born on July 11, 1767.
3. Two languages, Finnish and Swedish, are used in Helsinki, the capital of Finland.
4. The Washington National Monument, a towering obelisk made of white marble, is a famous landmark in the nation's capital.
5. Honolulu, best known to the traveler for Waikiki Beach, has consistently pleasant weather.
6. Libya, a country in North Africa, is a leading producer of oil.

◇ **PRACTICE 17, p. 145.**

1. None of the pedestrians *walking up and down the busy street* stopped to help or even inquire about the elderly man *slumped in the doorway of an apparently unoccupied building.*

2. Food *passing from the mouth to the stomach* goes through a tube *called the esophagus.*
3. Animals *born in a zoo* generally adjust to captivity better than those *captured in the wild.*
4. The children attended a special movie program *consisting of cartoons featuring Donald Duck and Mickey Mouse.*
5. One of the most important foodstuffs in the world is flour, *a fine powder made by grinding wheat or other grains.*
6. Nero, *Emperor of Rome from A.D. 54 to 68,* is believed to have murdered both his mother and his wife.
7. The conclusion *presented in that book* states that most of the automobiles *produced by American industry in the 1960s and '70s* had some defect.
8. Pictures *showing the brutality of war* entered the living rooms of millions of TV watchers on the nightly news.
9. The Indians *living in Peru before the discovery of the New World by Europeans* belonged to the Incan culture.
10. My uncle Elias, *a restaurant owner,* often buys fish and shellfish from boats *docked at the local pier.* Customers come from miles around to dine on a seafood feast *considered to be the best in all of the northeastern United States.*
11. Hundreds of volunteers went to a northern village yesterday to reinforce firefighters *trying to save a settlement threatened by a forest fire.* The fire started when a cigarette ignited oil *leaking from a machine used to cut timber.*
12. Researchers have developed a way to mark genes so that they glow in the dark, *a technique that scientists can use to follow specific genetic activity of cells within plants and animals.* This development, *announced by the National Science Foundation, the sponsor of the research,* should prove useful to scientists *studying the basic functions of organisms.*

◇ **PRACTICE 18, p. 146.**

1. . . . a lot of people **waiting** in a long line . . .
2. Students who **live** on campus . . . OR: Students (omit *who*) **living** on campus . . . .
3. . . . the librarian **who/that** sits at . . . OR: the librarian **sitting** at . . . .
4. . . . sister is Anna, **who** is 21 years old. OR: sister, Anna, is 21 years old.
5. . . . in Sapporo, **which** is a city . . . OR: . . . in Sapporo, (omit *that is*) a city . . . .
6. Patrick, **who** is my oldest brother, is married and . . . OR: Patrick, my oldest brother, **is** married and . . . .
7. The person **who sits/sitting** next to me is someone **who(m)/that/Ø** I've never met (omit *him*).
8. . . . a small city (omit *is*) located . . . OR: . . . a small city **which/that** is located . . . .
9. Last Saturday, I attended a party **given** by one of my friends. My friend, **whose** apartment is in another town, was very glad that I could come.
10. Dr. Darnell was the only person **who(m)/that/Ø** I wanted to see.
11. There are eighty **students from** all over the **world studying** English at this school. OR: . . . students from all over the world **who study** . . . *(no commas)*
12. The people **who(m)/that/Ø** we met on our trip last May are going to visit us in October.

13. Dianne Jones, **who used to teach Spanish**, has organized a tour of . . . .
14. . . . since I came **here, some of whom** are from my country. OR: . . . **here. Some of them** . . . .
15. People **who** (*also possible but not preferred:* that) can speak English can be . . . .

◇ **PRACTICE 19. Test A, p. 147.**

1. D	11. C
2. A	12. B
3. B	13. C
4. D	14. D
5. B	15. D
6. A	16. B
7. C	17. D
8. D	18. B
9. C	19. A
10. A	20. C

◇ **PRACTICE 20. Test B, p. 149.**

1. C	11. D
2. B	12. B
3. A	13. C
4. A	14. B
5. C	15. A
6. B	16. C
7. D	17. D
8. D	18. C
9. B	19. A
10. C	20. B

Chapter 14: GERUNDS AND INFINITIVES, PART 1

◇ **PRACTICE 1, p. 151.**
1. of asking
2. to seeing
3. of washing
4. for breaking
5. from opening
6. of talking
7. like having
8. to killing
9. about finishing
10. for locking . . . (for) making
11. of practicing

◇ **PRACTICE 2, p. 152.**
Expected completions:
1. I thanked my classmate for helping me with my homework.
2. The treasurer is responsible for balancing the checkbook.
3. The students complained about having too many tests.
4. I apologized for stepping on my friend's toe.
5. A bodybuilder is capable of lifting heavy weights.
6. A teacher is used to answering students' questions.

7. The rainy weather prevented us from going on a picnic.
8. All of the children participated in making decorations for their classroom.
9. Unauthorized persons are prohibited from entering a military base.
10. The little girl was excited about getting a new doll for her birthday.
11. I thanked the flight attendant for getting me a pillow.
12. The employees objected to being forced to work overtime.

◇ **PRACTICE 3, p. 152.**
Sample responses:
1. I *enjoy taking* long walks in the evening.
2. Pierre *avoids eating* spicy food.
3. I often *go jogging* in the morning.
4. When I *finished doing* the housework, I took a break.
5. Yoko *suggested changing* the time of our lunch date from 11:30 to noon.
6. I'm *considering going swimming* at the beach after work today.
7. The little girl *stopped crying* when I handed her her doll.
8. Mary and Bob *discussed going shopping* for new furniture sometime this week.
9. Tarik *mentioned having to go* to the doctor's office today.
10. Tom *delayed putting* his tools away until he had completely finished the job.
11. Would you *mind taking* this letter with you when you go to the post office?
12. The children *kept asking* for ice cream.
13. I *quit worrying about* my grade in my economics class after I passed the final exam.
14. Sam *postponed taking* his two-week vacation until August.

◇ **PRACTICE 4, p. 153.**
1. We spent all yesterday afternoon playing soccer.
2. All of us had a really good time playing soccer in the park yesterday.
3. Omar had trouble finding my house last night.
4. My mother caught some neighborhood kids trying to steal my bicycle yesterday.
5. When the boss walked into the office, all of the employees were standing at the window watching the parade on the street below. OR: All of the employees were standing at the window watching the parade on the street below when the boss walked into the office.
6. My father always said, "Don't waste your time reading novels when you could be learning something worthwhile from other kinds of books."
7. When Mrs. Smith checked on the children last night, she found them playing a game instead of sleeping.
8. When I opened the door, I found Susan lying on her bed crying. OR: I found Susan lying on her bed crying when I opened the door.

◇ PRACTICE 5, p. 153.

1. B	11. B
2. B	12. A
3. A	13. A
4. A	14. A
5. B	15. B
6. B	16. B
7. A	17. B
8. B	18. B
9. B	19. A
10. A	20. A

◇ PRACTICE 6, p. 154.

1. asked Jim to give
2. were warned not to park
3. reminded him to brush
4. are required to wear
5. advised me to consult
6. was ordered to leave
7. were expected to complete
8. reminded my husband to buy
9. advised me to get
10. were warned not to be
11. is permitted to use
12. asked her father to buy
13. encouraged our grandfather to write
14. was ordered not to shout

◇ PRACTICE 7, p. 155.

1. During the water shortage, the public *was asked to curtail* its use of water as much as possible.
2. Laura *reminded her roommate not to forget* to set her alarm clock for 6:00.
3. Mrs. Jones *allowed each of the children to have one* piece of candy.
4. The doctor *advised my father to limit* his sugar consumption.
5. My parents often *encouraged me to be* independent.
6. The children *were warned not to swim* in the lake without an adult present.
7. The police officer *ordered the reckless driver to pull over.*
8. Rose *invited Jerry to come* to her house Sunday night to meet her parents.

◇ PRACTICE 8, p. 156.

1. B	14. A, B
2. A, B	15. B
3. A, B	16. A
4. A, B	17. B
5. A, B	18. A
6. B	19. B
7. A, B	20. A
8. B	21. A
9. A, B	22. B
10. A, B	23. A
11. A	24. B
12. B	25. A, B
13. A, B	26. B

◇ PRACTICE 9, p. 157.

(The answers are included in the Practice.)

◇ PRACTICE 10, p. 158.

1. to refund	14. singing
2. to be	15. avoiding
3. to buy	16. to count
4. throwing	17. painting
5. to get	18. to get
6. to wear	19. paying
7. to visit	20. to keep
8. to be	21. taking
9. thinking	22. to know
10. to attend	23. moving
11. to leave	24. to watch
12. to cut	25. to keep
13. to ignore	

◇ PRACTICE 11, p. 160.

1. to operate	14. to see
2. to shoot	15. to go
3. having	16. taking
4. to go	17. to speak
5. getting	18. receiving
6. to attend	19. to meet
7. to come	20. getting
8. to turn	21. staying
9. to tell	22. to apologize
10. practicing	23. to obey
11. to clean	24. seeing
12. reading	25. to take
13. sending	

◇ PRACTICE 12, p. 161.

1. A	6. A	11. B
2. B	7. B	12. B
3. A	8. B	13. A
4. A	9. A	14. B
5. B	10. A	15. B

◇ PRACTICE 13, p. 162.

1. playing
2. (someone) to save
3. telling
4. to get
5. someone to take
6. staying
7. (someone) not to buy
8. giving
9. going
10. travel(l)ing
11. taking
12. (someone) to go swimming
13. being
14. hearing
15. to tell
16. being
17. eating
18. to know
19. to get
20. saying
21. seeing
22. (someone) to give
23. to hire someone to work

24. to tell someone to be/telling someone to be [with different meanings]
25. (someone) to practice speaking
26. (someone) to keep trying to call

◇ **PRACTICE 14, p. 163.**
1. It is cruel to tease animals.
2. Finding their house wasn't difficult.
3. It is important to vote in every election.
4. Meeting the king and queen was exciting.
5. It would be interesting to hear the other side of the story.
6. Seeing Joan awake early in the morning is unusual.
7. If you know how, floating in the water for a long time is easy.
8. It takes time and patience to master a second language.
9. It will take us ten hours to drive to Atlanta.
10. Diving into the sea from a high cliff takes courage.

Chapter 15: GERUNDS AND INFINITIVES, PART 2

◇ **PRACTICE 1, p. 164.**
1. Ø
2. in order
3. in order
4. in order
5. Ø
6. Ø
7. in order
8. in order
9. Ø
10. in order
11. in order
12. Ø . . . Ø

◇ **PRACTICE 2, p. 165.**
Possible completions:
1. to get
2. to find out
3. to be
4. to fight
5. to go
6. to stay . . . (to) read
7. to help
8. to learn
9. to slip
10. to walk
11. to walk
12. to be
13. to see
14. to hear

◇ **PRACTICE 3, p. 165.**
1. very
2. too
3. too
4. very
5. too
6. too
7. very
8. too
9. very
10. very

11. very . . . too
12. too
13. very
14. too
15. too

◇ **PRACTICE 4, p. 166.**
1. I didn't have enough time to finish my work yesterday.
2. Linda isn't well enough to go back to work.
3. Scissors are too sharp for very young children to use.
4. The streets in the old part of the city are too narrow for two-way traffic.
5. Jimmy isn't old enough to ride on the bus by himself.
6. Jules had to rewrite his composition because he made too many careless mistakes in grammar and spelling in the first one.
7. There aren't enough seats in the classroom for everyone assigned to this class.
8. We couldn't go to the musical because we waited too long to call the box office for tickets.

◇ **PRACTICE 5, p. 166.**
1. B   5. B
2. A   6. A
3. B   7. B
4. B

◇ **PRACTICE 6, p. 167.**
1. B   5. A
2. A   6. B
3. B   7. B
4. B   8. A

◇ **PRACTICE 7, p. 167.**
1. B   6. A   11. A
2. D   7. B   12. A
3. A   8. C   13. B
4. C   9. B   14. B
5. B   10. D   15. D

◇ **PRACTICE 8, p. 169.**
1. B   5. B
2. D   6. A
3. D   7. A
4. C

◇ **PRACTICE 9, p. 169.**
1. to be told
2. having written *(also possible:* writing)
3. being asked/having been asked
4. to have been given
5. being photographed
6. to have had
7. to be sent
8. to be told
9. to have recovered . . . to be
10. having had

◇ PRACTICE 10, p. 170.

1. My mother was angry about **my losing** (OR: **having lost**) my new watch.
2. We look forward to **their spending** their vacation with us.
3. No one can understand **Tony's failing** (OR: **having failed**) the economics test even though . . . .
4. I am upset about the **students being required** to pay an extra fee to use the laboratory.
5. The supervisor appreciated **Mary's working** (OR: **having worked**) late to finish the project.

◇ PRACTICE 11, p. 170.

1. D	6. D	11. D
2. A	7. B	12. C
3. C	8. C	13. B
4. A	9. D	14. C
5. A	10. B	15. A

◇ PRACTICE 12, p. 172.

1. practice
2. prevent
3. win
4. arrive
5. emerge *(also possible: emerging)*
6. perform *(also possible: performing)*
7. climb *(also possible: climbing)*
8. chirp *(also possible: chirping)*
9. explain
10. melt

◇ PRACTICE 13, p. 173.

1. C	6. B
2. A, B	7. A
3. A	8. A, B
4. A	9. A
5. C	10. A

◇ PRACTICE 14, p. 173.

1. B	11. B
2. A	12. A
3. B	13. A
4. C	14. C
5. C	15. D
6. D	16. D
7. D	17. D
8. B	18. B
9. B	19. D
10. C	20. C

◇ PRACTICE 15, p. 175.

1. to buy
2. opening
3. being asked
4. having
5. to wear . . . dressing
6. jumping . . . falling
7. being taken

8. to stop delivering . . . to fill
9. gazing . . . (in order) to cheer
10. having
11. being
12. to move
13. to help . . . resolve/to resolve . . . not to interfere
14. to apply
15. to learn . . . to discover . . . promoting
16. reminding . . . to lock . . . trying to remember
17. asking . . . forgetting
18. not to sign
19. notifying . . . to call
20. play
21. burning . . . coming
22. to be . . . (to) listen
23. thinking
24. tear
25. doing
26. going
27. to be admitted
28. take
29. translate
30. to say . . . understand
31. to begin
32. to be done
33. to discover
34. put
35. feel . . . to be intimidated
36. failing
37. twiddling
38. draw
39. laugh
40. open
41. sleeping
42. to pay
43. being . . . to expect
44. lying

◇ PRACTICE 16, p. 178.

1. to have . . . built . . . to do
2. watch . . . practice . . . finding
3. hearing . . . play . . . forgetting . . . making . . . to relax . . . enjoy
4. wasting . . . to fail . . . doing
5. Attending . . . embarrassing . . . to hide . . . get [parallel infinitives] . . . leave
6. recalling . . . being chosen . . . looking . . . laughing . . . acting . . . playing . . . being . . . achieving
7. cleaning/to be cleaned . . . sweeping/to be swept . . . washing/to be washed . . . dusting/to be dusted . . . Reading . . . doing
8. having been given . . . forming . . . to accept . . . going . . . being . . . having been exposed
9. Finding . . . to be . . . being exposed . . . staying . . . to avoid . . . to minimize . . . getting . . . to get . . . eat [parallel infinitives] . . . taking . . . to prevent catching
10. being inconvenienced or hurt [parallel passive gerunds] . . . to remind . . . to remove . . . to turn . . . to buckle ["buckle up" = connect one's seat belt] . . . to shut . . . to fill . . . to forget to do . . . driving . . . (to) avoid making . . . being instructed . . . to perform . . . being reminded to carry

PRACTICE 17. Test A, p. 181.

1. A	11. B
2. B	12. D
3. D	13. B
4. A	14. B
5. B	15. C
6. D	16. C
7. C	17. D
8. D	18. C
9. D	19. A
10. A	20. B

PRACTICE 18. Test B, p. 183.

1. D	11. D
2. D	12. A
3. A	13. C
4. B	14. D
5. B	15. A
6. C	16. C
7. C	17. D
8. C	18. C
9. B	19. A
10. A	20. D

Chapter 16: COORDINATING CONJUNCTIONS

PRACTICE 1, p. 185.

1. fresh and sweet
2. apples and pears
3. washed and dried
4. am washing and drying
5. happily and quickly
6. biting and tasting
7. to bite and (to) taste
8. delicious but expensive
9. apples, pears, and bananas
10. red, ripe, and juicy

PRACTICE 2, p. 185.

1. *(no commas)*
2. Jack was calm, quiet,★ and serene.
3. *(no commas)*
4. The children sang, danced,★ and played games.
5. *(no commas)*
6. Tom, Tariq,★ and Francisco joined in the soccer game.
7. I told the children to sit down, be quiet,★ and open their reading books.
8. *(no commas)*
9. *(no commas)*
10. Our waitress's tray held two cups of coffee, three glasses of water,★ and one glass of orange juice.
11. *(no commas)*
12. *(no commas) [Answer to question: larger]*

PRACTICE 3, p. 186.

1. **I:** for his intelligence, cheerful disposition, and **honesty**
2. **C:** was a lawyer and a politician
3. **I:** smoothly and **quietly**

4. **C:** Barb studies . . . and works
5. **C:** is plentiful and relatively inexpensive
6. **I:** enjoy visiting Disneyland and **touring** movie studios
7. **C:** are usually interested in but a little frightened by
8. **I:** Fainting can result from **either** a lack of oxygen or a loss of blood.
9. **I:** how to write . . . , organize . . . , and **summarize**
10. **C:** not coffee but chocolate
11. **I:** Not only universities but **also many government agencies** support medical research.
12. **C:** explains why water freezes and how the sun produces heat
13. **C:** need light, a suitable climate, and an ample supply *(also possible:* of water and minerals*)*
14. **C:** With their keen sight, fine hearing, and refined sense of smell *(also possible:* hunt day or night*)* *(also possible:* of elk, deer, moose, or caribou*)*
15. **I:** by telling jokes and **making** funny faces
16. **C:** is always understanding, patient, and sensitive
17. **C:** Not only the post office but also all banks close
18. **I:** Walking briskly for 30 minutes or **running** for 15 minutes

PRACTICE 4, p. 187.

1. D	5. F
2. A	6. E
3. B	7. H
4. G	8. C

PRACTICE 5, p. 187.

1. knows	5. know	9. agrees
2. know	6. wants	10. are
3. knows	7. like	11. realizes
4. know	8. has	12. think

PRACTICE 6, p. 188.

1. Many people drink **neither coffee nor alcohol**.
2. Barbara is fluent in **not only Chinese but also Japanese**. OR: . . . not only in Chinese but also in Japanese.
3. I'm sorry to say that Paul has **neither patience nor sensitivity** to others.
4. She can **both sing and dance**.
5. . . . you should talk to **either your teacher or your academic counselor**. OR: . . . talk either to your teacher or to your academic counselor.
6. Diana is **both intelligent and very creative**.
7. You may begin working **either tomorrow or next week**.
8. Michael told **neither** his **mother nor his father** . . . .
9. . . . requires **not only balance and skill but also concentration and mental alertness**.

PRACTICE 7, p. 189.

1. . . . cooking. **My** wife . . . .
2. . . . cooking, *(optional comma)* but my wife . . . .
3. . . . that book. **It's** very good.
4. . . . that book, but I didn't like it.

★ The comma before *and* in a series is optional.

5. *(Add no punctuation.)*
6. . . . the door. **M**y sister answered . . . .
7. . . . the door, *(optional comma)*
8. . . . materials. **T**hey are found in rocks and soil.
9. . . . are minerals. **T**hey are found in rocks, soil, and water.
10. . . . by plane, *(optional comma)* or you can go . . . .
11. *(Add no punctuation.)*
12. . . . all night, so he declined . . . .
13. . . . invitation to dinner. **H**e needed to . . . .
14. . . . howling outside, yet it was warm . . . .
15. . . . answer the phone, for I didn't want . . . .
16. . . . went camping. **I**t rained the entire time.
17. . . . under construction, so we had to take . . . .
18. . . . win the championship, yet our team won . . . .
19. . . . at the theatre late, but the play had not yet begun. **W**e were quite surprised.
20. . . . from one central place. **M**ost central heating systems service only one building, but some systems heat a group of buildings, such as those at a military base, a campus, or an apartment complex.

◇ PRACTICE 8, p. 189.

I spent yesterday with my brother. **W**e had a really good time. **H**e's visiting me for a couple of days, so I decided not to go to work yesterday. **W**e spent the day in the city. **F**irst I took him to the waterfront. **W**e went to the aquarium, where we saw fearsome sharks, some wonderfully funny marine mammals, *(optional comma)* and all kinds of tropical fish. **A**fter the aquarium, we went downtown to a big mall and went shopping. **M**y brother doesn't like to shop as much as I do, so we didn't stay there long.

I had trouble thinking of a place to take him for lunch, for he's a strict vegetarian. **L**uckily I finally remembered a restaurant that has vegan food, so we went there and had a wonderful lunch of fresh vegetables and whole grains. **I**'m not a vegetarian, yet I must say that I really enjoyed the meal.

In the afternoon, *(optional comma)* it started raining, so we went to a movie. **I**t was pretty good but had too much violence for me. **I** felt tense when we left the theater. **I** prefer comedies or dramas. **M**y brother loved the movie.

We ended the day with a good homecooked meal and some good talk in my living room. **I**t was a good day. **I** like spending time with my brother.

◇ PRACTICE 9, p. 190.

Some of the most interesting working women of the American West in the nineteenth century were African-American women. **M**ary Fields was one of them. **S**he had been born a slave in the mid-1800s in the South but moved west to the Rocky Mountains as a free woman in 1884. **H**er first job

was hauling freight. **S**he drove a wagon and delivered freight in the valleys and mountains of Montana. **S**he was tall, strong, *(optional comma)* and fast on the draw. **S**he didn't hesitate to protect her wagon of goods with her gun.

She drove a freight wagon for many years. **T**hen in her late fifties, *(optional comma)* she opened a restaurant, but her business failed. **I**n her sixties, *(optional comma)* she became a stagecoach driver carrying the U.S. mail. **B**ecause of outlaws, driving a mailcoach was dangerous, yet her mailcoach always arrived safely. **I**n her seventies, *(optional comma)* she opened her own laundry business. **S**he continued successfully in that business until her death in 1914.

Mary Fields deserves our respect and can be seen as a role model for young women, for she rose above unfortunate circumstances and became a determined, hardworking, *(optional comma)* and successful businesswoman.

Chapter 17: ADVERB CLAUSES

◇ PRACTICE 1, p. 191.

1. We'll all take a walk in the park after <u>Dad finishes working on the car</u>.
<u>After Dad finishes working on the car</u>, we'll all take a walk in the park.
2. <u>Since Douglas fell off his bicycle last week</u>, he has had to use crutches to walk.
Douglas has had to use crutches to walk <u>since he fell off his bicycle last week</u>.
3. <u>Because I already had my boarding pass</u>, I didn't have to stand in line at the airline counter.
I didn't have to stand in line at the airline counter <u>because I already had my boarding pass</u>.
4. Productivity in a factory increases <u>if the workplace is made pleasant</u>.
<u>If the workplace is made pleasant</u>, productivity in a factory increases.
5. <u>After Ceylon had been independent for 24 years</u>, the country's name was changed to Sri Lanka.
Ceylon's name was changed to Sri Lanka <u>after the country had been independent for 24 years</u>.
6. Ms. Johnson regularly returns her e-mail messages <u>as soon as she has some free time from her principal duties</u>.
<u>As soon as Ms. Johnson has some free time from her principal duties</u>, she regularly returns her e-mail messages.
7. Tariq will be able to work more efficiently <u>once he becomes familiar with the new computer program</u>.
<u>Once Tariq becomes familiar with the new computer program</u>, he will be able to work more efficiently.
8. <u>When the flooding river raced down the valley</u>, it destroyed everything in its path.
The flooding river destroyed everything in its path <u>when it raced down the valley</u>.

PRACTICE 2, p. 191.

1. The lake was calm. Tom went fishing.
2. Because the lake was calm, Tom went fishing.
3. Tom went fishing because the lake was calm. **He** caught two fish.
4. Tom went fishing because the lake was calm and caught two fish.
5. When Tom went fishing, the lake was calm. **He** caught two fish.
6. The lake was calm, so Tom went fishing. **He** caught two fish.
7. Because the lake was calm and quiet, Tom went fishing.
8. The lake was calm, quiet, and clear when Tom went fishing.
9. Mr. Hood is admired because he dedicated his life to helping the poor. **He** is well known for his work on behalf of homeless people.
10. Microscopes, automobile dashboards, and cameras are awkward for left-handed people to use. **They** are designed for right-handed people. **When** "lefties" use these items, they have to use their right hand to do the things that they would normally do with their left hand.

PRACTICE 3, p. 192.

1. C	5. C	9. C
2. C	6. D	10. A
3. D	7. B	11. D
4. C	8. B	12. A

PRACTICE 4, p. 193.

1. My registration was canceled <u>because I didn't pay my fees on time</u>.
   <u>Because I didn't pay my fees on time</u>, my registration was canceled.
2. <u>Now that Erica has qualified for the Olympics in speedskating</u>, she must train even more vigorously. Erica must train even more vigorously <u>now that she has qualified for the Olympics in speedskating</u>.
3. We decided not to buy the house on Fourth Street <u>since it's directly below flight patterns from the nearby international airport</u>.
   <u>Since the house on Fourth Street is directly below flight patterns from the nearby international airport</u>, we decided not to buy it.

PRACTICE 5, p. 193.

1. even though
2. because
3. Because
4. Even though
5. Even though
6. Because
7. even though
8. because
9. even though
10. because
11. Even though
12. because
13. Even though . . . because
14. even though . . . because

PRACTICE 6, p. 194.

1. C	4. C	7. C
2. C	5. C	8. C
3. C	6. C	9. I

PRACTICE 7, p. 194.

1. Let's not go to the park if <u>it ~~will rain~~ rains tomorrow</u>.
2. (no change)
3. (no change)
4. I'll send you an e-mail <u>if I ~~will have~~ have some free time tomorrow</u>.
5. <u>If we don't leave within the next ten minutes</u>, we ~~are~~ will be late to the theater.
6. <u>If we ~~will leave~~ leave within the next two minutes</u>, we will make it to the theater on time.

PRACTICE 8, p. 194.

1. doesn't approve . . . approves
2. can afford . . . can't afford
3. is raining . . . isn't raining
4. don't understand . . . understand

PRACTICE 9, p. 195.

1. In case . . . with me, I'll . . . .
2. **We'll** . . . in case you need to call us.
3. **In** case you find that you need help with it, she'll be . . . .
4. **My** boss . . . in case the company . . . .
5. **In** case I'm not back . . . dinner, I put the . . . .
6. **In** the event that Janet . . . tomorrow she will . . . .
7. **You'd** better . . . in the event that you run out of cash.
8. **My** family . . . the country in the event that there is civil war.
9. . . . safe side, I always . . . carry-on bag in the event that the airline loses my luggage.
10. **She** has already . . . speech in the event that she wins it tonight.

PRACTICE 10, p. 196.

1. B
2. A
3. B
4. B
5. A
6. B

PRACTICE 11, p. 196.

1. pass
2. not going to go
3. rains
4. only if
5. always eat
6. even if
7. won't
8. don't wake
9. if
10. Don't borrow

◇ **PRACTICE 12, p. 197.**

1. Only if you help me **can I finish** this work on time.
2. If you help me, **I can finish** this work on time.
3. Only if I am invited **will I go**.
4. If I am invited, **I will go**.
5. Only if I am hungry **do I eat**.
6. If I am hungry during the morning, **I** usually **eat** some fruit.
7. Only if you know both Arabic and Spanish **will you be considered** for that job.
8. Only if the refrigerator is empty **does John go** to the market.
9. Only if you promise not to get angry **will I tell** you the truth about what happened.
10. If you can't learn to communicate your feelings, **I won't marry** you.

◇ **PRACTICE 13, p. 197.**

1. B	7. D
2. C	8. B
3. D	9. C
4. A	10. C
5. B	11. D
6. C	12. A

Chapter 18: REDUCTION OF ADVERB CLAUSES TO MODIFYING ADVERBIAL PHRASES

◇ **PRACTICE 1, p. 199.**

1. Since opening . . . .
2. . . . before leaving the room.
3. While herding his goats . . . .
4. Before marching into battle, ...
5. After meeting/having met the movie star . . . .
6. . . . keys after searching through . . . .
7. When first brought . . . .
8. Since (being) imported into Australia many years ago, the rabbit . . . .

◇ **PRACTICE 2, p. 199**

1. While <u>Sam</u> was driving to work in the rain, <u>his car</u> got a flat tire.
   → *(no change)*
2. While <u>Sam</u> was driving to work, <u>he</u> had a flat tire.
   → *While driving to work, Sam had a flat tire.*
3. Before <u>Nick</u> left on his trip, <u>his son</u> gave him a big hug and a kiss.
   → *(no change)*
4. Before <u>Nick</u> left on his trip, <u>he</u> gave his itinerary to his secretary.
   → *Before leaving on his trip, Nick gave . . . .*
5. After <u>Tom</u> had worked hard in the garden all afternoon, <u>he</u> took a shower and then went to the movies with his friends.
   → *After having worked hard in the garden all afternoon, Tom took . . . .*
6. After <u>Sunita</u> had made a delicious chicken curry for her friends, <u>they</u> wanted the recipe.
   → *(no change)*

7. Before <u>a friend</u> tries to do something hard, <u>an American</u> may say "Break a leg!" to wish him or her good luck.
   → *(no change)*
8. <u>Emily</u> always straightens her desk before she leaves the office at the end of the day.
   → *Emily always straightens her desk before leaving the office at the end of the day.*

◇ **PRACTICE 3, p. 200.**

1. a. leaving . . . b. left
2. a. invented/had invented . . . b. inventing/having invented
3. a. working . . . b. was working
4. a. flies . . . b. flying
5. a. studied/had studied . . . b. studying/having studied
6. a. learning . . . b. learned
7. a. is taken . . . b. taken
8. a. taking . . . b. take
9. a. was driving . . . b. driving

◇ **PRACTICE 4, p. 201.**

1. Not wanting to disturb his sleeping wife, Larry tiptoed out of the room.
2. *(no change)*
3. Misunderstanding the directions to the hotel, I arrived one hour late for the dinner party.
4. *(no change)*
5. Misunderstanding my directions to the hotel, the taxi driver took me to the wrong place.
6. Remembering that she hadn't turned off the oven, Ann went directly home.
7. *(no change)*
8. Living in the Pacific Northwest, where it rains a great deal, my family and I are accustomed to cool, damp weather.

◇ **PRACTICE 5, p. 201.**

1. E	7. I
2. J	8. H
3. A	9. C
4. G	10. K
5. B	11. F
6. L	12. D

◇ **PRACTICE 6, p. 202.**

1. arriving at the airport
2. reaching the other side of the lake
3. investigating the cause
4. learning the problem was not at all serious
5. being told she got it

◇ **PRACTICE 7, p. 202.**

1. I	6. I
2. C	7. I
3. I	8. I
4. C	9. I
5. I	10. C

PRACTICE 8. Test A, p. 204.

1. B	11. A
2. D	12. D
3. C	13. C
4. C	14. A
5. C	15. B
6. A	16. D
7. D	17. B
8. B	18. A
9. C	19. C
10. D	20. C

PRACTICE 9. Test B, p. 206.

1. D	11. B
2. B	12. C
3. A	13. B
4. D	14. D
5. C	15. A
6. C	16. D
7. D	17. A
8. B	18. C
9. B	19. D
10. A	20. A

Chapter 19: CONNECTIVES THAT EXPRESS CAUSE AND EFFECT, CONTRAST, AND CONDITION

PRACTICE 1, p. 208.

1. because of
2. because
3. because of
4. because
5. because of
6. because
7. because
8. because of

PRACTICE 2, p. 208.

1. because
2. Therefore
3. Therefore
4. because
5. Because
6. therefore

PRACTICE 3, p. 209.

PART I.
1. Because
2. ... rained. Therefore, we ...
3. because of
4. ... town. Therefore, all ...
5. because of
6. Because the hurricane ... town, all ....
7. because of

PART II.
8. Due to his poor eyesight, John ....
9. Since John has poor eyesight, he ....
10. ... eyesight. Consequently, he ....
11. ... heights. Consequently, she ....

12. due to
13. ... overweight. Consequently, his doctor ....
14. Since a diamond ... hard, it can ....

PRACTICE 4, p. 209.

1. Edward missed the final exam. **T**herefore, he failed the course. (*also possible:* ... exam; therefore, he failed ....)
2. (*no change*)
3. Edward missed the final exam. **H**e simply forgot to go to it. (*also possible:* ... exam; he simply ....)
4. Because we forgot to make a reservation, we couldn't get a table at our favorite restaurant last night.
5. The waitress kept dropping trays full of dishes. **T**herefore, she was fired. (*also possible:* ... dishes; therefore, she was ....)
6. The waiter kept forgetting customers' orders, so he was fired.
7. (*no change*)
8. The needle has been around since prehistoric times. The button was invented about 2000 years ago. The zipper wasn't invented until 1890.
9. It is possible for wildlife observers to identify individual zebras because the patterns of stripes on each zebra are unique. **N**o two zebras are alike. (*also possible:* ... are unique; no two zebras ....)
10. (*no change*)

PRACTICE 5, p. 210.

1. such
2. so
3. so
4. such
5. such
6. so
7. so
8. such
9. so
10. so

PRACTICE 6, p. 210.

1. It was *such* a nice day *that* we took a walk.
2. The weather was *so* hot *that* you could fry an egg on the sidewalk.
3. She talked *so* fast *that* I couldn't understand her.
4. It was *such* an expensive car *that* we couldn't afford to buy it.
5. We're having *such* beautiful weather *that* I don't feel like going to class.
6. Grandpa held me *so* tightly when he hugged me *that* I couldn't breathe for a moment.
7. There were *so* few people at the meeting *that* it was canceled.
8. The classroom has *such* comfortable chairs *that* the students find it easy to fall asleep.
9. Ted was *so* worried about the exam *that* he couldn't get to sleep last night.
10. Jerry got *so* angry *that* he put his fist through the wall.
11. I have *so* many problems *that* I can use all the help you can give me.

12. The tornado struck with *such* great force *that* it lifted automobiles off the ground.
13. His handwriting is *so* illegible *that* I can't figure out what this sentence says.
14. David has *so* many girlfriends *that* he can't remember all of their names.
15. *So* many people came to the meeting *that* there were not enough seats for everyone.

◇ PRACTICE 7, p. 211.

1. Rachel turned on the TV *so that she could watch* the news.
2. Alex wrote down the time and date of his appointment *so that he wouldn't forget* to go.
3. Nancy is carrying extra courses every semester *so that she can graduate* early.
4. Jason is tired of work and school and is planning to take a semester off *so that he can travel in* Europe.
5. Suzanne lowered the volume on the TV set *so that she wouldn't disturb* her roommate.
6. Whenever we are planning a vacation, we call a travel agent *so that we can get* expert advice on our itinerary.
7. It's a good idea for you to learn how to type *so that you can type* your own papers when you go to the university.
8. Lynn tied a string around her finger *so that she wouldn't forget* to take her book back to the library.
9. Ed took some change from his pocket *so that he could buy* a newspaper.
10. I turned on the TV *so that I could listen* to the news while I was making dinner.
11. I unplugged the phone *so that I wouldn't be interrupted* while I was working.
12. Yesterday Linda was driving on the highway when her car started making strange noises. After she pulled over to the side of the road, she raised the hood of her car *so that other drivers would know* that she had car trouble.

◇ PRACTICE 8, p. 212.

1. D	6. C	11. A
2. A	7. A	12. B
3. C	8. C	13. B
4. D	9. B	14. C
5. D	10. C	15. D

◇ PRACTICE 9, p. 213.

1. Annie told the truth, but no one believed her.
2. Annie told the truth. **However**, no one believed her. *(also possible: . . . the truth; however, no one . . . .)*
3. Even though Annie told the truth, no one believed her.
4. *(no change)*
5. Annie told the truth, yet no one believed her.
6. Annie told the truth. **Nevertheless**, no one believed her. *(also possible: . . . the truth; nevertheless, no one . . . .)*
7. In spite of the fact that Annie told the truth, no one believed her.
8. *(no change)*

9. Even though all of my family friends have advised me not to travel abroad during this time of political turmoil, I'm leaving next week to begin a trip around the world.
10. Some people think great strides have been made in cleaning up the environment in much of the world. **However**, others think the situation is much worse than it was twenty years ago. *(also possible: of the world; however, others think . . . .)*

◇ PRACTICE 10, p. 213.

1.
  a. Even though
  b. Despite
  c. Despite
  d. Despite
  e. Even though
2.
  a. In spite of
  b. Although
  c. Although
  d. In spite of
  e. In spite of
3.
  a. Despite
  b. Although
  c. Despite
  d. Although
  e. Despite
4.
  a. In spite of
  b. Even though
  c. in spite of
  d. even though
  e. in spite of
  f. even though
  g. even though
  h. in spite of

◇ PRACTICE 11, p. 215.

1. B	6. H
2. E	7. A
3. J	8. G
4. F	9. I
5. C	10. D

◇ PRACTICE 12, p. 216.

1. Red is bright and lively, *while* gray is a dull color.
OR
While red is bright and lively, gray is a dull color.

2. Jane is insecure and unsure of herself. Her sister, *on the other hand*, is full of self-confidence. *(also possible: . . . of herself; her sister, on the other hand, is . . . .)*
OR
Jane is insecure and unsure of herself. *On the other hand*, her sister is full of self-confidence. OR
Jane is insecure and unsure of herself. Her sister is full of self-confidence, *on the other hand*.

3. A rock is heavy, *while* a feather is light. OR
While a rock is heavy, a feather is light.

4. Some children are unruly, *whereas* others are quiet and obedient. OR
Whereas some children are unruly, others are quiet and obedient.

5. Language and literature classes are easy and enjoyable for Alex. Math and science courses, *on the other hand*, are difficult for him. *(also possible: . . . for Alex; math and science courses, on the other hand, are difficult . . . .)* OR
   Language and literature classes are easy and enjoyable for Alex. *On the other hand*, math and science courses are difficult for him. OR
   Language and literature classes are easy and enjoyable for Alex. Math and science courses are difficult for him, *on the other hand*.

6. Strikes can bring improvements in wages and working conditions. *However*, strikes can also cause loss of jobs and bankruptcy. *(also possible: . . . conditions; however, strikes can . . . .)* OR
   Strikes can bring improvements in wages and working conditions. Strikes can also, *however*, cause loss of jobs and bankruptcy. OR
   Strikes can bring improvements in wages and working conditions. Strikes can also cause loss of jobs and bankruptcy, *however*. OR
   Strikes can bring improvements in wages and working conditions. Strikes can also, *however*, cause loss of jobs and bankruptcy.

◇ **PRACTICE 13, p. 216.**
1. even though/although
2. due to/because of
3. even though/although
4. Nevertheless/However
5. Even though/Although
6. In spite of/Despite
7. Therefore
8. on the other hand/however
9. because of/due to
10. Although/Even though
11. because/since
12. Even though/Although
13. because of/due to
14. Therefore
15. Although/Even though *(also possible:* While)
16. Because/Since

◇ **PRACTICE 14, p. 217.**
1. You should (had better/have to/must) eat less and get more exercise. Otherwise, you won't lose weight.
2. The children have to (had better/should/ must) finish all of their chores. Otherwise, they cannot watch TV tonight.
3. You have to (must/should/had better) speak up now. Otherwise, the boss will go ahead . . . .
4. You must (had better/should/have to) stop at the store on your way home from work. Otherwise, we won't have anything . . . .
5. You had better (have to/should/must) think it through very carefully. Otherwise, you won't come up . . . .
6. We have to (had better/should/must) catch fish this morning. Otherwise, we're going to have beans for dinner again.
7. You should (had better/have to/must) get someone to help you. Otherwise, it's going to be very . . . .

8. Maria had better (should/has to/must) find a way to convince the boss that the error was unavoidable. Otherwise, she'll probably lose her job.

◇ **PRACTICE 15, p. 218.**
1. passes
2. doesn't pass
3. passes
4. passes
5. doesn't pass
6. passes
7. docsn't pass
8. doesn't pass
9. must/has to pass
10. had better (must/has to) pass

◇ **PRACTICE 16. Test A, p. 219.**

1. C	14. A
2. A	15. C
3. C	16. B
4. C	17. A
5. A	18. A
6. C	19. B
7. C	20. B
8. B	21. B
9. D	22. B
10. A	23. D
11. B	24. A
12. C	25. C
13. B	

◇ **PRACTICE 17. Test B, p. 221.**

1. B	14. A
2. A	15. A
3. D	16. B
4. B	17. D
5. C	18. C
6. D	19. A
7. C	20. B
8. C	21. A
9. C	22. D
10. B	23. A
11. C	24. A
12. B	25. A
13. B	

Chapter 20: CONDITIONAL SENTENCES AND WISHES

◇ **PRACTICE 1, p. 223.**
1. were . . . would take
2. would accept . . . were
3. will explode/explodes . . . throw
4. were . . . would call . . . (would) talk
5. is . . . will be canceled
6. consisted . . . would be

◇ **PRACTICE 2, p. 223.**
1. had told . . . would have given
2. wouldn't have gotten/got . . . had remembered
3. had known . . . wouldn't have voted
4. would have gotten/got . . . had used

5. had written . . . wouldn't have lost
6. would you have taken . . . had known

◇ **PRACTICE 3, p. 224.**
1. had . . . wouldn't have to
2. Would people be . . . had
3. send . . . will arrive
4. had brought . . . wouldn't have had
5. felt . . . would drop
6. have . . . will always rise . . . flood OR: always rises . . . floods
7. discover . . . will call
8. had known . . . would have stayed up . . . (would have) finished

◇ **PRACTICE 4, p. 225.**
1. If I hadn't been sick yesterday, I would have gone to class.
2. If Alan ate breakfast, he wouldn't overeat at lunch.
3. Kostas wouldn't have been late to his own wedding if his watch hadn't been slow.
4. I would ride the bus to work every morning if it weren't always so crowded.
5. If Sara had known that highway 57 was closed, she would have taken an alternative route.
6. Camille could have finished unloading the truck if someone had been there to help her.

◇ **PRACTICE 5, p. 225.**
1. weren't raining   would finish
2. had eaten . . . wouldn't be
3. hadn't left . . . would have
4. would have answered . . . hadn't been studying
5. hadn't been shining . . . wouldn't have gone
6. wouldn't ache . . . hadn't played
7. wouldn't stop . . . weren't running
8. had eaten . . . wouldn't have to have
9. hadn't been playing . . . would have heard
10. weren't closing . . . wouldn't have to leave

◇ **PRACTICE 6, p. 226.**
1. If the wind **weren't blowing** hard, I **would take** the boat out for a ride.
2. I **wouldn't feel** better now if you **hadn't talked** to me about my problems last night.
3. If Ann **hadn't carried** heavy furniture when she helped her friend move, her back **wouldn't hurt** now.
4. If Paulo **weren't working** on two jobs right now, he **would have time** to help you with your remodeling.
5. If I **had been working** at the restaurant last night, I **would have waited** on your table.
6. If Diane **hadn't asked questions** every time she didn't understand a problem, she **wouldn't have** a good understanding of geometry now.
7. If a fallen tree **hadn't been blocking** the road, we **would have arrived** on time.
8. Rita **wouldn't be** exhausted today if she **had gotten** some sleep last night.
9. If Olga and Ivan **had been paying** attention, they **would have seen** the sign marking their exit from the highway.
10. If the doctor really **cared** about his patients, he **would have explained** the medical procedure to me before surgery.

◇ **PRACTICE 7, p. 227.**
1. Should you need
2. Were I you
3. Had I been offered
4. Should anyone call
5. Were I
6. had they known
7. were she
8. Had I not opened

◇ **PRACTICE 8, p. 227.**
1. Were I your age, I'd do things differently.
2. Should Bob show up while I'm away, please give him my message.
3. Had my uncle stood up to sing, I'd have been embarrassed.
4. Were she ever in trouble, I'd do anything I could to help her.
5. Should the manager question these figures, have her talk to the bookkeeper.
6. I wouldn't have known about your new job had I not talked to your mother. [*Had* and *not* are not contracted in the omitted-*if* pattern.]

◇ **PRACTICE 9, p. 227.**
1. . . . I hadn't forgotten to tell him that she needed a ride.
2. . . . I hadn't had your help.
3. If I hadn't opened the door slowly . . . .
4. . . . he could have gotten/got time off from work.
5. . . . he had told his boss about the problem.

◇ **PRACTICE 10, p. 228.**

1. D	11. C
2. B	12. A
3. D	13. B
4. D	14. D
5. C	15. C
6. A	16. B
7. C	17. B
8. B	18. B
9. C	19. A
10. D	20. C

◇ **PRACTICE 11, p. 229.**
1. would have . . . hadn't spent
2. would have been hit . . . hadn't pulled
3. would have been (*also possible:* could have been)
4. would think
5. would have done (*also possible:* could have done)
6. wouldn't say . . . meant
7. would have graduated (*also possible:* could have graduated)
8. had been driving fast . . . would have been
9. travels . . . always spends

◇ **PRACTICE 12, p. 230.**
1. were
2. had been made
3. had . . . met
4. were
5. hadn't heard
6. didn't have/hadn't

7. didn't exist
8. had happened
9. were
10. were
11. had stopped
12. had appeared

◇ **PRACTICE 13, p. 231.**
1. were shining
2. had gone
3. had driven
4. could swim
5. would stop
6. had won
7. had gotten
8. hadn't quit
9. were
10. would sing
11. could bring
12. had offered

◇ **PRACTICE 14, p. 232.**
1. had not missed
2. A: would stop   B: were shining
3. had gone . . . could paint
4. hadn't moved . . . had taken
5. would stop
6. hadn't paid
7. A: would hurry   B: would relax
8. hadn't invited
9. B: hadn't been elected   A: hadn't voted
10. A: could buy   B: grew
11. A: weren't . . . were   B: were . . . were
12. A: would meet   B: disagreed . . . could prove
13. had told
14. would go

◇ **PRACTICE 15, p. 233.**
1. had been run
2. would look
3. had had
4. hadn't been driving
5. wouldn't have slid
6. step ["step on the gas" = accelerate the car]
7. hadn't taken
8. wouldn't have lost
9. hadn't lost
10. would have had
11. had had
12. wouldn't have to pay
13. hadn't been driving
14. wouldn't have run into
15. wouldn't be
16. were/was
17. would take
18. stay
19. would stay
20. weren't/wasn't
21. could go
22. I'll fly
23. I'll take
24. could drive
25. would be

◇ **PRACTICE 16. Test A, p. 235.**

1. B	11. C
2. C	12. B
3. C	13. B
4. A	14. B
5. C	15. D
6. B	16. C
7. D	17. D
8. B	18. B
9. D	19. D
10. A	20. A

◇ **PRACTICE 17. Test B, p. 237.**

1. D	11. D
2. D	12. B
3. A	13. D
4. C	14. C
5. B	15. B
6. A	16. A
7. D	17. B
8. B	18. D
9. A	19. C
10. C	20. A

Appendix: SUPPLEMENTARY GRAMMAR UNITS

◇ **PRACTICE 1, p. A1.**

       S   V   O
1. Airplanes have wings.

        S   V   O
2. The teacher explained the problem.

      S   V O
3. Children enjoy games.

   S   V   O
4. Jack wore a blue suit.

        S   V   O   S   V
5. Some animals eat plants. Some animals eat
        O
other animals.

                          S
6. According to an experienced waitress, you
   S   V   O
can carry full cups of coffee without spilling

them just by never looking at them.

◇ **PRACTICE 2, p. A1.**

       VI
1. Alice arrived at six o'clock.

     VT
2. We drank some tea.

   VI
3. I agree with you.

   VI
4. I waited for Sam at the airport for two hours.

5. They're staying at a resort hotel in San Antonio, Texas. [VI over "staying"]

6. Chanchai is studying English. [VT]

7. The wind is blowing hard today. [VI]

8. I walked to the theater, but Janice rode her bicycle. [VI, VT]

9. Amphibians hatch from eggs. [VI]

10. Rivers flow toward the sea. [VI]

◇ **PRACTICE 3, p. A2.**

1. Jim came to class without his books.
2. We stayed at home during the storm.
3. Sonya walked across the bridge over the Cedar River.
4. When Alex walked through the door, his little sister ran toward him and put her arms around his neck.
5. The two of us need to talk to Tom, too.
6. Animals live in all parts of the world. Animals walk or crawl on land, fly in the air, and swim in the water.
7. Scientists divide living things into two main groups: the animal kingdom and the plant kingdom.
8. Asia extends from the Pacific Ocean in the east to Africa and Europe in the west.

◇ **PRACTICE 4, p. A2.**

1. Jack put the letter in the mailbox. [S V O PP]

2. The children walked to school. [S V PP]

3. Mary did her homework at the library. [S V O PP]

4. Chinese printers created the first paper money in the world. [S V O PP]

5. Dark clouds appeared on the horizon. [S V PP]

6. Mary filled the shelves of the cabinet with boxes of old books. [S V O PP PP PP]

◇ **PRACTICE 5, p. A2.**

1. Jack opened the heavy door slowly. [ADJ ADV]

2. Chinese jewelers carved beautiful ornaments from jade. [ADJ ADJ]

3. The old man carves wooden figures skillfully. [ADJ ADJ ADV]

4. A busy executive usually has short conversations on the telephone. [ADJ ADV ADJ]

5. The young woman had a very good time at the picnic yesterday. [ADJ ADV ADJ ADV]

◇ **PRACTICE 6, p. A3.**

1. quickly
2. quick
3. polite
4. politely
5. regularly
6. regular
7. usual
8. usually
9. well
10. good
11. gentle
12. gently
13. annually
14. annual
15. bad
16. badly

◇ **PRACTICE 7, p. A3.**

1. Sue **always takes** a walk in the morning.
2. Tim **is always** a hard worker.
3. Beth **has always worked** hard.
4. Jack **always works** hard.
5. **Do you always work** hard?
6. Taxis **are usually** available . . . .
7. Youssef **rarely takes** a taxi . . . .
8. I **have often thought** about . . . .
9. Yuko **probably needs** some help.
10. **Have you ever attended** the show . . . ?
11. Al **seldom goes** out . . . .
12. The students **are hardly ever** late.
13. **Do you usually finish** your . . . ?
14. In India, the monsoon season **generally begins** in April.
15. . . . Mr. Singh's hometown **usually receives** around . . . .

◇ **PRACTICE 8, p. A4.**

	L.VERB	+ ADJ
1.	Ø (no linking verb in the sentence)	
2.	looked	fresh
3.	Ø	
4.	Ø	
5.	tasted	good
6.	grew	quiet
7.	Ø	
8.	Ø	
9.	Ø	
10.	smells	delicious
11.	Ø	
12.	got	sleepy
13.	became	rough
14.	Ø	
15.	Ø	
16.	sounded	happy
17.	turns	hot

	L.VERB	+	ADJ
18.	Ø		
19.	Ø		
20.	appears		certain
21.	seems		strange

◇ PRACTICE 9, p. A5.

1. clean
2. slowly
3. safely
4. anxious
5. complete
6. wildly
7. honest
8. thoughtfully
9. well
10. fair
11. terrible
12. good
13. light
14. confidently
15. famous
16. fine

◇ PRACTICE 10, p. A6.

	Question word	Auxiliary verb	Subject	Main verb	Rest of question
1a.	Ø	Can	Bob	live	there?
1b.	Where	can	Bob	live	Ø?
1c.	Who	can	Ø	live	there?
2a.	Ø	**Is**	**Don**	**living**	there?
2b.	Where	**is**	**Don**	**living**	Ø?
2c.	Who	**is**	Ø	**living**	there?
3a.	Ø	**Does**	**Sue**	live	there?
3b.	Where	**does**	**Sue**	live	Ø?
3c.	Who	Ø	Ø	**lives**	there?
4a.	Ø	**Will**	**Ann**	live	there?
4b.	Where	**will**	**Ann**	live	Ø?
4c.	Who	**will**	Ø	**live**	there?
5a.	Ø	**Did**	**Jack**	live	there?
5b.	**Where**	**did**	**Jack**	live	Ø?
5c.	**Who**	Ø	Ø	**lived**	there?
6a.	Ø	**Has**	**Mary**	**lived**	**there?**
6b.	**Where**	**has**	**Mary**	**lived**	Ø?
6c.	**Who**	**has**	Ø	**lived**	**there?**

◇ PRACTICE 11, p. A7.

1. When are you going to the zoo?
2. Are you going downtown later today?
3. Do you live in an apartment?
4. Where does Sue live?
5. Who lives in that house?
6. Can you speak French?
7. Who can speak Arabic?
8. When did Olga arrive?
9. Who arrived late?
10. What is Ann opening?
11. What is Ann doing?
12. What did Mary open?
13. Who opened the door?
14. Has the mail arrived?
15. Do you have a bicycle?
16. What does Alex have in his hand?
17. Do you like ice cream?
18. Would you like an ice cream cone?
19. What would Joe like?
20. Who would like a soft drink?

◇ PRACTICE 12, p. A8.

1. How long has Pierre been living here?
2. Which (city) is farther north, London or Paris?
3. Whose is it?
4. What have you been doing?
5. Who answered the phone?
6. How do they plow their fields?
7. How long have you had it?
8. What kind of bird is that?
9. Why were you late for work this morning? (OR: How come you were late for work this morning?)
10. How long did it take you?
11. What time/When did he finally get home?
12. How do you take it?
13. What is the population of the United States?
14. Which (coat/one) do you like better (, the red one or the black one)?
15. How did you get there?
16. Who(m) should I address it to? *(formal:* To whom should I address it?)
17. How far (How many miles) is it from here to Los Angeles?
18. Who is going to be at the meeting tonight?
19. How often (How many times a week) do people in your country have rice?
20. Where did you get that silly looking hat?
21. What does "apologize" mean?
22. How many edges are there on a cube? . . . . How many edges are there on a pyramid?
23. What does he look like?
24. What is she like?

◇ PRACTICE 13, p. A10.

1. How do you take your coffee?
2. What kind of dictionary do you have? (have you?/have you got?)
3. What does he do for a living?
4. Who was Margaret talking to?/To whom was Margaret talking?
5. How many people showed up for the meeting?
6. Why could none of the planes take off?
7. What was she thinking about?/About what was she thinking?
8. How fast/How many miles per hour (OR: an hour) were you driving when the policeman stopped you?
9. What kind of food do you like best?
10. Which apartment is yours/Where is your apartment?
11. What is Oscar like? *(also possible:* What kind of person/man is Oscar?)
12. What does Oscar look like?
13. Whose dictionary fell to the floor?
14. Why isn't Abby here?
15. When will all of the students in the class be informed of their final grades?

16. How do you feel?
17. Which book did you prefer?
18. What kind of music do you like?
19. How late is the plane expected to be?
20. Why did the driver of the stalled car light a flare?
21. Which pen do you want?
22. What's the weather like in July?
23. How do you like your steak?
24. How did you do on the test?
25. How many seconds are there in a year?

◇ **PRACTICE 14, p. A11.**
1. How much money do you need?
2. Where was Roberto born?/In what country/city was . . .?/What country/city was Roberto born in?
3. How often do you go out to eat?
4. Who(m) are you waiting for? *(very formal and seldom used:* For whom are you waiting?)
5. Who answered the phone?
6. Who(m) did you call?
7. Who called?
8. How much gas/How many gallons of gas did she buy?
9. What does "deceitful" mean?
10. What is an abyss?
11. Which way did he go?
12. Whose books and papers are these?
13. How many children do they have? *[British or regional American:* How many children have they?]
14. How long has he been here?
15. How far is it/How many miles is it to New Orleans? ["New Orleans" has at least two commonly used pronunciations. Whatever pronunciation your students are familiar with is correct.]
16. When/At what time can the doctor see me?
17. Who **is** her roommate?
18. Who **are** her roommates?
19. How long/How many years have your parents been living there?
20. Whose book is this?
21. Who**'s** coming over for dinner?
22. What color **is** Ann's dress?
23. What color **are** Ann's eyes?
24. Who can't go . . . ?
25. Why **can't Bob** go?/How come **Bob can't** go?
26. Why **didn't you**/How come **you didn't** answer . . . ? *(formal and rare:* Why **did you not** answer the phone?)
27. What kind of music do you like?
28. What don't you understand?
29. What **is** Janet **doing** right now?
30. How do you spell "sitting"? [*you* = impersonal pronoun]
31. What **does** Tom **look like**?
32. What **is** Tom **like**?
33. What does Ron do (for a living)?
34. How far/How many miles is Mexico from here?
35. How do you take/like your coffee?
36. Which (city) is farther north, Stockholm or Moscow?/Of Stockholm and Moscow, which (city/one) is farther north?
37. How are you getting along?

◇ **PRACTICE 15, p. A12.**
1. Haven't you seen . . . ? No.
2. Don't you feel . . . ? No.
3. Wasn't he . . . ? No.
4. Didn't Mary tell . . . ? No.
5. Don't Janet and you work . . . ? Yes.
6. Isn't that . . . ? Yes.
7. Wasn't she . . . ? No.
8. Isn't she . . . ? Yes.

◇ **PRACTICE 16, p. A13.**
1. don't you
2. have you
3. didn't she
4. aren't there
5. have you
6. don't you *(also possible but less common:* haven't you)
7. won't you
8. doesn't he
9. shouldn't we
10. can they
11. are they
12. isn't it
13. did they
14. aren't I/am I not
15. isn't it

◇ **PRACTICE 17, p. A13.**
1. He's
2. Ø
3. He's
4. Ø
5. She'd
6. Ø
7. She'd
8. Ø
9. We'll
10. They're
11. It's
12. It's
13. Ø
14. Ø
15. We're
16. Ø
17. She's
18. She'd
19. She'd . . . we'd
20. Ø . . . he'd

◇ **PRACTICE 18, p. A14.**
1. I don't have any problems. I have no problems.
2. There wasn't any food on the shelf. There was no food on the shelf.
3. I didn't receive any letters from home. I received no letters from home.
4. I don't need any help. I need no help.
5. We don't have any time to waste. We have no time to waste.
6. You shouldn't have given the beggar any money. You should have given the beggar no money.

7. I don't trust anyone. I trust no one/no-one.
8. I didn't see anyone. I saw no one/no-one.
9. There wasn't anyone in his room. There was no one/no-one in his room.
10. She can't find anybody who knows about it. She can find nobody who knows about it.

◇ PRACTICE 19, p. A15.

1. We **have no** time to waste. OR: We **don't have any** time to waste.
2. I **didn't have any** problems. OR: I **had no** problems.
3. I **can't do anything** about it. OR: I **can do nothing** about it.
4. You **can hardly ever understand her** when she speaks.
5. I **know neither** Ann **nor** her husband. OR: I **don't know either** Ann **or** her husband.
6. **Don't ever drink** water from . . . . OR: **Never drink** water from . . . .
7. . . . I **could barely hear** the speaker.

◇ PRACTICE 20, p. A15.

1. **Hardly had I stepped** out of bed . . . .
2. **Never will I say** that again.
3. **Scarcely ever have I enjoyed** myself more . . . .
4. **Rarely does she make** a mistake.
5. **Never will I trust** him again because . . . .
6. **Hardly ever is it** possible to get . . . .
7. **Seldom do I skip** breakfast.
8. **Never have I known** a more . . . .

◇ PRACTICE 21, p. A15.

1. for	6. to	11. to
2. about	7. of	12. of
3. of	8. to	13. for
4. with	9. for	14. of
5. from	10. to	15. with

◇ PRACTICE 22, p. A16.

1. in	9. to . . . for
2. for	10. about
3. in	11. from
4. from	12. of
5. to	13. with
6. for	14. with . . . about
7. with	15. to
8. to . . . to	

◇ PRACTICE 23, p. A16.

1. of	6. of	11. from
2. of	7. to	12. in
3. of	8. for	13. with
4. for	9. (up)on	14. with
5. to	10. from	15. in

◇ PRACTICE 24, p. A17.

1. of	6. with	11. from
2. to	7. to	12. in
3. with	8. for	13. about
4. with	9. to	14. to
5. in	10. from	15. from

◇ PRACTICE 25, p. A18.

1. for	7. with	12. from
2. at	8. (up)on . . .	13. with . . .
3. for	(up)on	about
4. to	9. for	14. with
5. in	10. about	15. from
6. of	11. with	

◇ PRACTICE 26, p. A19.

1. from	6. with	11. of
2. of	7. for	12. from
3. to	8. for	13. to
4. with	9. in . . . at	14. with
5. to . . . for	10. to	15. with . . . of

Special Workbook Section: PHRASAL VERBS

◇ PRACTICE 1, p. A22.

1. up
2. away/out
3. out/off
4. up
5. off [A "raincheck" is a ticket that admits you to the theater another time without additional payment.]
6. up
7. out [from a library; "I.D." is an abbreviation for identification card.]
8. about
9. up
10. back . . . out of

◇ PRACTICE 2, p. A23.

1. in
2. on . . . off
3. back
4. in/by (also possible: over)
5. out
6. out
7. up
8. up . . . away/out
9. out . . . back [Note: One "fills out" a large item such as an application form, but "fills in" a small space such as a blank in an exercise. Also: "fill up" (British) = "fill in" (American).]
10. up ["catch up with him" (American) = "catch him up" (British)]
11. on
12. out

◇ PRACTICE 3, p. A24.

1. up
2. in . . . over
3. up
4. after/for
5. up
6. out
7. up
8. down
9. up
10. out

◇ PRACTICE 4, p. A25.

1. out/around
2. in/into . . . out
3 along
4. off
5. after
6. in
7. off
8. up
9. out
10. over

◇ PRACTICE 5, p. A25.

1. through [= finish a task]
2. up
3. out ["got dizzy" = had a whirling sensation in the head; *revive* = return to normal breathing; "out cold" = unconscious, in a faint]
4. over ["passed out" = fainted, became suddenly unconscious]
5. up
6. out [= make a line through it with pen or pencil]
7. back
8. on
9. on . . . off
10. into . . . out
11. on . . . off
12. on . . . off

◇ PRACTICE 6, p. A26.

1. on/up
2. over . . . in . . . over
3. up
4. up
5. away/on
6. on
7. over
8. out
9. out of
10. off . . . in
11. up
12. about . . . along with

◇ PRACTICE 7, p. A27

1. into
2. off
3. on
4. back [They are talking on the telephone.]
5. out
6. out . . . across/upon
7. up
8. into . . . out
9. up
10. on/off/out

◇ PRACTICE 8, p. A29.

1. after
2. out
3. up . . . out
4. up [= get ill or sick]
5. up
6. in [= into his office for an appointment]
7. out/into
8. down
9. out ["crash a party" = come without being invited, an impolite act]
10. away

NOTES

NOTES

NOTES

NOTES

NOTES

NOTES

NOTES

NOTES

pastperfect   past   presperfect present   future

Tense (Время)

	past	present	future
simple	studied	study	will study
perfect	had studied	have studied	will have studied
progressive	was studying	is studying	will be studying
perfect progressive	had been studying	have been studing	will have been studying

be
is are
was were

perfect   have + (v3)

go went (gone)
study studied (studied)

be + (Ving)

perfect progressive
have (had) + been + Ving

progressive

be